The Iconoclastic Imagination

The Iconoclastic Imagination

Image, Catastrophe, and Economy in America from the
Kennedy Assassination to September 11

NED O'GORMAN

The University of Chicago Press
Chicago and London

Ned O'Gorman is associate professor of communication and a Conrad Humanities Scholar at the University of Illinois at Urbana-Champaign.

The University of Chicago Press, Chicago 60637
The University of Chicago Press, Ltd., London
© 2016 by The University of Chicago
All rights reserved. Published 2016.
Printed in the United States of America

25 24 23 22 21 20 19 18 17 16   1 2 3 4 5

ISBN-13: 978-0-226-31006-0 (cloth)
ISBN-13: 978-0-226-31023-7 (paper)
ISBN-13: 978-0-226-31037-4 (e-book)
DOI: 10.7208/chicago/9780226310374.001.0001

Library of Congress Cataloging-in-Publication Data

O'Gorman, Ned, author.
    The iconoclastic imagination : image, catastrophe, and economy in America from the Kennedy assassination to September 11 / Ned O'Gorman.
        pages ; cm
    Includes bibliographical references and index.
    ISBN 978-0-226-31006-0 (cloth : alk. paper)—ISBN 978-0-226-31023-7 (pbk. : alk. paper)—ISBN 978-0-226-31037-4 (ebook)   1. Social perception—United States. 2. Neoliberalism—United States. 3. Iconoclasm—United States. 4. Disasters—United States—Public opinion. 5. Kennedy, John F. (John Fitzgerald), 1917–1963—Assassination—Public opinion. 6. Challenger (Spacecraft)—Accidents—Public opinion. 7. September 11 Terrorist Attacks, 2001—Public opinion.   I. Title.
    E839.044 2015
    302'.12—dc23
                                                                                2015014457

♾ This paper meets the requirements of ANSI/NISO Z39.48–1992 (Permanence of Paper).

For Linda, an Imago Dei

Why should we assume everything as we imagine it, as we make up our minds to imagine it? A thousand things may happen in reality which elude the subtlest imagination.

—FETYUKOVITCH in *The Brothers Karamazov*

How does one stand
To behold the sublime?

—WALLACE STEVENS, "The American Sublime"

Contents

Preface

This book consists of an inquiry into a history, indeed several histories. It is not, I want to stress at the outset, a history in and of itself. I offer no overarching narrative account of its main concern, the neoliberal imaginary. Rather, in the series of essays that follow, I build on historical narratives established by others as well as a range of primary sources as I consider a number of different histories and sketch out several typologies in an inquiry into the significance of neoliberalism as cultural and political discourse in the United States, one that I argue not only offers a positive vision of the unrepresentable but a negative ideology, perhaps even theology, that is iconoclastic. Historically, I locate the neoliberal imaginary at the conjunction of those catastrophic, "where-were-you-when?" events that have punctuated American life every fifteen years or so since the Kennedy assassination (and even earlier, in Pearl Harbor) and the emergence of free-market economics in social philosophy and public policy. More generally, I argue that the neoliberal imaginary entails a discourse of transcendence that appeals to invisible, unrepresentable orders as the overarching means of organizing and safeguarding society.

By *imaginary* I mean, following Charles Taylor's notion of a "social imaginary," a way of conceiving of and imagining one's social existence. Taylor characterizes a social imaginary as "much broader and deeper than the intellectual schemes people may entertain when they think about social reality in a disengaged mode." Rather a social imaginary concerns "the ways people imagine their social existence, how they fit together with others, how things go on between them and their fellows, the expectations that are normally met, and the deeper normative notions and images that underlie these expectations."[1] Neoliberalism can be said to have begun in the late 1930s and 1940s as an effort among American and European intellectuals to recuperate liberalism for a depression-wrecked and war-torn West. But its key assumptions and most poignant critiques reached both backward and forward in time. Neoliberalism as a social philosophy tapped into long-standing arguments and anxieties within the liberal tradition about the status and significance of representation in society and about the role of (im)personal rule; at the same time it would go on to inform and invigorate Cold War discourses about society, economy, and nationhood, especially in its appeal to impersonal and invisible mechanisms for ordering society. This forward movement has been traced in intellectual histories and, even more, in accounts of revolutions in policy in the 1970s and 1980s. In this book, however, I follow it into a broader social imaginary, arguing that neoliberalism can be conceived of as a distinct way of imagining social existence, reflected especially in and around discourses of disaster and energized by what are perhaps best called *aesthetic* anxieties, as they have to do with the sense and sensibility of our social and political lives.

At the heart of this book are three critical studies of texts peculiar to three American disasters, or where-were-you-when? events: the Zapruder film of Kennedy's assassination, Ronald Reagan's rhetorical response to the *Challenger* explosion, and CNN's coverage of September 11. I approach each as an "icon of an iconoclasm," attempting, as others surely have, to come to grips with their significance in American political culture. That significance, I argue, can be considered both in terms of the long history of iconoclasm and in terms of a recent history in the American imaginary (and the imagination of America), particularly as it relates to neoliberal social orders. The starkest argument of this book is that in the forty or so years after the Kennedy assassination, in concurrence with the rise of neoliberalism, the most powerful way for publics to see "America" was in the destruction of its representative symbols, or icons, because it was in such catastrophes that the impossibility of any image adequate to representing America, and social processes more generally, was asserted.[2] The more nuanced argument of the book is that this phenomenon was the product of complex histories that can be traced as far back as the theological controversies of the Byzantine Empire over icons and iconoclasm and extended forward through the Protestant Reformation, the confrontations of the Enlightenment and Romanticism with "the sublime," and indeed to the recent (say, post-1968) rise of neoliberalism against the backdrop of the Cold War.

In reflecting on the neoliberal imaginary, this book thus entails inquiries into several histories: where-were-you-when? events, iconoclasm, sublimity, and American political culture in the Cold War and after. It combines historical, philosophical, and critical modes of argument to reflect on these histories and on the broader problem of unrepresentable social orders. In this it works analogically, considering the relations among economy (specifically, forms of capitalism), technology (especially moving-image camera technologies), national security (especially in the Cold War), ideology (liberalisms), and rhetorics of catastrophe. The *image*, I argue, is integral to these analogical relations. We saw in the years after 1963 a marked change in the status of the image in American political culture, a product of numerous inter-animating factors: social, economic, political, technological, ideational, aesthetic, and moral. This change I characterize as an iconoclastic turn, but it is also presented as a neoliberal turn. This book thus offers an account of an era and its political culture. At the same time, it also entails an inquiry into the neoliberal imaginary and an argument for an intimate relationship between neoliberalism and iconoclasm.

Still, I have been quite conflicted about expecting so much from the term *neoliberalism*. Neoliberalism has been, it seems, named, critiqued, and challenged sufficiently enough.[3] Moreover, it is a notoriously fuzzy concept. Is this ground that only fools dare to tread? Finally, there is the problem of its contemporaneousness; the term itself seems now to be slipping, even if the underlying structural changes it represents, as well as the particular habits of public discourse that have developed with those changes, persist. Nevertheless, despite these reservations, I have not been able to wrest free of neoliberalism, either as a concept or as a problem for recent American political culture. Neoliberalism, for all of its slipperiness, is not a concept that I, and I would venture *we*, can simply do without.

I have three main reasons for saying so. First, the persistence of recognizable neoliberal structures and discourses in the wake of the global economic disaster of 2008 means that the neoliberal turn, however 1980s-minded it might now seem to be, cannot simply be dismissed as a thing of the past. Second, even if we would leave neoliberalism to the recent past, the sorts of things I want to say about it have not, as far as I know, been said. Indeed, I think we have neglected an important aspect of its social purchase. Specifically, I will argue that a pivotal organizing binary within neoliberalism is that between *visible* and *invisible* orders, such that neoliberalism is motivated by aesthetic anxieties, broadly understood, as much as economic ones. This binary organized the neoliberal imaginary in America as it was forged in the fire of the Cold War, at least as much as those oft-noted oppositions between individualism and collectivism, and between state-centric and market-centric views of social order. Indeed, the latter two binaries can be seen as subsets of the former. Neoliberalism thus represents far more than an economic theory and agenda; it entails, as Milton Friedman proclaimed as far back as 1951, a kind of social faith, and indeed a national one—a faith in the power of invisible orders to organize and sustain American society in a hostile and dangerous world.[4] This then leads to my third reason for wanting to hold on to the term *neoliberalism*. As a distinct social philosophy formed in the twentieth century, it articulates a more general problem in late modernity: modernity, in its self-reflexivity, may undermine democratically oriented liberalism by eroding the conditions of possibility for *representation*—seen paradigmatically in the image—so that unrepresentable, invisible powers (markets, state security activities hidden behind the legal and paralegal apparatuses of state secrecy and/or bureaucratic walls, and indeed historical destiny itself) become the objects of social faith over and against representable orders. At issue in neoliberalism is thus not only what Nicholas Mirzoeff has formulated as "the right to look," but the political and aesthetic conditions of possibility for such a right to be realized.[5]

Therefore, this is a book about neoliberalism and about much more. It is an essay on the conditions of possibility for democratic liberalism to survive, let alone thrive. In thinking about image, catastrophe, and economy together—and in conjunction with a range of political, aesthetic, and theological histories—I consider what is at stake in the image, in the destruction of the image, and above all in the image of the destruction of the image.

Before commencing, a broad overview of the book's chapters will be helpful, as in them I range widely, from more philosophical discussions of liberalism to critical studies of texts peculiar to the three where-were-you-when? events. After an introduction presenting the major themes and issues of these essays, the book proceeds in three parts, corresponding to the three key terms of my study: *image, catastrophe,* and *economy*. Part 1, consisting of two chapters, addresses the question of the status and significance of the image in liberal and neoliberal cultures by offering a typology of liberal versus neoliberal theories of legitimation crisis and suggesting their relationship to older theories of iconoclasm and sublimity. In chapter 1, I contrast Jürgen Habermas's theory of legitimation crisis with that of Friedrich Hayek in *The Road to Serfdom,* arguing that while the former is concerned with the poverty of social meaning, the latter is typified by a concern with the artificial overproduction of meaning. Then, in chapter 2, I consider anticipations of the neoliberal conception of legitimation crisis in both theologies of iconoclasm and theories of the sublime. In this way, part 1 situates the neoliberal imaginary within longer histories of political, aesthetic, and theological anxieties.

In part 2, "Catastrophe," I reflect on representations of sudden and spectacular violence in America in light of neoliberalism, iconoclasm, and sublimity, examining the Zapruder film of Kennedy's assassination in chapter 3, Ronald Reagan's rhetorical response to the *Challenger* explosion in chapter 4, and CNN's coverage of September 11 in chapter 5. Here, at the heart of the book, I consider ways of seeing (more often, not seeing) America during the Cold War and after through images of the destruction of images. These chapters attend not only to the explicit rhetoric of the texts I consider, but also to subjectivities of spectatorship and the aesthetic logics of the technologies of representation in and against which they are situated. Here I suggest analogous relationships between neoliberal anxieties about social meaning, forms of spectatorship, and various new media, not in order to offer a theory of the production of the neoliberal imaginary but to suggest something of its materialization. These chapters together argue that where-were-you-when? events have been so meaningful in America because in them we have been paradoxically presented with the appearance of invisible orders that summon our social faith.

Part 3, "Economy," takes up the themes of part 2 as it reframes the economic genealogy of neoliberalism in aesthetic, indeed political-aesthetic, terms. In chapter 6, I return to the central anxiety of Hayek's *The Road to Serfdom*: the transfiguration of the liberal warfare state into the totalitarian state, and I consider Eisenhower's New Look (as the president's national security platform was branded) in light of this anxiety. I argue that nuclear deterrence and, more broadly, the Cold War, entailed the institution of invisible emergency orders in both the service and spirit of economy as a means of safeguarding the nation against a transfiguration into a militant "aesthetic state"—what I would prefer to call the "iconic state." Then in chapter 7, I consider the more general problem of the place of the *artificial* within the history of liberalism and the liberal state, returning in this final chapter to the legitimation problem with which the book begins: the overproduction of social meaning.

Some of these essays will be more useful to some readers than others. The book is deliberately designed to give readers leeway in deciding what to read closely and what to pass over more lightly. At the same time, I offer the book as a whole—the pages that follow contain a sustained, if broad, argument concerning the relationship between iconoclasm, neoliberalism, and catastrophe. In the conclusion, I attempt to provide a part to represent this whole in the form of reflection on the pivotal features of the neoliberal imaginary.

Introduction

On November 22, 1963, John F. Kennedy was shot, and the world was shocked. The pattern felt familiar, but its form was not yet apparent: in a massive display of communications power, a violent event in some other part of the world breaks in on the ordinary rituals of being through media channels, producing collective trauma on a national, indeed international, scale. From then on, we are told, everything will be different. We are conscious of the "world-historical." We find ourselves at a point where history suddenly turns.

I grew up in the Midwestern United States in the 1970s and 80s, well after Kennedy's assassination, yet I still felt the traumatic rupture of that event. It was memorialized in my home in a gold-and-black gift box, in which my mother had placed a well-kept stack of magazines and newspapers from the dark autumn of 1963. It is quite possible that it was at that black box that I first became aware of the violence of history. In any case, I vividly recall feeling its consequence on January 28, 1986, when the space shuttle *Challenger* exploded, and I felt that I, too, could now lay claim to a where-were-you when? event, that I knew at last (with my parents and grandparents) the shudder of the world-historical violent spectacle. In the 1990s, I anxiously, if barely consciously, awaited its return. I wondered how it would appear. I wondered when the moment to change all subsequent moments would again break in. The anxiety was aroused on April 20, 1999, in a parking lot in suburban St. Louis when I first heard about the Columbine shooting. But the massacre, though tragic, did not regenerate the world-historical story I knew. Then came September 11, 2001, and the form was now all too apparent. In fact, as Jean Baudrillard suggested shortly after September 11, it was the obviousness of the form that gave rise to the event.[1]

September 11 thus meant for me, as for others, an awareness of what Hayden White once called "the content of the form." It is not just the plot-line of the story that is meaningful, White argued, it is also the form or structure of its telling.[2] The formal aspect of a story has its own significance. The sudden spectacle of violence on September 11 had a familiar form, a structure that itself possessed meaning, inasmuch as it had been memorialized in black-and-gold boxes like my mother's and recalled in the innumerable answers that have been given to the where-were-you-when? question. This awareness was not entirely new to me; again, it was in the black box, so to speak. But now the awareness was such that it called for thought. "One must take one's time," Baudrillard wrote with typical irony.[3] Indeed, for me, very soon after watching replays of the World Trade Center's destruction, I wondered why this where-were-you-when? event resonated with the others like it that had come before, especially Kennedy's assassination and the *Challenger* explosion. Why do these bloody and fiery spectacles mean so much? From where does the power of images of destruction come? What sort of history do they construct? What sort of world do they destroy? The only remaining question was, where to begin?

The Content of the Form

As will be apparent in the pages that follow, I could never fully settle on the answer to that last remaining question. Indeed, I know there are so many beginnings that the long history of the collective shudder before sudden, spectacular violence has the form of a big, bent vortex, where every turn—and almost everywhere there is a turn—is yet a birth and beginning. At the same time, the Kennedy assassination, the *Challenger* disaster, and September 11 share a trait that marks a distinctive and perhaps more profound beginning: each event is an icon of an iconoclasm. That is, in each instance we have a common form: a widely acknowledged icon—an object created both to materialize and "symbolize" the ideal—is spectacularly destroyed in a mass-mediated moving image. Each disaster was thus a kind of perverse simulacrum, conspicuously—one might even say doubly—artificial, as human-made forces destroyed human-made icons.[4] Indeed, each event created a crisis in iconicity—not only as an icon was destroyed, but also as the moving image of that destruction became itself in a certain sense iconic.

That this mass-mediated form is in part the product of a generic technological artifice, the motion-picture camera, means that in one sense it can be said to have its beginning in the advent and development of cinematographic techniques and technologies, stretching back to the age of Muybridge and Marey. Such early motion-picture developments allowed for the circulation of moving images of the destruction of the image. They offered the possibility of a live and, indeed, a kind of living (Muybridge made animals "alive" through the illusion of motion) record of the spectacular destruction of icons. But it was not until November 22, 1963, that this capacity was fully realized by Abraham Zapruder's 8mm Bell & Howell Zoomatic Director Series Model 414 PD. This is not to say that motion-picture cameras had never before captured the spectacular destruction of an iconic image. Motion picture units were widely active in World War II, leaving ample footage of the destruction of sites in Europe and elsewhere that could be justly called iconic; newsreels regularly featured scenes of such destruction and violence, bringing "an unmistakably cinematic dimension into the imagination of disaster."[5] And in the 1950s, the mushroom cloud was fantastically superimposed in public information films over such monumental sites as Manhattan and the Pentagon. Indeed, we can trace the moving image of the destruction of the image back to those turn-of-the-century Edison films of landmarks destroyed by the Galveston cyclone. But the Zapruder film was different in the sense that its subject, John F. Kennedy, was, from very early on in his public career, a carefully crafted icon in a newly televisual, Cold War age, one part of a larger communications revolution. He was, more than his presidential predecessors, a state administrator who was also an explicit image formed both to embody and represent higher, national ideals on the global stage. His assassination was thus an act of iconoclasm as well as murder. The moving record of this iconoclastic national act was indeed something new, and it would introduce—as I argue in the pages that follow—a new way of talking about the image in, and *of,* America, one that would be repeated and revised after the *Challenger* explosion and September 11. Zapruder can thus be seen as inaugurating not only a new form of political experience but also a new political aesthetic.

A chapter from the mid-century conservative critic Richard Weaver is helpful as I begin to outline the content of this form. Writing in 1953, the early but hot days of the Cold War, Weaver offered an account of "ultimate terms" in the public discourse of his time. Terms like *progress, science, modern,* and *America,* he explained, constituted "god terms"—that is, "that expression about which all other expressions are ranked as subordinate and serving dominations and powers." The force of the god term, he argued, "imparts to the others [terms of the culture] their lesser degree of force, and fixes the scale by which degrees of comparison are understood."[6] Weaver contrasted god terms with the "devil terms" of his day, epithets like *fascist, communist,* and *un-American,* arguing that the latter worked as the negative form of the former.[7] Cold War culture in America, he suggested, stood between these god terms and devil terms, which together created not only a common vocabulary of value but a referential hierarchy from which to make collective claims and, as Weaver would write, embody "an order of desire."[8] For Weaver, god terms thus stood like icons in the cathedral of America's Cold War, as objects of desire and indexes of ideals.

But Weaver noted a third type of vocabulary, one less conspicuous in his time than god terms and devil terms, but potentially emerging and perhaps more powerful. These he called "charismatic terms," describing them as, "terms of considerable potency whose referents it is virtually impossible to discover or to construct through imagination." Terms like *freedom, democracy*, and indeed *the United States* functioned in this way, Weaver suggested. Such terms "seem to have broken loose somehow and to operate independently of referential connections." They compel, impel, and indeed in some sense *mean*, but "without reference," and hence it seems that they derive their power neither from reason nor imagination, but from collective will or political powers.[9] Here Weaver struggled to describe a free-floating symbolic system, one that to him seemed just as potent (if not more so) as the god and devil terms, but more problematic because the logic of its order seemed to resist any conventional navigational guides.

A more recent chapter from a cultural history of the United States since the advent of the Cold War suggests something of the historical fate of Weaver's charismatic terms. In a survey of Cold War presidential rhetoric, Daniel T. Rodgers observes that Ronald Reagan brought a rhetorical revolution, especially as he turned from the heroic, bipolar themes of his Cold War predecessors to a new rhetoric of "belief." Rodgers writes, "On the axis of 'belief,' Reagan's speechwriters broke up and recast the rhetorical formulas of Cold War political culture. The story of peril, leadership, and resolve was replaced by a different plot. This one moved from initial confidence to momentary despair ... [and] finally to a 'revolution of hope' restored."[10] *Belief in what*? That was not so clear, and for Reagan, it was beside the point. As Rodgers argues, Reagan "invested belief itself" with extraordinary power; his was a project not in soul searching, but in "psychic restoration." America was presented "as a country of timeless confidence, in which past and present met on a field of eternally positive thinking."[11] The "future" of Ronald Reagan was not so much the object of belief as it was its subject: the future was a future of belief in which America was to believe. Just believe.

Indeed, in the wake of the age of Reagan and amid the enthusiasms of deconstruction, Frederic Jameson published a monumental essay entitled "The Cultural Logic of Late Capitalism," which reappeared as the first chapter of his 1991 *Postmodernism*.[12] In that essay, Jameson argued that the postmodern form of late capitalism was characterized first by a "depthlessness," or flatness, both in theory and in the "culture of the image"; second, by "a consequent weakening of historicity"; and, third, by "a whole new type of emotional ground tone" anticipated in eighteenth-century theories of the sublime.[13] Taken together, his arguments assert that to experience the postmodern was to feel what we couldn't represent or even imagine, *not*—Jameson argued—as a utopian or catastrophic culmination of history, but as precisely that which cannot be contained by history. The future of the postmodern was accessed affectively rather than temporally or historically; it was, to draw on an old Aristotelian distinction among types of rhetorical proof, a matter of pathos rather than logos or ethos.

Weaver, Rodgers, and Jameson each pointed to a form or, as the case may be, a formlessness that in some sense signifies but in a manner beyond representation—which is to say, each of them observed a discourse that operates beyond the icon, even the image. For whereas the image is the product of record (the *datum*) and/or projection (the *phantasm*), the discourse that Weaver sensed in 1953, that Rodgers observed in the Reagan of the 1980s, and that Jameson wrote so densely about in 1991 was the product of dogmatic powers that appealed neither to reason nor imagination, but to sheer *belief*. Here was a political culture of the cult of the unrepresentable and unimaginable, at first, it seems, competing with other images and idioms, but by the time of Reagan strangely regnant. Such is the content of the form that I explore in the icons of iconoclasm discussed in this book.

Transcendence and Transformation

My argument is that the content of the form of the where-were-you-when? event, condensed in the moving image of the destruction of the image, is charismatic in the sense that Weaver struggled to articulate. Moreover, I argue that this charismatic quality feeds off and is related to the discourse that Reagan spoke so fluently—that of neoliberalism. This discourse, in turn, can be approached through the theoretical idioms of both eighteenth-century theories of the sublime and postmodern thought.

Thus the essays that follow attempt to consider the still relatively recent advent of the spectacular moving image of the destruction of the image in light of broader historical developments in political aesthetics. My approach is theoretical, historical, and above all critical. Like Weaver, I aim to identify and explicate a basic rhetorical structure and direction. Like Rodgers, I aim to contribute to a history of American political culture in the Cold War and beyond. Like Jameson, I am concerned with the relationships among cultural logic, economy, and theory. But I am more preoccupied than the former two thinkers—and perhaps even the third—with the complex historical threads of this charismatic discourse of belief, which seem to me to be at once peculiar to US political culture in the last fifty-plus years and loaded with historical resonance and precedence. To do some justice to this complexity, I approach this discourse from three senses of history—as long, short, and medial.

My long history attempts to provide an account of the meaning of the destruction of images in patterns of belief and rhetoric across broad swaths of historical time. Here, I work to present persisting aspects of culture that inform the significance of relatively recent images of the destruction of images. The long histories I am concerned with here are those of iconoclasm, sublimity, and liberalism, each in some sense *discourses of transcendence*. In chapter 1, I begin with the problem of political legitimation in (neo)liberal societies, focusing specifically on the artificial character of social meaning as a distinct problem in (neo)liberalism. My aim here is to introduce neoliberalism as simultaneously a variation of, an alternative to, and a critique of liberalism. In chapter 2, I pursue this discussion into the subjects of iconoclasm and sublimity. I first look at a theological vocabulary developed in the Byzantine Empire with which to talk about the image as icon, idol, and token. This vocabulary was a response to the crisis of iconoclasm, which I show was not only an act but also an *argument* asserting that the image was not only insufficient to and unnecessary for belief, but that the image was in fact adverse to true belief. The subsequent history of iconoclasm in the Protestant Reformation extended this dogma in both theological and political directions that pitted word against image, positing for each not merely a different phenomenology but fundamentally opposed ontologies and epistemologies. The *word*, itself morphing into a kind of charismatic term, gained for radical Protestants not only a distinct personal piety and doctrinal purity, but also a means of culture critique and political protest before regnant authorities, institutions, and ideologies, and their respective logics of representation.

Thus, I turn in chapter 2 to the discourse of the sublime. Sublimity has not only a long but also a varied history, dating back to antiquity. In its Ur-source, the ancient text *Peri Hypsous* (*On the Sublime*, attributed to Longinus), we see a rhetoric imagined that rejected the norms of the deliberative assembly in favor of a discourse comparable to the monumental form of the Colossus, that great icon of the Roman Empire.[14] In the seventeenth-century the popularization of *Peri Hypsous* by Nicolas Boileau-Despréaux became part and parcel, in the words of one critic, of "a kind of conspiracy to protect the ineffable."[15] This conspiracy reached a high point in the eighteenth and nineteenth centuries, when images of ruins and ruined images took on a peculiar fascination. In fact, as I will show, the logic of sublimity came to closely resemble that of iconoclasm, and in Kant the two seem to be identified. Both shared not only an interest in the fragmented image, but a more fundamental conviction that the material of culture—whether in the form of icons, institutions, or traditions—cannot legitimately contain the transcendent(al). This theme, of course, was challenged by the various romanticisms of the eighteenth and nineteenth centuries, but never unequivocally, as these romanticisms too participated in the conspiracy to protect the ineffable. These long histories of iconoclasm and sublimity are historic threads that I weave together in the following pages.

My short history, on the other hand, concerns the iconoclastic where-were-you-when? events themselves: Kennedy's assassination, the *Challenger* disaster, and September 11. In the middle chapters, I consider their integration into what would become a dominant discourse—that of neoliberalism. At the same time, by approaching these events through criticism, I intend to include within my discussion the *new* (*neo*, "recently born"). The new is a constituent component, and not merely an incidental aspect, of the meaning of catastrophe, which always includes a sense of the end of some order and the birth of a new one (*katastrophê*, "overturning").[16] Despite the retrospective efforts of pundits and panels to assert that each event could have been, should have been, predicted—thus transforming history into something more like a series of causes and effects legible to hard science—the power of these collective communicational events is found in part in their unpredictability and thus in their potential unintelligibility—hence the sublime. My sense of short history is meant to reckon with the world-historical—that is, transformations, unexpected and sometimes radical, in the nature of our world that thus engender transformations in our identities. The production of meaning in light of a world-historical event will not be satisfactorily accomplished in the strict terms of the past, as conservative thought tends to do. Nor can such meaning be exhausted by the terms of the laws of history (or historical inevitability), as radicals and progressives have been known to attempt. Neither approach accounts for the power of the new in these events. Rather, such events entail a *discourse of transformation*. In each episode I consider (in chapters 3, 4, and 5), I thus offer an account of a discourse of transformation.

The juxtaposition of transcendence and transformation brings me to medial history. As the phrase suggests, medial histories have some of the attributes of long histories, and some of short histories. They reflect patterns of ideology, rhetoric, and so on that can be seen across a broad swath of history, yet they display something of the new, novel, and unanticipated that is characteristic of short histories. This book foregrounds three medial histories: (1) that of America's Cold War, which inaugurated a transformation not only in the global image of the United States, but in its self image; (2) that of the iconoclastic where-were-you-when? event itself, as Kennedy's death, the *Challenger* explosion, and September 11 are *considered together* as part of a common history; and (3) that of what is frequently called neoliberalism by cultural critics, political economists, and historians.

The Cold War grew out of the tensions and instabilities wrought by the unprecedented worldwide upheaval of World War II, which left the United States (more than the USSR) in a place of unprecedented power. The Cold War thus entailed for Americans in both official and unofficial capacities a reappraisal of what it meant to be American and, correspondingly, of what America was all about. For many non-Americans, similar issues were at play. Given the power and presence of the United States in much of the world, the image of America was contested in vital, and sometimes violent, ways. The Cold War thus was a crucible in which the character, dynamics, and impressions of American power were tried and tested.

The second medial history, that of the iconoclastic where-were-you-when? event, is part of both this Cold War context and a larger cultural history in the United States that serves as a backdrop to my study, one that Kevin Rozario has referred to as a "culture of calamity." Working from the "catastrophic logic of modernity" to a more focused consideration of the particular power of catastrophe in the United States, Rozario argues modernity's cyclical patterns of "ruin and renewal, boom and bust, destruction and construction" have had peculiar purchase in the United States, where there has been "a widespread conviction, born of beliefs and experience, that calamities are instruments of progress."[17] Such optimistic narratives would seem to have a difficulty in encompassing such traumas as presidential assassinations, televised instances of spaceship blow-ups, or terrorist attacks; indeed, in a certain sense they do. But as I show in the pages that follow, such narratives have managed not only to sneak in but to provide an overarching structure of meaning for the where-were-you-when? event—but less by suggesting that such traumas are instruments of progress and more by suggesting that American progress is not hindered by such spectacular catastrophes, that these violent spectacles do not represent America, that the meaning of America is found *beyond* material and visible manifestations.

Neoliberalism represents such a discourse of transcendence. Yet, viewed analytically, neoliberalism is a far more fine thread to follow than the where-were-you-when? events or even the culture of calamity. It has been characterized by a charismatic translucence—what is neoliberalism, what makes it new, and to what extent can it be said to be anything more than a particular, if radical, economic theory? As neoliberalism is central to the problem with which I wrestle in the chapters that follow—most overtly in chapters 1 and 7—some coloring is in order. Therefore, in the remainder of this introduction, I look more closely at the political-cultural logic of neoliberalism, taking some time to reflect on this and several other concepts integral to my argument. My goal here is less to define than to present ways of working with and thinking about the key terms of my study, and to anticipate in the process the sorts of arguments I will make.

The Neoliberal Imaginary

To what does *neoliberalism* refer? What are its particular aspects and attributes, and how does one account for its emergence? These questions are interrelated: here I begin with some background on the term, consider its aspects, and then proceed to consider some of the general attributes that typify what I call the neoliberal imaginary. I conclude with some general claims to set the stage for the chapters that follow.

The term *neoliberalism* in its contemporary use appears to have its origins in and around the Colloque Lippmann held in Paris in 1938 and attended by the Austrian economists (at the time working at the London School of Economics [LSE]) Friedrich Hayek and Ludwig von Mises, as well as others among the liberal intelligentsia in Europe and America—figures like Michael Polanyi, Raymond Aron, and, the meeting's namesake, Walter Lippmann. The Colloque Lippmann was held to consider how to revolutionize liberalism in light of the catastrophes of world war, economic depression, fascism, and communism. Its nominal occasion was the publication of Lippmann's 1937 *An Inquiry into the Principles of the Good Society*, where the author—building off conversations he had had at the LSE with Hayek and Mises—argued for considerable constraints to be placed on the scope and power of government planning in favor of greater freedom for market forces. Seen as something of a coup by free-market advocates, Lippmann's *Inquiry* provided grounds for a strong philosophical critique not just of communism and fascism, but of Roosevelt's New Deal and more moderate forms of European socialism. At the same time, Lippmann was careful to state in the book that he was not calling for a return to the full-bore, laissez-faire capitalism of the nineteenth century, which he suggested represented an abuse of market forces and hindered, rather than furthered, individual liberty. Rather, his was a call for the "reconstruction of liberalism" where "law and public policy" are adapted to ensure that the market is "preserved and perfected as the prime regulator of the division of labor."[18] The Colloque Lippmann was a seminal event with regard to the entrance of the principles of Austrian economics into American political-economic thought. It began a process of networking, collaboration, and advocacy that achieved, in historian Angus Burgin's words, "the great persuasion," a persuasion that worked its way through the well-known Mt. Perelin Society and culminated with the "radical liberal" free-market advocacy of Milton Friedman, which extended market triumphalism beyond business into fields like education, medicine, and social welfare.[19]

The effectiveness of this persuasion rested in part, as Burgin argues, on the efforts and arguments of advocates like Hayek and Friedman. But there was also the matter of the particular social and cultural contexts in which this persuasion became great. Every great persuader knows that her success depends upon accommodating the message to the basic assumptions, beliefs, and dispositions of the audience. Persuasion in this sense is an inherently conservative social activity, even when the ends being sought are quite radical. We might ask, then, to what cultural conventions did neoliberalism appeal, especially as it ascended to preeminence in the 1970s and 80s? If, with Burgin and others, we attribute the stunning success of free-market advocacy in part to the tireless efforts of economists like Hayek and Friedman, we must nevertheless ask how those efforts were culturally realized—indeed, to the point where they took on a life of their own.[20] For this we must look beyond the economists and their theories to the culture of their achievements.

In fact, for all that has been written about neoliberalism, relatively little attention has been given to the political culture in which it took hold or to its own critiques of political culture. Rather, we have been largely content to locate neoliberalism within the broad historical context of globalization, late capitalism, or, for some, postmodernism, where neoliberalism is sometimes the cause of these large-scale historical processes and at other times merely of their ideological cover. I am skeptical of the causal arguments. At the same time, I am reluctant to approach neoliberalism as the manifestation of an underlying historical phenomenon or movement.[21] Rather, I think neoliberalism can be approached as both a particular development within liberal social philosophy and as a distinct cultural achievement, a social imaginary.

In referring to neoliberalism as a social philosophy, I differ from the view that describes it, in David Harvey's words, as "a theory of political economic practices," and instead follow recent work like Burgin's on the intellectual history of neoliberalism that exposes its broader ideational aspects.[22] While neoliberal thinkers no doubt have made and still make theoretical claims—that is, claims about how things work—they have been, especially among the first generation, invested in issues of *how things should be*, and therefore represent a distinct normative project, a social philosophy. As a social philosophy, neoliberalism was conceived not only within the rarefied halls of Austrian economics, but also as an iconoclastic gesture against the dominant political cultures of twentieth-century Europe and America. Indeed, neoliberalism took aim at a kind of triptych of grotesque images of the state. In the late 1930s and 1940s, its most immediate and pressing critiques were against the police and fascist states. The former would violently and arbitrarily rule much of Europe in the 1940s, and the latter, of course, seemed to be the primary cause of all the chaos. But neoliberalism was also set against the image of the liberal welfare state and, as things turned out in the 1930s and 40s, its mirror image, the liberal warfare state. Both engendered centralized polities, and both depended on the practices and epistemologies of planning.

In each of these three images of the state—the police state, the fascist state, and the welfare/warfare state—neoliberals critiqued not just state planning and the overextension of its coercive power, but the attempt to organize society around *visible*, and we might even say *material*, manifestations of social power. In his foundational text, Lippmann represented this threat as that of "centralization," "concentration," and "collectivism," each of which entailed a turn "from the liberal to the authoritarian conception of society."[23] Liberal society, he warned, was giving itself over to the "gods of the machine" and "the providential state." "The contemporary collectivist," he wrote with typical flair, appealed to "one of the most enchanting myths which ever captured the human imagination. From the marriage of knowledge with force a new god is to be born. Out of the union of science with government there is to issue a providential state, possessed of all knowledge and of the power to enforce it."[24] Nevertheless, Lippmann continued, "though the ruler may think he has his patents from God, he does not have the wisdom or the power of God."[25] By contrast, "the men who made the modern world" were liberators, acting from "an evolution from the religious convictions that all men are persons and that the human person is inviolable."[26] Theirs was a progressive project:

> It was the energy released by this progressive emancipation which invented, wrought, and made available to mankind all that it counts as good in modern civilization. No government planned, no political authority directed, the material progress of the past four centuries, or the increasing humanity which has accompanied it. It was by a stupendous liberation of the minds and spirits

and conduct of men that a world-wide exchange of goods and services and ideas was promoted, and it was in this invigorating and sustaining environment that petty principalities were coalesced into great commonwealths.[27]

Neoliberalism as a social philosophy thus drew not just on economic theory, but on a particular vision of society organized around the liberation of the human spirit before the centralized and concentrated idols of the age. It represented an attempt to disenthrall Americans and Europeans from the pseudo-powers of planning, technocracy, and indeed technology—the "gods of the machine"—and reinvigorate mind and spirit as the true sources of progress and modernization.

If neoliberalism as a social philosophy was born out of such a Reformation-like spirit amid an age of planning, it became integral to a broader social imaginary amid the somewhat different crises of the Cold War that entailed a similar crisis in visions of capitalism. Critics of neoliberalism have typically identified this crisis as the breakdown of the Keynesian-based Bretton Woods system beginning in the late 1960s.[28] I think, however, the most significant crises predate this, as they have to do with the character of American global power. In fact, Keynesianism was a point of significant anxiety in Washington and the United States more broadly in the late 1940s and 1950s. Indeed, as we will see, well before the fiscal and economic crises of the early 1970s, the advocacy by someone like Friedrich Hayek of "free markets" over and against the interventionist state spoke in profound and powerful ways to an American public worried about the totalitarian potential of the warfare state and, by extension, of the welfare state. Moreover, both Truman and Eisenhower were full of worry about deficit spending and inflation, and the latter was committed to a global free-market vision in both policy and ideology.

Indeed, the contest between Keynesianism and anti-Keynesianism in Cold War America took place amid the conflagrations of American imperialism. The United States arose out of World War II with unprecedented global power. The question for America's leaders, newly convinced of a Soviet-led communist expansionist agenda, was how to exercise American power globally without becoming embroiled in the imperial misadventures of old Europe or even *looking* like an imperial power. Newly formed global institutions like the United Nations and the International Monetary Fund were a significant part of the equation here. But so was a more elusive factor, what Eisenhower referred to as the "image of America." American power would be symbolic power, not to the exclusion of military, economic, and diplomatic initiative, but rather in the sense that it would seek to influence the world and indeed win the Cold War through ideals and ideas, particularly historically liberal ideals and ideas, among which Eisenhower placed free enterprise.

That this contest for the image of America took place amid a global transformation—indeed revolution—in communication technologies and their related economies only exacerbated the problems. The rise of television represented the most conspicuous transformation. But the 1950s and 1960s also saw the rise of early forms of computing and digital architecture, as well as the development of early satellite technologies. These innovations, combined with old technologies like film, radio, and newsprint, contributed to the conspicuous presence of the *image* in the Cold War—not just as a means of representation, but as a point of social, cultural, and indeed geopolitical anxiety. Thus, in 1962, Daniel Boorstin published *The Image: A Guide to Pseudo-Events*, in which he critiqued the "thicket of unreality which stands between us and the facts of life."[29] The manifold deceptions of which Boorstin complained were inseparable from the constant staging of the Cold War. Boorstin worried that Americans might come to actually believe the deceptions, forgetting enduring truths. Two years later Marshall McLuhan took a bit more celebratory stance toward the new place of the image, presenting the Cold War itself as "an electric battle of information and images that goes far deeper and is more obsessional than the old hot wars of industrial hardware."[30] The Cold War, McLuhan concluded, was a "war of the icons."[31]

As James Simpson has recently argued, however, there was a profound iconoclastic aspect to this iconographic war, as spirit was pitted against, and indeed elevated above, matter as the central aesthetic object of American identity.[32] Thus Simpson examined the efforts in the 1950s and 1960s by the Central Intelligence Agency (CIA) to propagate, of all things, abstract expressionism as part of this iconographic war. The appeal of abstract art, as former CIA officers since have explained, was found in its aesthetic associations with "freedom of expression and . . . intellectual achievement, without any rigid barriers."[33] The abstract could be aesthetically and ideologically contrasted with socialist realism, which looked, next to abstract expressionism, "even more stylized and more rigid and confined than it was," according to the CIA.[34] To be sure, President Eisenhower himself would pit American artists, "free to create with sincerity and conviction," against those in states where "artists are made the slaves and the tools of the state," and "progress is arrested and creation of genius is destroyed."[35] Just as Lippmann had several decades before contrasted the creative, spiritual power of true liberalism with the rigid, mechanistic aesthetic of "collectivism," in fighting the Cold War, America pitted the abstract and ineffable against the concrete and oppressive.

In this context, neoliberalism—which posited invisible *principles* and *processes* as the regulating agents of society rather than external and "artificial" *persons* and *plans*—enjoyed a kind of aesthetic advantage over Keynesian technocracy with respect to a major front in America's Cold War, even as Keynesian thinking informed postwar global economic institutions.

Thus, more than an economic theory, more even than what Wendy Brown has called a "political rationality," neoliberalism could be incorporated into a social imaginary, a way of imagining social existence and expectations together with, in Charles Taylor's words, "the deeper normative notions and images that underlie these expectations."[36] In this respect, the contours of neoliberalism might be extended as far as the contours of culture itself.[37] To begin with, neoliberalism represents, in keeping with Burgin's account in *The Great Persuasion*, a *rhetoric*, where the ideas, arguments, and, indeed, the argumentative methods and styles of academics and other advocates pushed for free-market policies in the postwar period to extraordinary effect.[38] But if the culture of the rhetorical achievements of men like Hayek and Friedman was to become itself a cultural achievement, then neoliberalism became something more than a rhetoric; it became a cultural convention, an imaginary entailing broader discursive, rhetorical, and ideological patterns that, to quote David Harvey on the matter, have taken hold of "ways of thought to the point where [they have] become incorporated into the common-sense way many of us interpret, live in, and understand the world."[39]

Hence, in considering the "great persuasion" that would become neoliberalism, we find ourselves considering far more than political and economic arguments. We find ourselves amid a political culture, its pivotal events, and its peculiar histories—so much so that neoliberalism is but one history among several that I consider. In this book, as I turn my attention to matters seemingly tangential to neoliberalism per se, I do so in order to draw together the threads that would give power to a neoliberal imaginary. Above all, I find in the shock, awe, and sublimity of those iconoclastic where-were-you-when? events discourses of transcendence that articulate a neoliberal imaginary.

The Disestablishment of the Mundane

In accounting for what he calls the "culture of calamity" in the United States, Rozario finds *economy* a particularly powerful rhetorical resource for the optimism with which Americans have frequently approached their disasters. Citing a history of economic thought that extends back to John Stuart Mill and moves forward through Joseph Schumpeter and Alan Greenspan, Rozario observes that capitalism has long been thought of as benefiting from cycles of destruction and renewal (something, he notes, that David Harvey, Neil Smith, and Edward Soja have also asserted).[40] But even more significant for my argument here, Rozario shows how this particular economic logic has roots in theology, particularly theologies of divine providence that offered to Americans "a durable faith in the 'blessings of disaster,' according to which ruptures and crises were grasped by elites as opportunities for political and economic renovation."[41] In the pages that follow, I extend Rozario's argument into theologies of the icon and iconoclasm, which then become means of considering a larger question at stake in neoliberal discourse: the (il)legitimacy of *representation*. The neoliberal imaginary is not only rooted in a historic theology of providence—as Rozario suggests—it has drawn its life as well from a widespread, historic, Protestant-inspired critique of the adequacy of images and other forms of representations to legitimately picture providential—read, *social*—processes.[42]

All this is not to say, however, that neoliberalism represents merely an imaginary (as if that were not enough). It represents as well a development or set of developments within capitalism: thus the question of the relationship between culture and capitalism presents itself—pursued at length, and sometimes with great elegance, in fields ranging from cultural studies to geography and sociology. Taken together, culture and capitalism can be said to produce a *condition*, a particular type of existence. It is not among the explicit aims of this book to further theoretical inquiry into how culture and capitalism are related or how they might together produce a condition. I take this as a starting point. Still, I do take several positions relevant to the questions entailed here, and want to speak to them as I bring this introduction to a close.

First, in considering the neoliberal imaginary one cannot help but be struck by the ways in which its rhetorics, rhythms, and logics resemble the processes, logics, and technologies of late capitalism. It does indeed seem that the capitalist engine and rhetorical and cultural invention hum together, as what we see in neoliberal markets can look a lot like what we see in neoliberal discourse and the broader culture of which it is a part. I take these resemblances seriously, offering analogy (*ana-logos*, side-by-side rationalities) not only as a critical method but as a pivotal aspect of the power of the neoliberal imaginary itself. Nowhere is the analogous relation between neoliberal discourse and neoliberal capitalism clearer than in that likeness shared between the "creative destruction" of capitalism and what I argue is the iconoclastic logic of neoliberal discourse. At the very least it is apparent that one by-product of the creative destruction of capitalism has been the destruction of local institutions, traditions, and artifacts, or what anthropologists have referred to as "material culture." So too capitalist creative destruction, as Schumpeter suggested it would, has made havoc of markets themselves, creating new markets out of the ruins of old ones and in the process destroying material culture of a different sort—namely, all those consumer goods rendered quickly obsolete or dispensable by virtue of "innovation."[43] The discourse of consumerism thus has its iconoclastic aspects, trashing the artifacts of yesteryear in the name of the god of innovation.

But there is another significant way in which the neoliberal imaginary finds an analog in neoliberal capitalism. The latter is typified by a capacity to make everything commensurable with the value of money, where money itself takes on a kind of self-referentiality, so as to create a comprehensive system, a closed world. Neoliberal discourse, as I explore in the chapters that follow, shares this appetite for a comprehensive commensurability, and this appetite is at the heart of the assault of neoliberal discourse on the distinctly *political*. It has often been observed that neoliberalism would displace the political with the economic; this is indeed a project that reaches not only back to early neoliberal advocates like Lippmann and Hayek, but much further to the genesis of classical liberalism itself in the eighteenth century. But what is less noted is the particular means by which this displacement would be achieved—namely, through a critique of *representation* and its close political kin, *publicity*. Despite an illustrious history of efforts to eradicate representation from the political—most notably by Rousseau—to attack representation is to attack the political. In F. R. Ankersmit's words, "all politics presupposes the self-awareness of the political collectivity that is paradigmatically exemplified by (political) representation."[44] Representation is the means by which we come to grasp our political (and indeed historical) existence; without it we have nothing to "get hold of," and without anything to get hold of, it is hard to conceive of a politics. Contemporary economic reality is so difficult to grasp in part because it eludes representation, systematically and structurally so.[45] The free-market system would be unrepresentable, or sublime; at the same time, everything that appears in it is but a token of the invisible order, having no mimetic or symbolic, let alone intrinsic, relationship to what it represents.

This relentless capacity of advanced capitalism to make everything convertible and thus unrepresentable is, of course, a source of its peculiar power. A similar power, less noted, is enjoyed by neoliberal discourse. The latter exploits resemblances across distinct domains so as to suggest their common participation within what Ankersmit refers to as a *tertium*, or "third" realm, itself ultimately unrepresentable.[46] Here the neoliberal imaginary is itself a kind of closed world that relies on a system of conversions—moving freely, for example, from a political ethic of individualism to a radical commitment

to consumer participation within the market, or from the flat macroeco-
nomic calculus of game theory to the flat architecture of the digital.[47] Such
movements, it need not be stressed, are achieved not through apodictic reasoning; it is not even a matter of representing one thing in terms of another.
Rather they are achieved through a form of identification, where, as Kenneth Burke writes, two or more things are made "consubstantial," or part of
the same substance (or *tertium*).[48] That neoliberal discourse has pretended to
explain not just economic realities, but an entire moral and historical universe is due in large part to the power of identification. Such power has, since
the advent of eighteenth-century classical economics, become paradigmatically *economic*: markets and money facilitate relentless identifications. Yet,
as Burke argued, any identification leaves open the possibility of division.[49]
The process of identification assumes a difference of one sort or another.
Therefore, neoliberal discourse, though paradigmatically economic, always
remains potentially political: to draw identities is to border the space of representation where one thing is approached in or through another, the two
remaining distinct. This space is intrinsically capable of being politicized
inasmuch as representation depends on discrimination or judgment with
respect to the relation between the representation and the represented, and
those judgments can be brought into public view to be contested among
citizens, or among citizens and their representatives. Similarly, as W. J. T.
Mitchell has noted, to assert the "unimaginable" and "unspeakable" is to all
but "insist on talking about it, depicting it, and trying to render it in increasingly vivid and literal ways."[50]

Indeed, the discursive character of representation is part of what makes
the dream of identification so powerful, and it is this dream that neoliberalism promises to fulfill by transforming the political into the economic: an
order of algorithms, a set of fixed rules that finally mend our broken political life. Government, we are told, is supposed to represent the wills of individuals, but repeatedly fails to do so; there is, however, a mechanism that can
efficiently achieve identification between the will of the citizen and individual
goods. Indeed, we can finally move *beyond* politics and representation altogether and enter a realm of pure consubstantiality and efficient identification.
This realm, on the one hand, is characterized by a certain tokenization of the
realm of representation: all signs are merely arbitrary images, tools rather
than meaningful symbols beneath a transcendent economic order. Neoliberalism thus entails an iconoclastic critique of politics. At the same time, it
is a realm imbued with the aura of the sublime, an unrepresentable *tertium*
that converts all that is solid into air. Neoliberalism is thus a discourse of the
sublimely unrepresentable. And this is what makes it both so powerful and so

problematic for democratic politics: for neoliberalism would transcend the iconic indexes of a political culture to locate the basis of social order in an invisible realm beyond debate.

One wishes this were but a challenge to democracy from the right flank. But if neoliberalism helped undercut the institutional and epistemological bases of the welfare state, postmodernism took a seat in the ruins—sometimes ambivalently, sometimes playfully, but rarely mournfully. Even as a new and powerful generation of neoliberals like Friedman and Alan Greenspan turned from empiricist confidence to philosophical commitments and principles (Friedman drawing on the thought of the Austrians, and Greenspan on a combination of Austrian thought and Randianism), a cluster of epistemologically meek ideas, arguments, and postulates arose with postmodernism. To be sure, postmodernists, as Lyotard suggested, worked apart from "preestablished rules," while neoliberal thinkers instead sought inviolable ones.[51] But neoliberals and postmodernists alike left epistemological confidences floundering somewhat helplessly in the old reflecting pools of the academy. Indeed, neoliberalism and postmodernism, though tending to operate at countervailing political poles, were both theories and conditions that were willfully nonrepresentational. Early neoliberal theorists turned variously to deontological maxims or to game theory—both of which presumed the impossibility of any representation adequate to actual social and economic processes.[52] Postmodernists (a reference, admittedly, that can be as flexible as neoliberalism can be), meanwhile, contented themselves with the surface, giving up "big, high spaces" that sought depth and communal meaning to the "big, low space" that "is a space for crowds of anonymous individuals without explicit connection with each other."[53] Here were what Hayek would call *kosmoi*, several steps removed, if not entirely unmoored, from historical or empirical grounds, set free either by *a priori* principles subject in the end only to a faith, or by a psychology leading to skepticism, or by hypotheses refutable only through repeated (just how often was not clear) failure to predict, or by the prison house of language, or by the free interplay of the symbolic. Here were sublime *kosmoi*, we might say, removed from *Welt* or "world," and sublime sciences finally divorced from the vestiges of Baconian *scientia*. Thus what Milton Friedman wrote of economic theory in 1953 could well have been written of postmodern theory thirty years later: "The construction of the hypothesis is a creative act of inspiration, intuition, invention; its essence is the vision of something new in familiar material. The process must be discussed in psychological, not logical categories; studied in autobiographies and biographies, not treatises on scientific method; and promoted by maxim and example, not syllogism of theorem."[54] Logic and science alike would make some claim to represent a truth, either apodictically or empirically. But neoliberal and postmodern theories made no such truth claims: they held up no mirror to nature. From where, then, did the power of this peculiar knowledge come? From the sublime.

Thus, to return to the cultural diagnoses of Weaver, Rodgers, and Jameson with which I began this chapter, American political culture witnessed in the course of the Cold War the development of a kind of cultural conspiracy to protect the ineffable. What I am calling the neoliberal imaginary was as much a product of this conspiracy as it was its cause, and it seems to have had help from the academy and some sectors of the art and architecture worlds in the form of postmodernism. What was achieved here, however, was not the establishment of a transcendent order as much as *the disestablishment of a mundane one.* Democracy has arguably never been achieved, and the tale I tell in the pages that follow hardly amounts to the story of the loss or "decline" of democracy. Rather, it concerns the development of a significant challenge to the conditions of possibility for democracy, as *invisible*—more than transcendent, properly speaking—means and mechanisms came to be associated in the course of the second half of the twentieth century in America with the preservation and progress of America, or with its postmodern denouement. But invisible orders, by their very nature, escape view, and therefore representation, and thus the principle means by which politics, above all democratic politics, functions. Democratic possibilities, and the possibility of democracy, do not depend on everything becoming public. They do require, however, *iconicity*—representations that appear, and appear to represent that which they are not.

PART I

Image

The Neoliberal Legitimation Crisis

It was a black-and-white tapestry. The dress, prepared and pressed for this most ominous of occasions, hung solidly on the shoulders of Elizabeth Eckford as she walked outside Central High School in Little Rock, Arkansas, on September 4, 1957. The dress had been made especially for the day, and pressed that morning as images of crowds gathering at Central High played on the Eckford family's television set. The dress, like the crowds, had been crafted to communicate: the lower part of the skirt, like the depths of the American republic in and for which Eckford stood, was fashioned in checked black-and-white (fig. 1). The skirt flowed outward, reaching toward the bystanders, bodyguards, belligerents, and photographers that would surround her—as if to remind them too that the threads of history, though individually indistinct, when combined together create patterns that intrude into our civic spaces. The many images of Eckford that day—published in newspapers and magazines and shown on television—similarly communicated, spreading out into the republic and into the world, causing some to feel outrage, others spite, others perplexity, and others even a curious indifference.

For President Eisenhower, however, the images caused alarm. Quietly watching from his vacation spot in Newport, Rhode Island, in early September, they gave ample indication of the mob violence that would ensue that month. Eisenhower himself was "profoundly ambivalent" about the 1954 Supreme Court decision that had led to integration efforts in Arkansas and elsewhere; he preferred an approach consistent with "free enterprise" that balked at any "coercive" measures on the part of the federal government with respect to race relations.[1] In fact, he had insisted in a July 1957 news conference, only two months before Eckford donned her checked dress, "I can't imagine any set of circumstances that would ever induce me to send Federal troops into a

FIGURE 1. Elizabeth Eckford in her dress outside Central High School in Little Rock, Arkansas. (Photo courtesy of Will Counts Collection: Indiana University Archives.)

Federal court and into any area to enforce the orders of a Federal court, because I believe that [the] common sense of America will never require it."[2] So much for common sense, Eisenhower must have later figured. On September 24, he authorized his secretary of defense to use "the armed forces of the United States as he may deem necessary" to put down the willful "obstruction of justice," and thus uniformed troops with helmets and rifles appeared in Little Rock amid an Eisenhower presidency that, as we will see later, was bent on overcoming such martial iconographies.[3]

It was an extraordinary measure, one—as Eisenhower explained in a televised address the evening of September 24—that had everything to do with the repair of "the image of America." Little Rock was doing a "tremendous disservice . . . to the nation in the eyes of the world." It was, he continued "difficult to exaggerate the harm that is being done to the prestige and influence, and indeed to the safety, of our nation and the world."[4] In the black-and-white images of racial hatred coming out of Little Rock, we were witnessing, Eisenhower suggested, an American crisis of global proportions, as all Cold War crises involving the "image of America" would be.

Of course, Eisenhower was right to see in the images of violence against Elizabeth Eckford and other activists a challenge to the image of America. He was wrong, however, to claim to be able to speak for its authenticity. It had been sewn from the bottom up, so to speak, and there its authenticity would be arbitrated. The pictures Eisenhower and countless others saw were "image events," but ones fashioned out of years of struggle for civil rights and recognition.[5] When Eckford put on that checked black-and-white dress, she offered it, and herself, as a kind of image of America. Reflecting on its significance, political philosopher Danielle Allen has written,

> The dress reports on the gap between ideals and actualities, and also on the importance of symbols to the efforts of democratic citizens to deal with that gap. Although her fellow citizens across the country did not, Elizabeth knew that the integration of the public school system would require a made-from-scratch reweaving of the relationships among citizens. When she made the dress, she expressed the autonomy of the democratic citizen who desires to be sovereign and to effect new political orders but also must confess her own disempowerment. She had at her disposal the means to reconstitute not the "fabric" of society but only her daily uniform, and hers alone.[6]

Lest we retroactively romanticize the moment, it needs to be said that the spitting, the shouting, the slurs and shoving—all frozen in the chemistry of film—were also expressions of citizens seeking to effect, or at least protect, a social and political order. These were also images of America. Indeed, none of this was accidental. Here we had the black-and-white tapestry of America woven in discordant threads. The result was a crisis that, as Hannah Arendt suggested in her immodest essay "Reflections on Little Rock," challenged the legitimacy of the entire "political and historical framework of the Republic."[7]

It is little wonder that Eisenhower, trying to manage the ideology of the Cold War and offer to the world a new look at America, saw in these images an attack on the image of America. His militaristic intervention in Little Rock was decided upon, very likely *only* decided upon, against this backdrop. Enemies of America, he claimed in his televised speech announcing his intentions to intervene, were seizing upon the discordant images of racial strife to "misrepresent our whole nation." Therefore, extraordinary emergency measures were necessary: a man, the president, would authorize another man, the secretary of defense, to send military men to Central High School so that it might be "demonstrated to the world that we are a nation in which laws, not men, are supreme." The logic here, though purportedly liberal and democratic, was Hobbesian and authoritarian. Indeed, Eisenhower retold the Hobbesian story in his televised address: "Unless the President did so, anarchy would result. There would be no security for any except that which each one of us could provide for himself."[8] Thus Eisenhower would offer to the world his own accidental image of America: the troops of the 101st Airborne escorting children to school (fig. 2).

FIGURE 2. Troops from the 101st Airborne escort the Little Rock Nine to school.

As the United States' first "total cold war" president, Eisenhower was caught historically and ideologically between two different political logics regarding the image of America, and the image more generically.[9] The first, what I will refer to as a liberal logic, takes the image seriously as a locus of political meaning and therefore invests a great deal of energy (even if that energy seems futile) in its production and control. The second, what I will refer to as a neoliberal logic, insists that too much meaning engenders political crises.[10] This neoliberal logic therefore critiques, even attacks, the role of the image in political life. In this chapter, I sketch out a typology of these two political logics by considering their respective theories of "legitimation crisis," for it is the question of political legitimacy, more than any other single question, that motivates the differences between the liberal and neoliberal political logics that I explore in this book.

Liberal and Neoliberal Legitimation Crises

In addition to neoliberalism, the cluster of political and economic phenomena that began to unfold in dramatic fashion in the 1970s—among them the breakdown of the Bretton Woods system of global monetary management, the rise of free markets as an ideological centerpiece in the discipline of economics, the political push for deregulation, an increasing global division of labor, the decline of unions, the minimization of substantive institutional investments by corporations, and corporate diversification—has been discussed under notions of advanced capitalism, late capitalism, globalization, reflexive modernity, and even postmodernism. Neoliberalism and its kin have been the subject of numerous analyses, ranging from those looking at the breakdown of the postwar liberal international system, to those concerned with the withering of the welfare state and social democracies, those about the dissolution of established cultures and traditional social institutions, and even those reflecting on the evaporation of the notion of history itself.[11] Moreover, there have been numerous attempts to define *neoliberalism*, a matter that I addressed in the introduction to this book. A common theme running through all these terminologies and analyses, however, is what Jürgen Habermas called in 1973— but two years after the "Nixon shock" and the same year as the fateful Arab oil boycott—the "legitimation crisis."[12]

In Habermas's view, the road to legitimation crises begins as the state, an administrative apparatus, expands the scope of its activities in order to serve the private goal of capitalist profit maximization by managing, in Keynesian fashion, the economy. But this expansion does not overcome the tensions and contradictions of a class-based society. Hence, met with its inevitable failures, the state appears as overreaching, unable to manage the demands it has assumed. As a consequence, it attempts "ideology planning"—the management of meaning in order to maintain legitimacy. But, as Habermas writes, "There is no administrative production of meaning."[13] That is, the sort of substantive meaning that lends legitimacy to government is derived, in Habermas's view, from culture (in a kind of bottom-up manner), not bureaucracies, and culture is "peculiarly resistant to administrative control."[14] Consequently, the state's effort to win legitimacy for itself through the management of meaning in ideology and symbol is "self-defeating."[15] At the same time, advanced capitalist societies tend to erode the cultural traditions that lent legitimacy to the state in the first place. Hence, advanced capitalist societies fall into legitimation difficulties, indicative of an even more basic "motivation crisis."[16] Capitalist interests, in turn, approach this crisis as a short-term opportunity to be exploited.

The legitimation crises of late capitalism that Habermas describes are rooted in the state's administrative overreach in the name of protecting profits, together with the erosion of traditional cultural forms of meaning under the joint pressures of rationalization and the irrational quest for unlimited capital expansion. The state ever tries to compensate for the thinning of meaning, but its efforts are seen through, which only compounds the state's legitimation difficulties. Economic metrics and language, Habermas suggests, represent an effort to compensate for the attenuation of political institutions with economic mechanisms:

We have seen now that the state cannot simply take over the cultural system, and that expansion of the areas of state planning actually makes problematic matters that were formally culturally taken for granted. "Meaning" is a scarce resource and is becoming ever scarcer. Consequently, expectations oriented to use values—that is, expectations monitored by success—are rising in the civil public. . . . The fiscally siphoned-off resource "value" [via taxes and expenditures] must take the place of the scanty resource "meaning." Missing legitimation must be offset by rewards conforming to the system. A legitimation crisis arises as soon as the demands for such rewards rise faster than the available quantity of value, or when expectations arise that cannot be satisfied with such rewards.[17]

That in the 1970s and especially the 1980s dominant forms of social science abandoned an institutional framework and replaced it with theories of the market is one indication of this broader legitimation crisis.[18] We might also look to the advent of the "post-bureaucratic organization," deliberately designed to replace traditional state and corporate bureaucracies with a flat, free-floating network of contractors, temporary workers, and managers tasked with measuring and monitoring organizational efficiency according to a market paradigm.[19] Indeed, the *market*, the god-term of neoliberalism, systematically as well as ideologically excludes from relevance not only political institutions, but a wide range of social structures. Instead, we are presented only with individuals (even corporate "individuals" in the United States!) acting in abstract exchange systems, and the occasional appearance of the state operating in an autocratically declared state of emergency to preserve or create markets. In this new, market-driven order, as Margaret Thatcher infamously declared, "there is no such thing as society."[20] It is arguable, as well, that there is within its confines no such thing as meaning, at least not meaning generated through representation.

Habermas offered in 1973 a poignant account of the legitimation difficulties felt by late twentieth-century advanced capitalist societies. Yet, several decades earlier the story of legitimation crisis had been told differently, and in fact far more effectually, by Friedrich Hayek. This neoliberal account of legitimation crisis not only differed from Habermas's liberal one, but also anticipated the cultural-political logic that began to take hold in the 1970s in the United States.

In the mid-1940s, as war was wrecking Europe, Hayek wrote a book warning socialist intellectuals in Great Britain (where he had been teaching at the London School of Economics) of the dangers of extending Britain's planned war economy into the postwar period. Published by the University of Chicago Press, *The Road to Serfdom* gained startling traction in the United

States, traction that left even Hayek surprised. When the editors of *Reader's Digest*, the most widely circulated magazine in America, read the book, they promptly published a condensation of the text as the lead article in their April 1945 issue.[21] The condensation—more of a re-creation of Hayek's text than a mere weaving of excerpts—was sent to newsstands as Hitler's forces were crumbling in Europe. This gave *Reader's Digest* editors room to turn their sights on the threat of Soviet Russia.[22] Indeed, the *Reader's Digest* version of *The Road to Serfdom* stressed "the extraordinary similarity in many respects of the conditions under 'communism' and 'fascism.'"[23] The magazine told its readers, "The question is whether we should create conditions under which the knowledge and initiative of individuals are given the best scope so that they can plan most successfully; or whether we should direct and organize all economic activities according to a 'blueprint,' that is, 'consciously direct the resources of society to conform to the planners' particular views of who should have what.'"[24] *Reader's Digest's* condensation was so successful that the magazine quickly found itself facing requests for more than one million reprints of the article, many of them ordered by corporate and political crusaders against the New Deal.

Earlier that year, *Look* magazine offered a cartoon version of *The Road to Serfdom*, which General Motors, led by Eisenhower's future secretary of defense, Charles Wilson, would reprint and disseminate as part of their "Thought Starter" series of publications. The *Look* version departed far enough from Hayek's original text that it hardly merited the same title. Nevertheless, it did present the outlines of a popularized version of the neoliberal account of legitimation crisis that Hayek articulated. Hayek had argued in *The Road to Serfdom* that the path to totalitarianism passes from the "will of the people" through a technocratic regime that progressively morphs into an autocratic one:

> It may be the unanimously expressed will of the people that its parliament should prepare a comprehensive economic plan, yet neither the people nor its representatives need therefore be able to agree on any particular plan. The inability of democratic assemblies to carry out what seems to be a clear mandate of the people will inevitably cause dissatisfaction with democratic institutions. Parliaments come to be regarded as ineffective "talking shops," unable or incompetent to carry out the tasks for which they have been chosen. The conviction grows that if efficient planning is to be done, the direction must be "taken out of politics" and placed in the hands of experts—permanent officials or independent autonomous bodies.[25]

In Hayek's original account, this autocratic, technocratic regime—in contrast with what Habermas would argue—*could* in fact win legitimacy through something like the administrative production of meaning. Propaganda, ora-tory, rallies, party pamphlets, and so forth could win broad assent among the people. (For Hayek, the capacity of the state to produce such meaning was seemingly affirmed both by fascism and by the war efforts of the Allies.)

In this respect, it is significant that the story in *Look* followed Hayek's logic quite closely, beginning not with the state's efforts to mediate capital-ist accumulation but with war. "War forces 'national planning,'" the account began. Thus, "you gladly surrender many freedoms" to planners who are put in power to regulate and regiment the war economy. However, as the planners go about their work, they come to cherish their power, encouraging its exten-sion beyond the war's end. They offer through wartime propaganda utopian visions of a postwar planned economy, and campaign to have politicians elected into office who will support those postwar plans. Yet, the planners soon find that they cannot themselves agree on any single plan, let alone a vi-sion for society. Therefore, they begin to vie for power. Citizens likewise fight over plans and policies, joining special interest groups to push for programs planned to serve their own interests over those of others.

Here begins a legitimation crisis of the order Habermas would later de-scribe, as planners, being in *Look*'s words "well-meaning idealists," are reluc-tant to force their plans through. They therefore begin to piece together a "patchwork plan" in the vain hope that they might establish a planned econ-omy that could satisfy most, if not all, citizens and interest groups. However, the patchwork plan, because it is so broken, requires an extra measure of per-suasion, leading the planners to make use of "a giant propaganda machine." The propaganda machine soon comes under the control of a party, and the party grows through it and "by fiery oratory" into a powerful force, one that captivates the imaginations of the "least educated" and "gullible." Meanwhile, the economy falls into shambles, and "everybody suffers." In an act of "des-peration," the planners "authorize the new party leader to hammer out a plan and force its obedience [*sic*]." The party and its leader assume authoritarian power. Soon they identify a "scapegoat minority" on which to blame social and economic ills and "inflame the majority." Opposition to the party is now "suicide," and "all freedom is gone." The planned economy has become a to-talitarian state, one that plans—as *Look* offered in a succession of frames—"your profession, . . . your wages, . . . your thinking, . . . your recreation," and, ultimately, "your disciplining."[26]

Of course, this dystopian scene of the totalitarian state, however cartoon-ish, had in general form, if not in exact detail, a real-world parallel in Nazi Germany—as *Look* recalled through its drawings of a Führer-like figure (fig. 3). Habermas too was profoundly aware of this historical possibility, seeing the

FIGURE 3. *Look* magazine's cartoon version of *The Road to Serfdom*, produced without Hayek's consultation, features a Hitler-like figure in command of the crowd.

totalitarian state as one possible perverse outcome of legitimation crises. But the Hayekian neoliberal account differed from the Habermasian liberal one in two significant respects.

First, in beginning with a state of war, the neoliberal version aligned the state with necessity (that seventeenth-century basis for the *raison d'état*). In a Hobbesian manner, a state of war forces the state to establish a planning regime—or, as the case might be, forces the establishment of an extraordinarily strong state. Importantly, the neoliberal account offered by Hayek did not refute this necessity. While it may be true that, as Hayek's biographer Bruce Caldwell writes, "Hayek's message was to be wary of . . . martial invocations," Hayek nevertheless strongly associated the powers of the state with the powers of waging war.[27] Indeed, his anxieties about the expansion of the state grew in part out of this association. Caldwell writes, "His specific fear was that, for a war to be fought effectively, the power and size of the state must grow. No matter what rhetoric they employ, politicians and the bureaucracies over which they preside love power, and power is never easily surrendered once the danger, if there ever was one, has passed."[28] But while Hayek *began* where Hobbes did with a state of war, he did not end with a Leviathan. Rather, he constructed an anti-Leviathan philosophy by associating war with politics rather than nature.

It is, Hayek maintained, the *artificial*, planned, and intentional quest for power that leads to social conflict both within a society and among societies. "Democracy," he would argue in *The Constitution of Liberty* (1960), "is the only method of peaceful change that man has yet discovered."[29] But "democracy is not yet liberty," he continued, and should not be the only, and not even the primary, means of social order in liberal societies, for democracy is itself the source of a myriad of social crises.[30] Rather, Hayek argued we should turn to economy, a "spontaneous order."[31] This unplanned order paradigmatically circumvents social conflict by replacing such conflict—whether of the violent sort or the democratic sort—between humans who have "plans" with market competition regulated by impersonal, spontaneous forces.[32]

Thus Hayek added to the dialectic between the state of war and artificial political power a third order—what he would at one point term the "cosmic" order (rather than "natural," the former to "convey a sense of admiration and awe"), which he strongly associated with a free-market economy.[33] Hayek thus had a far more benign view of "nature" or "cosmos" than did Hobbes, one that was in a certain sense reminiscent of Lockean and later eighteenth-century British senses of the state of nature, where humans were envisioned as being naturally social.[34] But though Hayek was fond of citing "British philosophers," his sense of a cosmic social order was more organicist, even romantic, than that of these philosophers, and certainly more informed by social evolutionism. Of Smith, David Hume, and Adam Ferguson, Hayek wrote, "They find the origin of institutions . . . not in contrivance or design, but in the survival of the successful." Thus, "what we call political order is much less the product of our ordering intelligence than is commonly imagined." Civilization has "evolved by a process of cumulative growth" quite apart from human reason and intentionality.[35]

But neoliberals like Hayek and Milton Friedman (at least the Friedman of the 1951 "Neo-Liberalism and Its Prospects") explicitly differed from their nineteenth-century laissez-faire predecessors in arguing for the state to play an intentional "police" role in maintaining conditions conducive to the spontaneous order of "the survival of the successful." Moreover, as they were writing on the heels of the Great Depression, they argued that the government could legitimately intervene in situations of "acute misery and distress," as long as it did not interfere with free-market alternatives.[36] Thus neoliberals contrasted their thinking with nineteenth-century laissez-faire thought by giving the state a well-defined, legitimate role as a protector of market forces and as a corrective power in situations of great social crisis. But the state must be limited to these roles; otherwise, it would be tempted to overreach, creating legitimation crises. In this neoliberal account, one form of legitimation crisis occurs when the methods and norms of the state police function—necessarily expanded in a state of emergency—are falsely and unnecessarily amplified in a state of relative normalcy. This was Hayek's worry in *The Road to Serfdom*: the warfare state morphs into a totalitarian state. A second form of legitimation crisis occurs when democratic constituencies, fueled by their special interests, demand that the state use its artificial mechanisms to meet desires left unsatisfied by the spontaneous market order. This would be Hayek's pronounced worry in the 1970s: that the welfare state would morph into an autocratic state serving select constituencies.[37] In either case, government extends its artificial order into realms reserved for spontaneous, evolutionary, and unplanned social order. In both cases, the state crosses the line of legitimacy. As Hayek summarized, "Government therefore owes its authority and has a claim to the allegiance of citizens *only* if it maintains the foundations of that spontaneous order on which the working of society's everyday life rests."[38] Within the parameters of legitimacy, the state was thus restricted to policing and emergency functions.

The second way in which the neoliberal account of the legitimation crisis differed from the Habermasian one has to do with the question of meaning. Hayek in *The Road to Serfdom*, and *Reader's Digest* and *Look* in their condensations, located the specific source of the totalitarian threat not in the contradictions of capitalism but in the inherent instabilities of parliamentary democracy and the consequent threat of the *overproduction of meaning*. While for Habermas, legitimation crises would be rooted in the state's inability to effectively produce meaning, despite its best propagandistic efforts, the neoliberal account worried about producing *too much* meaning, together with the inability of citizens to see through it. That is, it worried—to use the terminology on which I elaborate in chapter 2—about *idolatry*. *Look*'s cartoonish rendering of *The Road to Serfdom* made the point graphically, portraying a citizen surrounded by party propaganda, unable to get outside of it, let alone see through it. Here citizens end up in a posture of reverence, even worship (fig. 4). In a similar way, Hayek's original text wove together a tale of the overdetermination of meaning, as a myriad of sources, from the popular press to political prejudice and state propaganda, threaten to put "politics over economics" and planning over markets.[39] Hayek argued in *The Road to Serfdom* that late nineteenth-century liberal societies, too anxious to achieve the progress liberalism had set in motion, began lose faith in "the basic tenets of liberalism" and sought instead to engineer solutions to social problems by "collective and 'conscious' direction of all social forces to deliberately chosen

FIGURE 4. *Look* magazine's cartoon version of Hayek's *The Road to Serfdom* shows a "citizen" bowing before a *führer*-like figure.

goals,"[40] so that "the eyes of the people became fixed on the new demands" and, indeed, on new idols.[41]

Here again Hayek worried about the artificial. Whereas Habermas took the artificiality and arbitrariness of political order as *reason* for democratic deliberation—"Legitimacy means that there are good arguments for a political order's claim to be recognized as right and just"—Hayek found in the artificial and arbitrary character of political order reason for prioritizing nondeliberative, a priori market principles over parliamentary democratic processes. The market, he argued, unlike politics, is natural, spontaneous, impersonal, anonymous, and "blind."[42]

The problem of *vision* was at the center of Hayek's concern with meaning and critique of deliberative politics, as it was in Walter Lippmann's *The Good Society*. "It is impossible," Hayek argued, for planners "to gain a synoptic view" of all the relevant facts entailed in ordering a society economically.[43] Deliberation regarding the future entailed for Hayek the assumption, severely problematic, that planners could imagine particular social ends and the specific means to those ends. Thus the problem with most policy and nearly all planning, and therefore with any elevation of politics over economics in society, was, in this neoliberal account, inseparable from the limits of the imagination and, indeed, of the *image*—we cannot "picture" social processes.

This was true even for the economist, perhaps especially so. In his famous essay "The Methodology of Positive Economics," Milton Friedman would argue that every economic theory necessarily amounts to a "false image of reality."[44] It is impossible, Friedman argued, for even the economist to see economic processes as they exist in reality. Thus, he or she must knowingly construct false images of such processes and continuously expose them, negatively, to "repeated failure to be contradicted."[45] Economic hypotheses are tools for inquiry rather than representations of reality, he argued. They have use value, but they lack any substantive representational value. They are—again using the terminology I introduce in chapter 2—mere *tokens*. If we confuse them with icons—that is, representations of a reality—we find ourselves beholden to dogmatisms rather than reality. Friedman wrote of Alfred Marshall, "Marshall took the world as it is: he sought to construct [through economic theory] an 'engine' to analyze it, not a photographic reproduction of it."[46]

Therefore, far more than an argument pertaining to the relationship of politics to economics, Hayek and Friedman found in the limits of the powers of imagination the basis of economic science and, more broadly, a comprehensive, non-egoistic philosophy of individualism. To quote Hayek,

> This is the fundamental fact on which the whole philosophy of individualism is based. It does not assume, as is often asserted, that man is egoistic or selfish or ought to be. It merely starts from the indisputable fact that the limits of our powers of imagination make it impossible to include in our scale of values more than a sector of the needs of the whole society, and that, since, strictly speaking, scales of value can exist only in individual minds, nothing but partial scales of values exist—scales which are inevitably different and often inconsistent with each other.[47]

The market, via such spontaneous mechanisms as the price system and the division of labor, represents a means of social order that does not depend on vision, but on invisible forces. Any claim to picture social forces is illegitimate. Schumpeter also suggested that economics—in theory and practice—offers reliable mechanisms of *motion* (e.g., hypotheses and laws), but none of *representation*.[48]

Hence, Hayek suggested that the need for legitimation was itself, in an important sense, a problem. A society preoccupied with the question of legitimacy is a society as yet unconverted to the particular power of "impersonal and anonymous social processes" to bring its own distinct form of social order to the world.[49] Thus legitimacy was for Hayek, as for Hobbes and Habermas, an "artificial" problem; but for Hayek, unlike the latter two thinkers, this artificiality meant that legitimacy was a problem to be triumphed over rather than simply lived with as an integral feature of political society. Whereas

Habermas would argue that "it is realistic to speak today of legitimation as a permanent problem," Hayek saw it in important respects as an artificial problem and thus one to be overcome.[50]

Contrasting Hayek's position with that of John Rawls helps make even clearer the neoliberal approach to legitimation crises. Rawls's sense of social justice in *A Theory of Justice* applies to social institutions explicitly *designed*, including markets. A Rawlsian legitimation crisis would have the form of real or perceived rule-breaking when those in positions of social authority fail to or appear to fail to adhere to the principles of justice-as-fairness derived from the "original agreement" of a liberal society and built into the design of social institutions. Those principles, Rawls argues, have principally a "pure procedural" character; they are concerned not with specific, planned outcomes but with the construction of fair processes that can vouch for the justice of an outcome, whatever it is, by virtue of the fact that it was carried out fairly.[51] As others have noted, there are striking similarities between Hayek and Rawls in this emphasis on the justness of processes, procedures, or mechanisms, irrespective of outcomes; however, what separates the two is their respective stances toward the artificial character of society. Rawls's theory accepts on a fundamental level the artificial character of social institutions, rendering them problematic only insofar as they fail to meet the criteria of justice; Hayek, as I have argued, sees in the artificiality of society a threat to the very idea of justice. To put the matter a different way, Rawls sees the problem as one of how to design a just society, arguing, for example, with utilitarian theories only about the means and ends of such design, not about the need for design per se. Hayek sees the basic problem as the design of society itself, arguing for spontaneous order as an alternative.[52]

Democratic Vistas?

When Eisenhower considered the images of Elizabeth Eckford and the angry mobs in Little Rock, he found his "free enterprise" wishes for American race relations being challenged—we might even say *attacked*—by the performances of racial animosity and injustice in the American south. It was a problem to be overcome in an emergency policing manner. While Eisenhower was hardly a consistent neoliberal, his approach to the Little Rock crisis reverberated with the basic assumptions and arguments of the neoliberal theory of legitimation crisis then being developed: Little Rock was producing too much meaning— meaning that was itself determined at least in part by what Eisenhower probably thought was the overreach of government in social affairs vis-à-vis the Supreme Court. Little Rock was therefore creating a crisis *for* government, but one—importantly—derived as much from its effects on the image of America as from tensions in federal-state relations. Finally, though for Eisenhower the role of the federal government was at best murky with respect to racial injustice, it could unequivocally assume a policing function amid what was for the president a national emergency, if only an emergency resulting from the overproduction of meaning. At the same time, however, Eisenhower recognized in a much more liberal vein that part of what was at issue in Little Rock was the image of America, and that politics—or at least *geo*politics—would be contested in and through images. He was thus caught, as the liberal democratic tradition more generally has been, between iconophilic and iconoclastic politics.

Legitimacy is a *political* problem, and thus an *image* problem. "Only political orders can have and lose legitimacy; only they need legitimation," Habermas wrote. "Multinational corporations or the world market are not capable of legitimation."[53] Hayek's, and then Friedman's, and later Alan Greenspan's, respective concerns with replacing state mechanisms with market machines were part of the broader attempt to replace political orders with economic ones—and thus to remedy legitimation crises by narrowing the sphere of the political, which was inseparable, for these thinkers, from the scope and power of the state. This neoliberal project entailed shifting the social from the artificial to the natural (or "cosmic," as Hayek would put it), from the domain of the visible to that of the invisible, and from the domain of the beautiful to that of the sublime. In neoliberalism, we are met not so much with a conspiracy to protect the ineffable, but to assert, and indeed in some sense institute, the ineffable. This cannot but be an attempt to overcome politics—not the least, democratic politics.

It would therefore be nice to set neoliberalism over and against democracy and leave it at that. Neoliberalism would simply be the antidemocratic bugaboo. But this would misrepresent the situation, both historically and in the present. Neoliberalism—to recall the Hayek's organicism—grew out of the soil of liberal democracies. Thus, in important respects we must return to liberal democracy in considering its constitution, seeing it as a problem *within* larger liberal democratic and republican traditions. As we do, we find that neoliberalism has an equivocal relationship to liberal democracy. On the one hand, it represents a strong critique of deliberative democratic politics, but on the other hand it represents the realization of a certain liberal democratic desire for direct participation within the social forces that give order to our lives. Here again I think the *image* constitutes a pivotal point of contestation.

If in liberal democracies political legitimacy is to be in some sense derived from the people, it follows that the people must be able to *see* the political powers they authorize. Whether or not they see truly, accurately, or well is a secondary consideration. First they must be able to see. Therefore, it is a commonplace that publicity and representation are crucial to democratic political culture. *Publicity* here entails making things appear before the sight of citizens *qua* citizens. Its most basic form is what the ancient Greeks called *epideixis,* a kind of "showing forth" or "display," as distinguished from *apodeixis,* or logical demonstration—hence the difference between "public demonstration" and "mathematical demonstration."[54] (Margaret Thatcher purportedly once said "publicity is the oxygen of terrorism." What this statement altogether fails to consider is the fact that publicity is also the oxygen of liberal democratic societies. Terrorism is in this sense a parasitic phenomenon, seeking to kill that which feeds it. But Thatcher was also an enemy of publicity.)

Representation, as Frank Ankersmit has shown, is a subtler concept. Though we might think of it simply as making present that which is absent, this can be done in an array of contexts (e.g., political, semiotic, and artistic), through a variety of media (e.g., spoken or written words, paint, film, or governmental mechanisms), and according to distinct logics—most significantly what Ankersmit presents as "mimetic" versus "aesthetic" theories of representation. In mimetic political representation, "the representation of the people should reflect the people represented as accurately as possible."[55] On the other hand, aesthetic representation less mimics and more re-presents, substituting for that which is represented.[56] This substitution is inevitably imperfect; it is "broken," part of a political world "whose components are as irreducible to each other as a painting and what it depicts."[57] But it is nevertheless a legitimate representation, having a kind of metaphorical or analogical relationship to that which is being represented.

We can see from this distinction already just how much is at stake with regard to representation. When we speak of political representation, we often tend implicitly toward a mimetic conception of representation. We expect political representatives to reflect as accurately as possible the will of the people.[58] When they do not, they may get voted out; when they do not consistently and systematically, a legitimation crisis of one sort or another may occur. Indeed, because we tend to assume that political representation is mimetic, we may (with Habermas) see legitimacy as a permanent problem, since everywhere in liberal democratic societies representatives fail to live up to our expectations with respect to the will of the people.

But if such mimetic, seamless representation is never achieved, perhaps we should reconsider the nature of political representation. Though political representation may aspire to the power we (somewhat wishfully) tend to attribute to the medium of the photograph, simply recording its subject matter, Ankersmit suggests that its power is far more like that we attribute to painting, which re-presents its subject matter in a qualitatively different aspect. "We can only talk about [political] representation when there is a difference—and *not* an identity—between the representative and the person represented," Ankersmit writes.[59] But even in this "broken" world of political representation, a great deal is at stake. The question may no longer be framed in terms of accuracy or comprehensiveness, but it will nevertheless concern fidelity. If we follow Ankersmit in using the analogy of painting, we may ask to what degree the artist was faithful to her subject without asking at the same time to what degree she realistically mimicked it.

Legitimacy is thus, at a minimum, an *aesthetic* problem.[60] As such, a legitimation crisis will entail a crisis of the image, for the image is the paradigmatic form of representation. The image, in its broadest conception, is "any likeness, figure, motif, or form that appears in some medium or another."[61] It is not that there are no other means of public political representation—for example, statistical evidence or logical demonstration; it is that these other forms gain their public weight from the gravitational field of visual display. Again, the notion of political legitimacy assumes that the people must somehow be able to see the political powers they authorize.

Therefore, the legitimacy of the image, in a generic sense, is a condition *sine qua non* for democratic politics—and, arguably, for any sort of politics. A discourse that challenges this condition is a discourse that comes very near to challenging the political as such. Neoliberalism has done just this: its theory is premised on the inadequacy of any image, whether mimetic or aesthetic, to represent social processes. In Hayek's theory, this is at root a claim made on psychological and epistemological grounds.[62] In Friedman's approach, it is made more narrowly on methodological grounds.[63] Both of these enormously influential free-market advocates rested their case not precisely, as has often been assumed, on a dogmatic theory of limited government but on more sophisticated claims regarding the impossibility of representing social processes and future scenarios. Both therefore argued for the inherently false character of all images of society and its operations.

We might add a third category to Ankersmit's distinction between mimetic and aesthetic theories of representation. Anticipating a notion I discuss further in the next chapter, we can call it a *token* theory of representation, indeed of *non*-representation, where the image has an altogether accidental and arbitrary relationship to that which we might mistake for being represented. The function of the image here is not to represent a reality at all, but strictly to serve some pragmatic purpose, whether noble or base. It would be an "engine," rather than a "photograph." It has use value but no substantive representational value. We are already familiar with this phenomenon in language, which does not typically generate meaning, at the semantic level at least, through the mechanism of representation—even "broken" representation—but through repeated use ("meaning is use," Wittgenstein said). Here, the non-representational nature of the language enhances rather than undermines its efficiency. Similarly, Friedman argued that the hypotheses of economic science functioned in the same non-representational but still powerful manner, never positively related to economic processes, only negatively refuted through repeated predictive falsification. Economic hypotheses and assumptions remain valid as long as they are useful, or (better) as long as they are not repeatedly found to be useless.[64]

The neoliberal project relies on a token theory of non-representation. Here, images are not absent; indeed, they can be everywhere. But they are, as Nicholas Mirzoeff has observed more generally, typified by a *banality*: "Images ceased to be the subject of substantive debate."[65] Nevertheless, they are *useful* as fuel for theoretical and indeed economic engines. Friedman's argument regarding the inherent falsity but limitless usefulness of economic theories with respect to economic science echoes the function of money in a capitalist economy and now the function of "big data." In each case, representation is not the issue; rather, it is efficiency within economic or epistemic engines. If, as Ankersmit argues, the political is dependent on representation, the economic (both in theory and practice) offers the possibility of a non-representational social field.

Here we see the fraught character of neoliberalism. As I have suggested, and as I explore further in the following chapters, neoliberal discourse is a *political* discourse not only in its content but also in its form. It is aggressively mimetic in Ankersmit's sense, accounting for a wide array of social, technical, economic, and political phenomena according to a singular algorithm: that of *drawing identities*. Neoliberal discourse thus relies on the image both as a medium and mechanism of propagation. At the very same time, it challenges the legitimacy of the image as a medium of representation within the broader construction of social order, asserting instead the primacy of an invisible, perhaps even ineffable, economic order.

It is not accidental that liberal democratic culture has comprised the political context for neoliberalism's ascent. Liberal democracy has long been ambivalent about representation and thus about the image—an ambivalence related both to notions of direct democracy and to the rise of the economic as a distinct category for social thought. Today, there are significant ways in which certain democratic ideologies are invoked to underlie and energize neoliberalism, not the least a kind of romantic individualism of the self and a constitutionalism which, as James Tully has noted, is strangely Platonic in its quest for a "foundational, universal, and fixed background to democracy."[66] Moreover, as Nadia Urbinati and Mark Warren discuss, the Rousseauean democratic tradition has long been skeptical of representation, according it at best an instrumental (or token) status.[67] Rousseaueans and their kin would reject aristocratic intermediaries and tend to be suspicious of indirect discourse. They see democratic life as one where the *demos* must in some sense be present to itself, and where citizens participate directly in the social forces that determine their fates. Such Rousseauean perspectives thus sometimes strangely square with technocratic cynicism about democracy: both see real democracy as an imperfect but potent exercise in the manipulation of mass opinion, a practice that cannot be disassociated from integral discourses of a neoliberal age—advertising, marketing, public relations, and so forth—that at once frenetically deploy the image and deny the possibility of its representational fidelity.

Still, these tendencies of liberal democracy do not neatly harmonize it with the neoliberal project. To begin with, democracy is rooted in traditions and historic institutions designed by humans.[68] In this way, democracy cannot well sustain the fundamentally antitraditional and antihistorical evolutionary premises of neoliberalism, seen especially in the latter's peculiar brand of abstract individualism and market ideology. Democracy and neoliberalism are in tension not only in their respective approaches to tradition and history, but also in their orientation toward deliberation. Whereas neoliberalism ideally depends on the efficient operation of processes of exchange where all deliberation takes the form of free choice within a market context, democracy—even direct democracy—is a form of politics that depends on deliberation and debate.[69] That this is a truism does not make it any less true. It is precisely the deliberative aspect of democracy that neoliberalism attacks in attacking the representational fidelity of the image. In fact, democracy's detractors have long observed that the deliberative and "display" qualities of democracy seem to be of a piece. Hobbes, the great seventeenth-century antidemocrat, found in democracy's incessant contentiousness over public objects or images the cause of political upheavals, absurdities, aggressions, and fantasies. "In popular dominion," he protested, "there may be as many Neros as there are orators."[70] All speech was, for Hobbes, derived from sense and imagination, and produced the same.[71] In democracy, images are everywhere—in the form of what today might be called common visions, political imaginaries, or democratic vistas—and these images, Hobbes worried, stimulate political appetites, aggressions, and so on, until we end up in a civil war, maybe even another war of all against all.[72] This was, I suggested at the beginning of this chapter, the worry Eisenhower had amid the crisis at Little

Rock. The images of racial violence circulating in newspapers, magazines, and on newly bought televisions threatened to institute mob violence as the primary means of arbitrating social strife.

From the iconophilic perspective, however, images play a crucial role in bringing publics to look *at* and *beyond* complex processes of political vision and deliberation. In this vein, Robert Hariman and John Lucaites write of photojournalistic icons, "They are doing more than reproducing a structure of power. From an intermediate position within the social order, the icon provides a reflexive awareness of social forms and state actions that can lead to individual decisions and collective movements on behalf of democratic ideals."[73] As important, the image, in the generic sense I am invoking here, is critical to the discourse of justice, as it is only in and through representation that issues of political exclusion and inclusion, "voice" and power, equity and privilege can be contested. What Nancy Fraser writes of political representation traditionally conceived can be said of the role of the image in this most expansive sense within politics:

> Representation furnishes the stage on which struggles over distribution and recognition are played out. Establishing criteria of political membership, it tells us who is included, and who is excluded, from the circle of those entitled to a just distribution and reciprocal recognition. Specifying the reach of those other dimensions, representation enables us to pose the question of the frame. Thematizing boundary-making as a vehicle of exclusion, it points to yet another class of obstacles to justice: neither economic nor cultural, but political. Representation, accordingly, constitutes a third, political dimension of justice, alongside the (economic) dimension of redistribution and the (cultural) dimension of recognition.[74]

The image, like representation, is discrete, and this is one of its distinct political virtues. Inherently limited or bounded, the image allows us to consider questions of political justice or truth in terms of the frame. Images provide the discrete material of citizenship as objects about which and through which battles among political factions are fought, and around which the ongoing battle between ideological projection and critical reflection revolves.[75] Democracy is a political festival of display. Therefore, the conditions necessary for democracy to thrive would seem to include those needed for images to multiply. The image is the "first metaphor," the antidemocratic Nietzsche once said, thinking of all those appearances we meet with our eyes each day as primary vehicles of meaning.[76] In a democracy, they might well be the ultimate vehicles of meaning too, as it is through images that meanings are transferred, activated, sustained, or contested.

While I think the iconophiles have it right, I am less focused in this book on defending them than on exploring the fraught character of neoliberal discourse when it comes to the image and thus to politics. To put the matter boldly, though the age of market triumphalism may or may not be past, I think we remain today in important respects in the crosshairs of a contradiction with respect to the history of liberal democracy. Neoliberalism not only represents an effort to displace the political with the economic, but also carries forward an ideological iconoclasm familiar to liberal democracy itself, one where social and political institutions and their corresponding imaginaries are readily destroyed in deference to the invisible ideals. Neoliberal discourse not only generates distrust in cultural and political institutions, it also asserts more generally, and more importantly, that the meaning of politics and economy alike—or "political economy"—cannot truly be determined in the domain of image and imagination, but only in the realm of the unrepresentable.

What, then, of the destruction of the image? More precisely, what of the image of the destruction of the image? Such questions drive this book. As I consider relations among economy, technology, politics, ideology, and discourses of catastrophe, I home in on the problem of the image in a neoliberal order. More than arguing for a change in American political culture since the Zapruder film—an iconoclastic turn, a neoliberal turn—I am concerned with a social imaginary that is invested in invisible, unrepresentable orders. If scholars like Hariman and Lucaites have found in the image a wellspring of democratic culture, I'd ask: Can democracy survive the destruction of the image? It is a Hobbesian question for a Nietzschean world, a world where even language discards, dissolves, and destroys the image.[77]

The Iconoclastic Sublime

It has been fifty years now, and it is time to see Zapruder as an accomplice. For too long, he has been treated as a mere accessory, that Dallas business-man who showed up in Dealey Plaza on November 22, 1963, 8mm camera in hand, looking for a shot of the president. But that look contained an appetite, and while the appetite may have been naive, it was not innocent. It sought an image, an image to acquire, to store, to treasure—to possess like a jewel cut from the rock at some sacred spot in the Andes. Zapruder, like so many other Americans in the early 1960s, wanted the image, and wanted the im-age iconic. He wanted a visible representation of an invisible essence, some statuary figure to index a higher truth. Americans knew, of course, that the American way was superior to Soviet-style communism, to any form of com-munism for that matter. At least they thought they knew it. But wouldn't it be nice to see it, to find it manifest in a concrete and positive image, to stop searching for Eisenhower's vague "image of America" and to get a sign that seals the faith in certainty? So they built spaceships, and skyscrapers, and even a giant, multimillion-dollar steel arch on the banks of the Mississippi. And they elected a new president who, unlike his predecessor, could sit or stand, it didn't matter which, with a sterling smile next to a gloved wife with bouf-fant hair, together determined not only to remake the White House, but to remake America and America's image into an icon. Zapruder was right there with them, 8mm camera in hand, not just observant, but eager, even zealous.

He got far more than he expected, but not more than he wanted, or at least than his camera wanted. For if the image is wanted for what it cannot capture, if the camera wants not any image, but an icon, then the destruction of the icon is the perfect image. For destruction proves the point: what really matters can't be destroyed. Disaster vindicates spirit. If the material has a spiritual referent, then what could be more sublime proof of the supremacy of spirit over matter than a spirit that survives the destruction of its material icon? And so when Zapruder's camera turned toward the presidential motorcade that Dallas morning, it expected an image of an icon but got—tragically, ecstatically—all that it really wanted: the destruction of an icon. And, as if to set the value of iconoclastic image, upon acquiring it, Zapruder quickly nationalized it (even as he commodified it), selling all the rights to the film to *Life* for $150,000 within forty-eight hours of Kennedy's death.

Icons have long bid us to believe, to see in an image the reflection of a higher truth. Their suasive power has been sufficient to create concerns, anxieties, and antagonisms. Iconoclasts, however, have argued that the image is insufficient to the essence, that the fragment is truer than the icon, or at least more effective for communicating the truth. This debate, one for the ages, was reinvigorated in the post-1945 United States as cold warriors tried to shape the image of America at home and abroad, even as they put that image in grave jeopardy by means of a new, nuclear militancy.

Government, corporations, and private organizations often collaborated in the 1950s to produce icons of America. Everything from architecture to actors and appliances was used to symbolize the American spirit at home and abroad, creating a Cold War American culture that Beatriz Colomina has described as "enclosed by images."[1] Even so, Americans in the era sought the iconoclastic image just as much. "The sublime is now," Barnett Newman declared in 1948. "We are reasserting man's natural desire for the exalted, for a concern with our relationship to the absolute emotions. We do not need the obsolete props of an outmoded and antiquated legend. We are creating images whose reality is self-evident and which are devoid of the props and crutches that evoke associations with outmoded images, both sublime and beautiful. We are freeing ourselves of the impediments of memory, association, nostalgia, legend, myth, or what have you, that have been the devices of Western European painting."[2] But abstract expressionism was just the beginning of it. "Disaster," as Kevin Rozario writes of the era, "was now a media staple."[3] In the new mass media industries, spectacle sold. If America rose out of the ashes of World War II as a new global power, Americans, it seems, found in images of destruction and ruin a generative aesthetic, one that perhaps replayed for them their own Promethean fantasies. Thus, corporate cameras sought the iconoclastic image. *Life* magazine, the preeminent image-text of 1940s and 1950s America, made something of a market out of images of devastation, destruction, and disaster. Indeed, when the atomic bomb was dropped on Hiroshima, the magazine proclaimed it "the day men formally began a new epoch in their history," one where, like Prometheus, America would lift up "the worth and dignity of man" over "naked force."[4] And so an epochal image of violence and destruction, the mushroom cloud, came to signify not only the triumph of America, but the triumph of the human spirit.

There was a crucial Cold War message to be seen here—namely, that America is the land where spirit is the key to triumph. Thus Eisenhower, in his 1953 State of the Union address, told Americans that while the nation must be strong in arms and productivity, "We must be strong, above all, in the spiritual resources upon which all else depends." He explained: "We must be devoted with all our heart to the values we defend. We must know that each of these values and virtues applies with equal force at the ends of the earth and in our relations with our neighbor next door. We must know that freedom expresses itself with equal eloquence in the right of workers to strike in the nearby factory, and in the yearnings and sufferings of the peoples of Eastern Europe. As our heart summons our strength, our wisdom must direct it."[5] In a similar vein, social philosopher and commentator Will Herberg spoke for many Americans when he insisted that "only a transcendental faith that finds absolutes beyond the ideas, institutions, or allegiances of the world could meet the challenge of the demonic idolatry of communism without falling into idolatry itself."[6] America was the manifestation of absolute spirit, or the spirit of absolutes. But this meant that in an important respect America would be a kingdom divided against itself: for if everything depended upon spirit, what of all the postwar material, especially its Cold War militarism and consumptive materialism? Indeed, Americans seemed to want it both ways. They wanted icons: visible manifestations of invisible truths. But they also insisted that the essence of America could not be found in the proliferation of consumer goods and growing numbers of nuclear weapons.

In the next chapter I look at the circulation of the Zapruder film, reading it as an iconoclastic image by which America could be seen. I follow this up with considerations of Ronald Reagan's rhetorical response to the *Challenger* explosion, and CNN's coverage of September 11. In each instance, I argue, we are presented with an "icon of an iconoclasm." But this means that each was the expression of the convergence of two seemingly conflicting appetites, one iconic and the other iconoclastic. In this chapter, I consider the nature of these respective appetites in relation to each other. In an extension of the typological sketch begun in the previous chapter, I look at the iconic and iconoclastic appetites, especially as they came to be realized in the sublime. For if—as Newman, Herberg, Eisenhower, and Zapruder each suggested in their own idioms—the moment of the sublime in America is the *now*, then we would do well to reflect on the sublime.

Iconic and Iconoclastic Logics

Both the iconic and iconoclastic appetites are found at the intersections of image, politics, and theology. This is no place to delve into a thorough account of those intersections. Rather, I offer here a sketch of iconic and iconoclastic logics so as to suggest that when we address them, we are in fact approaching, in contests over the image, not only metaphysical matters but the very core of politics. For both the logic of the icon and that of its destruction entail claims about the relationship of power to representation.

To begin with the latter, iconoclasm, almost every theologically inspired iconoclast within Protestantism has begun with scripture, especially the prohibition against graven images: "And God spake all these words, saying, 'I am the LORD thy God, which have brought thee out of the land of Egypt, out of the house of bondage. Thou shalt have no other gods before me. Thou shalt not make unto thee any graven image, or any likeness of any thing that is in heaven above, or that is in the earth beneath, or that is in the water under the earth'" (Exodus 20:1–4, KJV). The logic of the command is significant. It does not, as might be assumed, reason Platonically, claiming that, because the being of God is immaterial and invisible, God must not be represented visibly. The biblical prohibition, that is, does not hinge on the essence of God in a metaphysical sense. Rather, the claim concerns power—indeed sovereignty: because God (*YHWH*) has liberated Israel from bondage to the Egyptians, Israel must not craft for themselves their own gods but worship *YHWH* only.

Indeed, in the theology of the Protestant Reformation, God could thus be the quintessential iconoclast. "God *hates* and is jealous of pictures," the sixteenth-century German protestant Andreas Karlstadt wrote.[7] Pictures, made by the mere hands of men, possess us with the desire to bow down and kneel. But "such honors"—such desire, devotion, reverence, respect—"belong to *me*," Karlstadt has God say.[8] Protestants like Karlstadt turned to other scriptures as their witness here: God, for example, declares in the Levitical proscription against idolatry, "I will destroy your high places, and cut down your images, and cast your carcases [*sic*] upon the carcases [*sic*] of your idols, and my soul shall abhor you" (Leviticus 26:30, KJV). Iconoclasm could thus be the performance of divine judgment, and divine judgment was a form of revelation. Iconoclasm, in the schema of Protestant theology, can therefore be approached as a species of apocalypse, or critical revelation.

But a critical revelation of what? To answer this question, we must first consider the significance of the icon. An icon is a likeness (Greek *eikôn* < *eikein*, "to be like"); therefore, it is an "image, figure, or representation," etched, cut, carved, painted, stamped, sketched, printed, exposed on film, or displayed electronically on a screen. But an icon may also be described, invoked, alluded to, and imagined. Thus, while in print an icon can be an illustration and in sculpture a crafted figure, in rhetoric it can be a vivid metaphor or description, and in semiotics, a sign that has a direct visual or logical relationship to that which it represents. And then there is the rather recent use of *icon* to mean a person or object that functions as a "representative symbol" of a history, a culture, a people, a movement, or an institution, especially one "considered worthy of admiration or respect."[9] Such an icon seemingly stands between artifact and archetype, material art and spiritual principle.

Theologians of the ninth-century Byzantine Empire tried to sort through similar possibilities by distinguishing among idols, tokens, and icons. Jaroslav Pelikan summarizes their schema as follows:

> An *idol* purports to be the embodiment of that which it represents, but it directs us to itself rather than beyond itself; idolatry, therefore, is the failure to pay attention to the transcendent reality beyond the representation. A *token*, on the other hand, does point us beyond itself, but it is an altogether accidental representation that does not embody what it represents. An authentic image, which came to be called *icon* in Greek and then in other languages, is what it represents; nevertheless, it bids us look at it, but through it and beyond it, to that living reality of which is an embodiment.[10]

The icon was thus not only a likeness, but also a representation, one that pointed beyond itself without thereby negating itself. Iconicity in the Byzantine Empire constituted a system of legitimate representation, circumscribed by illegitimate representations (the representational retardation of the idol, the arbitrariness of the token). The icon not only signified and revealed but also arbitrated or judged among images that could possibly claim to signify or reveal.

And this meant that iconic representation was a rhetoric, a means of suasion.[11] For the symbol, and the system of which it is a part, must be believed. The icon "bids us," to use Pelikan's language.[12] It bids us by heightening its own significance as a representation, dividing spirit from matter, and so establishing an ethos that entails as well an emotional appeal, or pathos, of respect for the icon's being and its being for others, both transcendent and immanent. Pope Gregory the Great's famous letter to Serenus (ca. 600) sought respect for the iconic representation: "What writing provides for people who read, paintings provide for the illiterate (*idiotis*); . . . paintings are books for those who do not know their letters."[13] Two centuries later, the Second Council of Nicaea (787) reinforced Gregory's argument for the legitimacy of icons by presenting them as rhetorics of desire: "Whenever they see through the impression of

icon, those who look at icons are led to the memory and desire of the pro-
totypes."[14] Indeed, everywhere in the Empire there were images appealing to
reason and appetite to teach, to move, and to delight.

If the icon is a rhetoric of legitimate representation—a means of both
revelation and arbitration—then iconoclasm is an attack on representation,
tout court, within a given domain. For iconoclasm does not merely redescribe
the icon as an idol or token. Such redescription can begin and end in speech
alone and is well within the legitimizing structure of the icon itself.[15] Iconoclasm does more than judge illegitimacy or inauthenticity. It entails an attack
not on the status of a particular icon, but on the logic and rhetoric of iconic
representation as such. Iconoclasm asserts the inability of a sign to point beyond itself without collapsing the signified into the being of the sign (idol), or
being merely an arbitrary sign (token). Indeed, *an iconoclastic cultural domain
leaves us only with a world of idols and tokens*. For iconoclasm holds that God
cannot be represented in an image, no matter how thoroughly regulated, and
still be respected. Iconoclasm is thus a critical revelation of the impossibility of
legitimate symbolic representation with respect to a given political, theological
domain. It is critical because it entails a judgment. It is a revelation because
it comes in the form of an unanticipated event. It reveals the impossibility of
legitimate symbolic representation because representation as such is under attack. And it concerns a political, theological domain because iconoclasm concerns the illegitimacy of any attempt to represent the sovereign power of God
in sensible form.

Thus, while sixteenth-century radical reformers like Karlstadt and Thomas
Müntzer, as well as more moderate reformers like Luther and Calvin, shared
a common theological concern about the false worship of images, the former
attacked religious images as such, whereas the latter merely sought to regulate
them.[16] Among Lutherans, for example, care was taken to exclude representations of Jesus from ecclesial spaces, including removing the figure of Jesus
from the cross, but Lutherans did not generally attack Church symbols as such.
Among Anabaptists and other radical reformers, especially later Calvinists,
concerns about misplaced reverence for and subservience to "graven images"
were transformed into theologically and politically motivated destructive acts
against "all the material culture of Christianity."[17] And here, in the violent attempt to overthrow orders of worship by assaulting the visible products of a
culture in the name of an invisible and immaterial order, we find a paradigmatic project not only of the Reformation, but of liberal modernity.

Both iconic and iconoclastic appetites have been formative for liberal democracies. The former is seen in the particular pressure that liberal societies
have put on political representation, above all through what Ankersmit has

identified as a pervasive assumption that representation should be mimetic—
that is, it should "reflect the people represented as accurately as possible."
Thus Ankersmit quotes John Adams's claim that political representation
"should be an exact portrait, in miniature, of the people at large, as it should
think, feel, reason and act like them."[18] Such mimetic political representation
is fundamentally iconic, in that the people, in looking to the representation
or representative, would be brought back to looking upon themselves and
so desire the democratic prototype through the medium of representation.
But liberal societies have looked to icons beyond political representation per
se. Nationhood, as Benedict Anderson has influentially argued, is imagined.[19]
It is thus frequently *imaged*; that is, it is given material form in representative
images—monuments, texts, spaces, seals, flags, presidents, soldiers, astronauts,
skyscrapers and so on—that bid us to look both *at* and *beyond* the prototypi-
cal ideas, values, or virtues that constitute the essence of the nation. Such representative images need not be designed to carry such rhetorical weight: they
can be adopted—we might even say anointed—by liberal cultures. Virginia's
Natural Bridge was adopted in the early nineteenth century as a representative symbol of a new American nationality, as was Alfred Eisenstaedt's "Times
Square Kiss" upon America's triumph in World War II.[20] Whether made to be
iconic or anointed as such, these icons, as Robert Hariman and John Louis Lucaites write of iconic photojournalistic images, "provide a basis for the reproduction of and critical reflection on public culture" as they circulate through
society. They thus offer means by which not only to see the nation, but to
worry about it, argue about it, and even re-imagine it.

   The iconoclastic appetite in liberal societies is aroused precisely at this
point. If every icon is potentially a point of contestation, then perhaps the
image should not be made to bear such weight. This, I suggested in the previous chapter, was at the very least an issue at play in Eisenhower's crisis at
Little Rock. It is also an aspect of what Hariman and Lucaites have described
as the "iconoclastic" suspicion of much liberal democratic theory with regard
to images, rooted in a "logocentrism" that implicitly or explicitly assumes
the superiority of the word over the image.[21] But while these iconoclasms are
rooted in worry and skepticism, a kind of distaste, there has been within liberal culture a more positive, or positively hungry, iconoclastic appetite that
took shape in the Enlightenment. The Enlightenment, as James Simpson argues (writing in the present tense so as to suggest the lasting significance of
its revolution) sees the image as a threat to its positive pursuit of reason and
order; it thus "neutralizes and commodifies images," through the invention
of the museum and the formal category of "Art," and more generally in a

"philosophical iconoclasm" preoccupied with ideology, "an idol that enthralls the naïve and that must be broken."[22] Thus the positive pursuit of a certain sort of truth—an Enlightenment-inflected universal, abstract, and absolute truth—drives a desire to get beyond the image and its apparent equivalent, ideology. No longer hostage to representation, this Enlightened society would be in full possession of its truths, having no need of iconic rhetorics other than as tokens to trade in the marketplace of cultural refinement or commodity pleasures.

Twice Destroying the Image

It is not only that, as Carlos Eire has written, in modernity "the religion of immanence was replaced by the religion of transcendence."[23] In addition, as the Enlightenment would reveal with great clarity, the crises of images in the sixteenth and seventeenth centuries concerned the status of symbolic representation—and mediation more generally—whether historical (Were history and tradition authoritative?), communicative (Can language be cleaned up and made more transparent?), or political (Is sovereignty to be dispersed among a demos that constitutes an administrative government, or is sovereignty contained within the absolute monarch?).[24] If iconoclasm was an attack on symbolic representation, we have seen since the Protestant Reformation an ongoing crisis of legitimate mediation.

But if the Reformation entailed theological crises with political purchase, modernity's crises have been political with theological undertones. As Alain Besançon has noted, here we come—almost inevitably, even if quite unexpectedly—to that which is, in the most technical sense, sublime about iconoclasm.[25] Indeed, in one of the most important technical accounts of the sublime ever written, that of Immanuel Kant in the *Critique of Judgment*, the logic of iconoclasm is clearly sublimated into a theory of the sublime. There we see the remarkable convergence of the iconic and iconoclastic appetites, as Kant begins with the desire for an image of the sublime, only to conclude that no such image is possible, thereby stimulating a desire for a superior faculty, that of reason. In Kant's sublime we have a kind of moving image that shows that it is impossible for an image to represent a destiny.

To see what is at stake in Kant's Enlightenment project, we need to begin with Edmund Burke's *A Philosophical Enquiry into the Origins of our Ideas of the Sublime and Beautiful* (1759), as this treatise not only left a powerful mark on Kant, but shows us an iconic logic inherent within neoclassical thinking about the sublime, a logic that was still rhetorical. Mary Wollstonecraft Shelley wrote of "the ideal and bold images that constitute the sublime."[26] Here she was following neoclassical criticism, especially the work of Nicolas Boileau-Despréaux, who saw literature principally in terms of vision and sought to *see* therein "esthetic truths."[27] So too sublimity, in Burke's modification of the neoclassical sublime, is founded in iconicity—that is, in the possibility of a representation of realities, especially ultimate realities like death or God, that is as direct as possible while still being mediated, and therefore a fiction. For example, of the effects of tragedy, which Burke closely couples to sublimity, he writes, "So it is certain, that it is absolutely necessary my life should be out of any immanent hazard before I can take a delight in the sufferings of others, real or imaginary."[28] What makes such "delight" possible in Burke's thinking is precisely the double movement we identified in the apprehension of the icon: the direct apprehension of an object or scene, and along with it the indirect apprehension of some greater reality or power. What Burke then explores in his study are the formal, circumstantial, and psychological conditions necessary for the most powerful iconic apprehensions one can conceive, which come down to "indirect" experiences of power that ultimately evoke the idea of God, or "direct" scenes of danger that evoke ideas of imminent death.[29]

Even so, Burke in his discussion of the sublime, like the reformers before him, never leaves the realm of political theology, nor does he attempt to. God is the ultimate power, and therefore sublime; God also has the power to execute death, and therefore a certain power over the sublime. Burke argues the same, in a kind of psychological transfer of powers, with regard to earthly political rulers, reminding his readers, "Sovereigns are frequently addressed with the title of dread majesty."[30] Nature, which constitutes a significant scene of the sublime for Burke, also is a locus of the godlike: "In the scripture," he writes, "wherever God is represented as appearing or speaking, everything terrible in nature is called up to heighten the awe and solemnity of the divine presence" (as if God needed nature to be terrifying).[31] Therefore, wherever Burke's liberal self, bent on its own preservation, finds itself—whether at sea, in the royal court, or in a cathedral—it may encounter an object of terror that fills the self with the apprehension of death or the divine, the decisive realities that, in Burke's view, ultimately prove the limits of the self's quest for its preservation and thus its need for political society.

The iconic—the art of simultaneously looking at and beyond an object—is therefore for Burke not just the foundation of the sublime, but the basis of what Ankersmit calls a "broken" view of politics, one that populates the political world with "representative symbols" even as it insists that their power is indirect and rhetorical, rather than immediate and literal.[32] Thus his harrowing protest against the French Revolution, published some thirty years

after his treatise on the sublime, condemns what he sees as the representational recklessness of the revolutionaries:

> But now all is to be changed. All the pleasing illusions, which made power
> gentle, and obedience liberal, which harmonised the different shades of life,
> and which, by bland assimilation, incorporated into politics the sentiments
> which beautify and soften private society, are to be dissolved by this new
> conquering empire of light and reason. All the decent drapery of life is to be
> rudely torn off. All the superadded ideas, furnished from the wardrobe of a
> moral imagination, which the heart owns, and the understanding ratifies, as
> necessary to cover the defects of our naked shivering nature, and to raise it to
> dignity in our own estimation, are to be exploded as a ridiculous, absurd, and
> antiquated fashion.[33]

It is not, as might be suspected, that Burke sees in the French Revolution the
transfer of politics from the realm of the beautiful to that of the sublime.
Rather, it is that he finds in revolutionary France a different sublime altogether, an iconoclastic sublime. Political icons were in revolutionary France
reduced to mere tokens and idols. The spirit of iconoclasm had prevailed, but
so did the sublime.[34]

If Burke presents an iconic foundation for the sublime, in his *Critique of
Judgment* Kant—who earlier, in his "precritical" phase, had written a small
treatise on the sublime and the beautiful to both imitate and correct Burke—
wrests the sublime from any lingering entanglements of neoclassicism and
re-founds it within the logic of iconoclasm.[35] Kant's "Analytic of the Sublime"
in the *Critique of Judgment* reads like a recapitulation of the radical reformers' iconoclastic theological tracts, save that the sublime takes the place of
the divine.[36] "We express ourselves incorrectly if we call any object of nature
sublime," he admonishes his readers.[37] "For no sensible form can contain the
sublime properly so-called."[38] In fact, Kant insists, the sublime is so precisely
as it transcends objective representation: "The feeling of the sublime may appear, as regards its form, to violate purpose in respect of the judgment, to
be unsuited to the presentative faculty, and as it were to do violence to the
imagination; and yet it is judged to be only the more sublime."[39] Thus, in
Kant's sublime, we do not look at a representation and beyond it, in two si-
multaneous movements; rather, we approach the sublime only as the representation is destroyed. Sublimity, for Kant, is an iconoclastic operation.

At issue is the transcendental, if not the transcendent; the authority of
reason, if not that of God. The Kantian analytic of the sublime is a means of
demonstrating in transcendental terms the legitimacy of the Kantian subject—or a rational humanity. The sublime, Kant tells us, generates respect

(*Achtung*) for human reason (or the supersensible destination of the subject via reason) by revealing its capacity to think totality, even as the human imagination cannot picture it.[40] Writing of sublime experiences in nature, Kant argues, "We may describe the sublime thus: it is an object (of nature) the representation of which determines the mind to think the unattainability of nature regarded as a presentation of ideas."[41] That is, when we come upon a sublime object in nature—a seascape, the starry skies, a vast canyon—we find ourselves striving to imagine (or "represent") its scope or scale, but fail in every effort. This is why we feel a type of pain before the "sublime object." Nevertheless, in this moment we find ourselves caught up in an event wherein, though we cannot imagine it, we think, through our (superior) faculty of reason, the idea of totality, infinitude, or the absolute.

In this way, in this event—which Kant portrays in a manner consistent with Burke as coming upon us, seemingly uncontrollably—is revealed something astounding about ourselves (transcendentally understood): our capacity, thus our end or destination, is both supersensible and supervisual. *What we cannot picture, we can nonetheless think.* And in so thinking, we find ourselves unmistakably in a position of superiority, indeed a kind of sovereignty, over nature:

> In this way nature is not judged to be sublime in our aesthetical judgments in so far as it excites fear, but because it calls up that power in us (which is not nature) of regarding as small the things about which we are solicitous (goods, health, life), and of regarding its might (to which we are no doubt subjected in respect of these things) as nevertheless *without any dominion over us and our personality to which we must bow* where our highest fundamental propositions, and their assertion or abandonment, are concerned. Therefore, nature is here called sublime merely because it elevates the imagination to a presentation of those cases in which the mind can make felt the proper sublimity of its destination, in comparison with nature itself.[42]

Whereas the iconoclasts of the Reformation said it is not *it* that is divine, but *He*, Kant says it is not *it* that is sublime, but *we*, or at least "the worth of humanity in our own person."[43]

Kant here, however, anticipates the objection of Burke and the pious. Has he not here violated the most fundamental principle of religion, that of subordination, even subjection, to the Godhead?[44] He writes,

> It appears to conflict with this solution to the concept of the sublime, so far as sublimity is ascribed to might, that we are accustomed to represent God as presenting Himself in His wrath and yet in His sublimity, in the tempest,

the storm, the earthquake, etc.; and that it would be foolish and criminal to imagine a superiority of our minds over the works of His and, it seems, even over the designs of such might. Hence it would appear that no feeling of the sublimity of our own nature, but rather subjection, abasement, and a feeling of complete powerlessness, is a fitting state of mind in the presence of such an object. . . . In religion in general, prostration, adoration with bent head, with contrite, anxious demeanor and voice, seems to be the only fitting behavior in presence of the Godhead, and hence most peoples have adopted and still observe it.[45]

Kant, in reply, urges a reformation not only in religious manners but in the symbolic dimensions of religion by drawing a contrast between religion and superstition. "The latter," he insists, "establishes in the mind, not reverence for the sublime, but fear and apprehension of the all-powerful Being to whose will the terrified man sees himself subject, without according Him any high esteem."[46] Hence, Kant reestablishes grounds for the reverence of the divine by positing that only a being free of subjection to representations can render due reverence to Being. Here we have, in a theory of the sublime, an iconoclastic theology.

But don't we need the sensible to arouse our emotions, to bind us to each other and to common objects of assent? Isn't what Burke wrote in the *Enquiry* of divinity true of political society as well?—"Whilst we consider the divinity in this refined and abstracted light, the imagination and passions are little or nothing affected."[47] Is not, we might add, political society constituted through the imaginary?[48] Haven't we turned to avenues, landscapes, maps, flags, heroes, myths, speeches, monuments, altars, and temples to witness common identities, to see ourselves as one among many, to construct the clubs, communities, and cults of which we are a part? Isn't the iconic, in other words, integral to identity, the stuff apart from which ideas and abstractions affect not?

That is, is not the iconoclastic impulse, though it may arouse us momentarily, fundamentally unsustainable? Kant's reply is biblical: "Perhaps there is no sublimer passages [*sic*] in Jewish law than the command, 'Thou shalt not make to thyself any graven image, nor the likeness of anything which is in heaven or in the earth or under the earth,' etc. This command alone can explain the enthusiasm that the Jewish people in their moral period felt for their religion, when they compared themselves with other peoples, or explain the pride which Mohammedanism inspires."[49] Here we come back to the triad of image, politics, and theology, where "image" is relegated to an inferior position with respect to the motive force of political society before the *idea*.[50] It is false, Kant claims, to suppose that the intensity of political associations depends on the power of symbols. Indeed, it is "childish," a symptom of our political immaturity.

> For where the senses see nothing more before them, and the unmistakable and indelible *idea* of morality remains, it would be rather necessary to moderate the impetus of an unbounded imagination, to prevent it from rising to enthusism, than through fear of powerlessness of these ideas to seek aid for them in images and childish ritual. Thus governments have willingly allowed religion to be abundantly provided with the latter accomplishments ["images and childish ritual"], and seeking thereby to relieve their subjects of trouble, they have also sought to deprive them of the faculty of extending their spiritual powers beyond the limits that are arbitrarily assigned to them and by means of which they can be the more easily treated as mere passive beings.[51]

The correlation between political culture and iconic culture, in Kant's view, is precisely the means by which political sovereigns have maintained the passivity of their subjects. Political liberty is liberation from the constraining powers of the image. Kant here remains true not only to the revolutionary implications of the Enlightenment he championed, but to his iconoclastic forbearers, for whom not only the character of devotion but the quality of community were correlated with the degree to which faith could transcend the sensible world of images, rituals, and the like.[52] The argument is not, therefore, for an austere faith (though this could certainly be an effect). To the contrary, it is made on behalf of a mature faith that no longer needs the propaedeutic devices of material culture to bring enthusiasm to assent.

Nevertheless, has Kant really transcended the sensible world? Isn't his theory of the sublime, which hinges on the confrontation of the subject with an object, like Burke's, still fundamentally iconic, requiring mediation? "We are bound," Burke argues, "by the condition of our nature to ascend to these pure and intellectual ideas, through the medium of sensible images."[53] But Kant insists that we are not so bound, that it is possible to pass directly to the sublime idea, unmediated. This possibility assumes the radical contingency, indeed arbitrariness, of the sensible world with respect to ultimate identity. ("The apprehension of an otherwise formless and unpurposive object gives merely the occasion through which we become conscious of such a state; the object is thus employed as subjectively purposive, but is not judged as such in itself and on account of its form [it is, as it were, a species *finalis accepta, non data*)].")[54] On the one hand, we might say that, for Kant, the object is always, at best, merely a token, the accidental representation that does not embody what it represents (for Kant, always in danger of becoming an idol). But yet, in another sense, the nature of the object in question as "formless and unpurposive" (*formlos oder ungestalt*) means that not even the concept of the token will fully suffice in explaining Kant's approach to the image. For what the sublime "employs" here is a particular type or category of image: the incoherent, fragmented, "formless" image.

The image in Kant's sublime is thus twice destroyed. Most obviously, it is destroyed in the violence to the imagination that constitutes for Kant the passage to the sublime: here the effort of the imagination to present to itself an image of totality ends in the destruction of any and all images. But there is also, prior to this, the fundamental Kantian insistence on the impossibility of the adequate representation or image of the sublime destination. When it comes to our highest and noblest apprehensions, the quintessentially human, there is no adequate form: Kant insists on the nonexistence of any image adequate to our destination. Hence, in this most profound sense, his thought is iconoclastic; for only in the breakdown, the destruction, of our "childish" belief in the image as such do we find an "object" useful for considering our destiny.

Thus Kant's sublimity offers the strongest possible counterargument to the logic and rhetoric of the icon, as well as an implicit rejoinder to a broken view of politics. We are not bound to the icons and institutions of political culture. They are merely the occasion for our political maturation. Moreover, they are fundamentally inadequate to our proper, legitimate destiny. This inadequacy, we might say, is the critical revelation of Kant's sublime.

It is a revolutionary idea, but it may turn out to support a surprisingly conservative politics. For it suggests, as Rousseau recognized, that the civil religious power of ideas and ideology can be a more powerful means of maintaining power than a strong iconic culture:

> There is therefore a purely civil profession of faith of which the Sovereign should fix the articles, not exactly as religious dogmas, but as social sentiments without which a man cannot be a good citizen or a faithful subject. . . . The dogmas of civil religion ought to be few, simple, and exactly worded, without explanation or commentary. The existence of a mighty, intelligent and beneficent Divinity, possessed of foresight and providence, the life to come, the happiness of the just, the punishment of the wicked, the sanctity of the social contract and the laws: these are its positive dogmas. Its negative dogmas I confine to one, intolerance, which is a part of the cults we have rejected.[55]

Thus Rousseau's political community is formed out of the conjunction of common social sentiments with simple truths. By this, political loyalty is measured and political membership arbitrated.[56]

Rousseau's state could not, however, reside in the ether. There would be institutions, material forms, images, and so forth. There would have to be.

But they would be only tokens (or idols if falsely revered). Governors would thus be "mere officials," tokens of sovereignty.[57] And religion—that is, traditional religion—would function within the state in a way that would not challenge the state's civil religion. Otherwise, such religious loyalties would be idolatrous, disrupting civil unity, and would need to be "driven from the State."[58] Yet, it is not idols, whether political or theological, that would be most aggressively driven from Rousseau's civil state, but icons. For Rousseau's state amounts to a social project in which the very cultural conditions necessary for iconicity would be constitutionally excluded: images could only have the status of tokens or idols. There would be no "middle ground," so to speak, no place for a mode of representation that requires simultaneously looking at and through an object. Images simply could not be legible, approachable, and viewable as icons. Rousseau's civil theology, like Kant's sublime, is in this most profound sense iconoclastic.

Such a civil theology would enjoy eruptions in Europe, particularly in France, but it would gain more lasting purchase in the United States, a nation seemingly founded and refounded, to use Garry Wills's cogent phrase, in "transcendental declarations."[59] Attempts to make for the icon a home in America have repeatedly been met by questions about the legitimacy of an American iconicity per se. Such questions have constituted a context in which American images have had to stake their existence and find their place. We can recall, for example, debates within nineteenth-century literary culture about the legitimacy of a representative American literature—not which literature, but whether such a literature should be at all.[60] More recently, we can think of the debates around so-called identity politics with respect to symbols, sites, stories, and monuments—debates that have been about not only what should be represented, but about whether such material representations really have a proper place at all. Perhaps above all we can see the fraught place of the icon in America in the discourse of the sublime, that "typical amalgamation of natural, technological, classical, and religious elements into a single aesthetic" in which a national character could be constructed as Americans looked *beyond* landscape and material culture to a transcendental realm of ideals with their corresponding emotions.[61] Thus Robert Bellah, in an influential 1966 reflection on John F. Kennedy's inaugural address, described "an elaborate and well-institutionalized civil religion in America," one that "provides a transcendent goal for the political process."[62] "At its best," he argued, American civil religion would be a "genuine apprehension of universal and transcendent religious reality as seen in or, one could almost say, as revealed through the experience of the American people."[63] It is hard to find an essay coming from the American academy in the 1960s that is more consensus-oriented than Bellah's. Nevertheless, he has since written that upon the publication of his essay, he was met with sharp accusations of "supporting an idolatrous worship of the American nation."[64] *Idolatry* or *iconicity?* Perhaps just mere tokenization?

Conclusion

America's Cold War was riddled with such dilemmas. As Eisenhower felt amid the pressures of Little Rock, the image was both an asset and a liability in the Cold War battle for hearts and minds. Enduring political institutions, economic productivity, technological ingenuity, and booming new social forms were exploited as indexes of the superiority of the American way. Cold warriors were, as a rule, hyperconscious of the importance of the image of America, both at home and abroad, for America's ability to fight communism. At the same time, by drawing attention to the image of America, they risked its demise in world opinion, as conspicuous consumption, nuclear militancy, and racial conflict variously made "America" look inauthentic, even idolatrous—an accusation some were all too eager to make.

Indeed, Eisenhower himself was quite worried about too much focus on any one image of America. America was bigger, and indeed better, than what any one image could contain.[65] Eisenhower had good reason to insist on this. Nuclear weapons could in fact look very idolatrous, as they would to Bellah, who warned in his essay on American civil religion against being "tempted to rely on our overwhelming physical power rather than on our intelligence."[66] More generally, for all the enthusiasm for American technological and industrial ingenuity in the postwar world, such purported strengths could make America look quite materialistic, and Eisenhower regularly expressed worry about American militarism and materialism, and about militaristic materialism. Thus, in his famous farewell address, offered just before the Kennedy inaugural that Bellah celebrated, Eisenhower urged Americans not to see America in the military-industrial complex he had helped build, but rather to look beyond it toward the principles and ideals of the nation.

In the speech America stood perilously at the edge of doom, as "threats, new in kind or degree, constantly arise."[67] Hence, arms, including nuclear arms, "must be mighty, ready for instant action, so that no potential aggressor may be tempted to risk his own destruction."[68] Economic productivity and military might were crucial for America's survival. Yet, Eisenhower suggested, a nuclear arsenal on constant alert meant US citizens needed to be equally alert to the misuse of such great power. "Only an alert and knowledgeable citizenry," he argued, "can compel the proper meshing of the huge industrial and military machinery of defense with our peaceful methods and goals, so that security and liberty may prosper together."[69] Eisenhower placed on American citizens not only the burden of seeing beyond America's militarism and materialism toward the ideals that economy and security were supposed to defend, but also the greater task of "meshing" militarism and materialism with pacific intentions. The charge, importantly, presupposed that America's militant, materialist culture had become unmoored from national purpose, that somehow spirit had become detached from matter. It had therefore become a citizenly duty to conjoin again what the necessities of the Cold War had split asunder. Just as nukes would force America's enemies into restraint, so a watchful American citizenry would restrain the manufacturers and operators of those nukes and would somehow "compel" the material of security and the ideal of liberty into cooperation. But this, Eisenhower suggested with his ominous words, could at best be only an uneasy cooperation; it would never represent an iconic harmony between material culture and national ideals.

Indeed, Eisenhower's charge could only compound the dilemma of the citizen-spectator looking for an image of America in the Cold War. For in summoning a watchful public, he called citizens to first peer into gaps. There was, to begin with, the vast space between a militant material culture and national ideals. But then there were greater historical expanses among a civic republican past, a techno-scientific, industrially driven present, and utopian visions of the future. Finally, there was the abyss of nuclear annihilation. Such gaps indeed put extraordinary pressure on US citizens to somehow force together and "mesh" matter and spirit, the real and the ideal. But such forced coupling already surrendered the icon to its own empty space.

Kennedy's election to the presidency, however, seemed to establish the return of an iconic logic in America's Cold War. Here was a president, unlike Eisenhower (and Kennedy's electoral opponent, Nixon), who could act as an image of America: youthful, energetic, bold, articulate, and equally comfortable in the worlds of politics and celebrity. The image of John F. Kennedy was never divorced from the ideals he forwarded. In the image of Kennedy, the world could see that American ideals were not mere code words for capitalist domination, but rather the expression of a desire to better humankind. Indeed, the Kennedy years now appear to be the high point of the image in America's Cold War. From the *Life* covers of the Kennedys to Jacqueline Kennedy's televised tour of the White House and George Tames's iconic "The Loneliest Job in the World," and even to the spy-plane images of the missile installations being constructed in Cuba, each step of the Kennedy presidency seemed to further confirm that the image could indeed function as a reliable and effective index of the truth of things.

Yet, there remained a lingering sense that this iconicity should only be taken ironically, as Kennedy was the first president to absorb the image, reflexively adapting the techniques and tenor of Hollywood to consciously produce, rather than only reveal, a "universal appeal."[70] Thus, in 1962, Daniel Boorstin lamented the rise of "pseudo-events" in America under the straight-forward title, *The Image*—as if it were the image itself that was the central problem in American political culture.[71] And so we come back to the roofless presidential limousine, to the pomp of parade and motorcade, and to Abraham Zapruder's appetite to capture an icon on film.

PART II

Catastrophe

3

Zapruder

There were no journalists at Dealey Plaza the morning of November 22, 1963, only a cluster of spectators, stretched thin on both sides of Elm Street, perched for a firsthand look at the president and his wife. Yet, like the professional press, a number of these citizen-spectators came with photographic equipment in hand, ready to track, snap, and shoot on cue. For these were watchful citizens, reminiscent of the sort Eisenhower had encouraged in his farewell address not yet two years earlier, but watchful with the gaze of a moviegoer rather than with the stare of a soldier. Still, their vigilance was sincere—they, like the most ardent cold warriors, knew the image mattered. They recognized, even if only implicitly, that a great deal depended on the capacity of an image to be that which we can both look *at* and *beyond* to that which the image embodies. The visual record of the president—made possible by the latest models of photographic technology, technique, and culture—would not just be a keepsake; it would be an icon that in its own peculiar way would be blessed and spirit-bearing.

To be sure, Zapruder provided America with an icon, a spectacular and paradoxical one, an image of the destruction of an image. Immediately upon hearing of the 8mm film, the publisher of *Life* magazine knew something extraordinary had been made and quickly sent corporate men and money to secure it. Abraham Zapruder had set out to make an icon to treasure and keep in his home. Instead he made one that would be treasured, kept, cut, copied, circulated, manipulated, and sold on the Cold War home front.

Art historian David Lubin has considered at length the film's internal quality in light of high art, film art, and Hollywood. As he follows the Kennedy's iconic images through the American cultural landscape, he describes Jack and Jacqueline as movie stars, and as the movie's stars. He presents

Zapruder's film as a three-act drama—Act 1: radiant couple appears in the limousine; Act 2: tragedy; Act 3: closure as the limousine disappears from the screen. Lubin reads the film as art, part classical tragedy, part domestic tragedy, part nihilist film, and part sad home movie.[1] For Lubin, these rich narrative resonances and the film's place within the discourses of political and cultural authority bring the Zapruder film to be properly named *Zapruder*— one of the "saddest movies ever made."[2]

Still, the Zapruder film had alternate careers, and highly contentious ones. It provided, in journalistic fashion, a firsthand look at the assassination. It was central to innumerable official and unofficial forensic investigations. And it served repeatedly as a proof text in jeremiads of American decline. In each case the film stubbornly challenged the country's citizens to make some sort of sense out of assassination violence. It is as if it appeared in American political culture to mock Kennedy's civil religious confidence in his inaugural: "In your hands, my fellow citizens, more than mine, will rest the final success or failure of our course."[3] Kennedy's assassination made sure of that, as Americans were confronted with the shocking image of the destruction of their president. Indeed, in post-1963 America the image of the Kennedys in the Zapruder film, like the image in Kant's sublime, was twice destroyed: in the event of the assassination represented so vividly on film, and then subsequently in the career of the film in a political culture of manipulation, suspicion, and incredulity.

What is perhaps most striking, however, about the history of the Zapruder film's circulation and presentations to American publics is that, despite the film's finality, destruction was never quite the last word. Rather, in the Zapruder film's presentation and representations, America is somehow always made to transcend assassination violence, as spirit surpasses matter. The image and the crises it engendered were reduced to mere tokens before a transcendental America. Born in a moment of national iconicity, the public career of the Zapruder film solidified an age of American iconoclasm.

The Kennedy assassination stands, along with Pearl Harbor, the *Challenger* explosion, and September 11, among a small group of modern American where-were-you-when? events. Indeed, it was the first principally visual one, the first mediated as an image event. Hence, Kennedy's violent death has been considered and contested in American culture at the intersection of two general strains of institutionalized publicity: that of the press (especially the television press) and the closely related entertainment industry, and that of the Cold War state. In tracing the career of the Zapruder film, two features of its publicity are conspicuous. First, citizen-spectators are repeatedly placed before the sublime object, asked to assume the subjective state of not only shock and terror, but also awe and reverence. Second, for all the reverence the film is made to summon, in its appropriation by political, corporate, and cultural institutions, Zapruder's camera acquires an ironic angle. Seeing the Zapruder film becomes not just about seeing an assassination, but knowingly seeing what is not seen, or—again recalling Kant's sublime—seeing the nonexistence of any image adequate to the rightful destination of America. Such visual irony, I argue, is integral not only to the meanings of assassination violence that are produced through the representation of Kennedy's violent death in the Zapruder film, but also to the neoliberal discourse that found greater purchase in the decades after the Kennedy assassination. It is as if the ironies that Kennedy himself so effortlessly introduced came to possess the image of his violent death and then the image of America.

The convergence of the transcendental and the ironic is necessary to neoliberal discourse. For neoliberalism posits, first of all, the impossibility of any image adequate to the representation of society or economy. Destruction—whether the creative destruction of markets or the violent destruction of political bodies—is thereby analogously related to the destruction of representations and thus incorporated into an ineffable process, a sublime becoming that calls for respect (*Achtung*), even reverence. Yet, at the same time, this neoliberal discourse also would wink at such destructions, so to speak, as destruction is viewed in an optimistic, even comic, frame, one that overcomes the finality of violence with processes of reconciliation, of which economic equilibration is but one sort of reconciliation, and "shock and awe" before American power another.

Lacunae

Three distinct ironies came to possess the Zapruder film. The first concerns its role in claims to journalistic, forensic, and narrative presence. Despite their absence from the scene of the crime, as Barbie Zelizer has shown, journalists have effectively taught their publics to see what was not seen by constructing a professional image that hinged on their role as "eyewitnesses" of Kennedy's assassination. As Zelizer writes, "Documenting one's presence at the events of Kennedy's death thus imparted much of the authority for retelling its story. . . . Attempts to construct presence where there was none, and imply presence through authoritative retellings, ultimately gave journalists an advantage over other groups of speakers."[4] Still, as Zelizer also shows, government panels, private investigators, and Hollywood directors vehemently challenged journalistic authority, staking their claims, too, on presence—and it was the images stripped from Zapruder's camera that they used to support their claims. Indeed, more than any other object that emerged from Dealey Plaza that November day, the Zapruder film has functioned as a medium of presence. To invoke it, let alone to show it, has been to claim legitimacy to tell the story of the president's death for a myriad of absentee public actors.

Still, that story has been far from straightforward; hence, the second irony. Despite the fact that the film included a full-color, tightly framed sequence of images portraying the explosive disintegration of the president's head, it had, as if made in Hollywood, a tantalizing omission: the first of the bullets to hit Kennedy does so when Kennedy's visage is hidden behind an obtrusive street sign. As in the script of any crime film, almost everything is disclosed, but the undisclosed leaves a yawning gap.

Finally, there is a third, more fundamental, irony in this, for presence is always elusive, if only because the present is always ephemeral. Susan Sontag remarks that photographic technology is a technology of acquisition, and acquisition is a means of control: "The photographic exploration and duplication of the world fragments continuities and feeds the pieces into an interminable dossier, thereby providing possibilities of control."[5] Yet, what does it mean to acquire or control the present? What does it mean to be present when the moment passes before it can be reckoned, even when that moment is artificially recorded? Isn't the quest for presence, like iconicity, futile, an attempt to determine in space and time the indeterminable? Are all attempts at presence practices in idolatry? Film scholar Leo Charney, reflecting on the thought of Martin Heidegger, Walter Benjamin, and Jean Epstein, has argued that such is the mantra of modernity: "We can never be present in a present."[6] And here, Charney argues, film is "emblematically modern," as it always tacitly, and sometimes explicitly, presents the dilemma of presence, not only by its "ceaseless forward movement," always leaving the present behind, but also in its very technical composition, as in film continuous motion is but "a chain of fragmentary moments:"[7] "This fragmentation marks the heart of film as re-presentation: because it is always fragmentary, always a string of moments, it is never complete and present. Re-presentation, in its very form, played into the evacuation of presence that characterized the modern. If there was no present, then re-presentation did not simply reiterate a previous presence. There was no present to re-present. Representation in this sense confirmed the artificiality and evacuation of presence in general."[8] Thus, film *proves* rather than challenges that "it is never possible to recapture the whole movement."[9] It consequently throws upon the spectator an emblematically modern burden, the burden of interpretation, of making a whole out of mere fragments.

Indeed, a series of gaps in disclosure typify the legacy of the Kennedy assassination and its representation in the Zapruder film. However the who, what, where, when, why, and how of the event are approached, debates over the Kennedy assassination keep turning up gaps, silences, fissures, cuts, and lacunae. Josiah Thompson, an ivy-league trained former college professor and a well-known independent assassination investigator, wrote of the Zapruder film in his 1967 book *Six Seconds in Dallas*, "If studied with the utmost care and under optimum conditions, it can yield answers to enormous questions."[10] However, in an interview thirty years after the publication of *Six Seconds*, Thompson sounded a quite different note, saying,

> I've been in the middle of [criminal investigations] for twenty-two years, [and] I've never remotely encountered a murder case where the more it's investigated, the less you know about what happened. I mean, that's bizarre. Usually in a murder case, you investigate it[, and] the more you investigate, the more coherence you get. More and more things fit; [you get] more and more confident about that. There may be residual doubts often about, perhaps, who did it? Or even why they did it; that seems to be the major problem. But as to what happened, no, never. That never happens. You always get greater and greater coherence. Whereas, with this case, you get greater and greater incoherence.[11]

To be sure, in the myriad of stories of Kennedy's assassination very little has been settled. Citizens have been left to make wholes out of fragments. What Epstein writes of cinema in general would seem to characterize the experience of watching the Zapruder film in particular: "Discontinuity becomes continuity only after penetrating the spectator. It is a purely interior phenomenon. . . . Within, there is an impression that, like all the others given by the senses, is an interpretation of the object—in other words, an illusion, a phantom."[12] Is the fantastic quality of Kennedy's assassination a product of the cinematic medium itself? Would its nature and meanings be perpetually unsettled because it was represented most vividly to us in fragments?

There is indeed something illusory about film, but it has less directly to do with its technique than with its social standing. Cinema—and now video, both analog and digital—promises to capture everything within its temporal and spatial scope, and this promise is made firm by its technological capacity to very nearly meet the challenge. But artificial records of human events in fact do not, and indeed cannot, capture the things that are so crucial to political life: contexts, motives, and—above all—meanings. Motion pictures are ideal for fictitious storytelling, where the viewer participates, as Epstein insisted, in the production of meaning. At the same time, the self-same technology can have and has had vital scientific use, deployed to record physical phenomena invisible to the naked eye (whether because of scale or speed). But both nonfictitious documentation of "real" events and the "scientific" record of human action rest on a profound illusion, the promise of representing in "fact" what can only be determined contingently in society (or sociality). In this way, the Zapruder film intruded into American political culture as a great illusion that would also be a means of profound disillusionment. But, as we will see, disillusionment was an opportunity—an opportunity to discredit the value of the image and institutions more generally, to insist, in a neoliberal vein, not merely that the image cannot fully contain the meanings that really matter, but that the image contains nothing that really matters.

For the fundamental vacancy that emerges from the Zapruder film is in the gap between ordinary human experience and the film as an extraordinary social product. As a social product, the Zapruder film has assumed the aura of a sacred text, and, as Edwin Black writes, "The sacred text . . . never completely yields up its secrets."[13] As evidence of presence, as the most valued piece of Kennedy-assassination evidence, and as a powerful filmic narrative, the Zapruder film has transcended its own commodification. And this elevated stature has enhanced its mystery. Black quotes Frank Kermode as follows: "Once a text is credited with high authority, it is studied intensely; once it is so studied, it acquires mystery or secrecy."[14] As a journalistic text, the film has served as a monument to the golden age of network reporting. As a forensic object, it has been no less mysterious. For example, a wave of "scientific" interpretations of the film concluded that the film is in fact the product of a government-designed hoax. Hence, it represents a more spectacular cover-up than we ever imagined.[15] As an aesthetic object, *Zapruder* has acquired all the mystery of Edvard Munch's *The Scream*. The fundamental gap or vacancy that emerges through *Zapruder*, however, is not principally journalistic, forensic, or aesthetic, but political. It is one between ordinary human political experiences and capacities, which are wed to the world of appearances and to speech, and what late-modern political culture can acquire, produce, and represent as "extraordinary," whether that be political violence or economic destruction.

I peer into this political gap in the following pages through a series of readings that focus on major public displays of the Zapruder film over an almost thirty-year period: its first public presentation, which occurred in the pages of *Life* in 1963; its presentation in the Warren Commission *Report of the President's Commission on the Assassination of President Kennedy* a short time later; its first televisual display on *Good Night America* in 1975; and its appearance in Oliver Stone's *JFK* in 1991. In these discrete discourses we see the interplay of image, vacancy, and interpretation, where the second term represents both the burden put on interpretation and the emptying of the image. I argue that such vacancy—as chaos, silence, cut, or lacuna—is destructive, but not merely so. Rather, it is productive too, productive of conditions that summon a transcendental order. The Zapruder film is repeatedly made to move through the destruction of the image to a more extraordinary lucidity, indeed, a higher truth.

Life's Zapruder

The twenty-six second color film captured in 486 eighteenth-of-a-second frames traces the president, his car, his wife, his company, and the positions and reactions of onlookers at the moment of Kennedy's fatal wounding. The film begins with the motorcade turning toward the camera onto Elm Street. The camera is elevated above and away from the street, so that it may follow the motorcade all the way down Dealey Plaza. The black convertible limousine moves slowly toward the camera as the president waves to the crowd. Jacqueline Kennedy, in a pink dress and matching pillbox hat, is at her husband's left side, camera-right, and Governor Connally sits with his wife in front of the president. The president stops waving as the car travels behind a street sign that stands between the camera and Elm Street. The camera moves right in expectation of the reemergence of the motorcade from behind the sign. When the convertible comes back into view, the president has both hands upon his chest, near his neck, and seems to be pulling at his shirt. Mrs. Kennedy is looking at him, her hand outstretched toward him. Governor Connally is looking back.

The camera acquires these movements via bright light provided by the sun. The gleaming black border of the car frames each figure beneath. A grassy green backdrop, peppered with spectators, lies behind the figures in the car. As the camera moves right, the car comes closer into view. Connally turns toward the president, apparently in distress, then leans back onto his wife and starts to fall back. Spectators are still cheering. The camera keeps the car steadily in its frame until the convertible's passenger side is directly centered before it. The car now fills the camera frame completely, so that its exact position on Elm Street can no longer be discerned. The president, however, is now prominently in view. He bends over. Mrs. Kennedy moves closer to him. As she draws near, however, pink flesh suddenly and explosively sprays out from the president's head. Mrs. Kennedy thrusts backward, looking startled and confused: she momentarily grabs the president's head as it falls, and then turns away and begins to climb out of the back seat of the convertible onto the rear trunk. His head falls toward her lap. She finds the trunk, climbs upon it, and begins to fall prostrate. A dark-suited man mounts the back of the car, meets Mrs. Kennedy, and pushes her back in the direction of her fallen husband. The car accelerates; it disappears behind a tree and then a street sign. The camera waits. The car reappears, but now at a distance; it presents itself only momentarily before disappearing again under a black, shadowy overpass.

One can only imagine what C. D. Jackson, at the helm of *Life*, thought when he first saw what he had acquired in November 1963. Within forty-eight hours of the president's death, amid a frenzy of media efforts to get access to the 8mm film, Zapruder sold all the rights to it to *Life* for $150,000. Jackson was a long-time compatriot of Henry Luce at Time, Inc. From the mid-1930s on, he oversaw at different times Luce's *Time, Life, Fortune*, and *Sports Illustrated*, and founded the international versions of *Time* and *Life*. However, he was not only a major media executive; he was a true-blooded cold warrior. In fact, during the 1950s, he was arguably the most influential propagandist of the Eisenhower administration, and before his work with Eisenhower, he had been president of the Council for Democracy, an economic and political warfare specialist in World War II, and a founder and director of Radio Free Europe. During the Eisenhower years, Jackson had moved in and out of government, working for the president and then for Luce. But the two jobs were never sharply divided. Even after Eisenhower left office, Jackson remained in touch with some of the goings-on in the Kennedy administration through friends and allies there, including Walt Rostow. Thus, upon Kennedy's violent death, Jackson was no doubt as conscious as anyone of the power an image of an assassination could have both in American political culture and in the Cold War world.

My own attempts to learn exactly how much direct editorial control Jackson took over the presentation of *Zapruder* in *Life* have been inconclusive.[16] However, at least one account has reported that Jackson, upon seeing the film, quickly determined that the public "was not ready" to see it in full.[17] Indeed, given Jackson's interest in directing public reactions toward spectacular political events and his years of experience in the enterprise, it is hard to believe that he, along with Luce, had anything but a strongly directive role in the production of *Zapruder* in *Life*. The intensely stylized and controlled pages of the issue reinforce this conclusion, as they mirror in gravitas and spectacle the typical Jacksonian propagandistic style.[18]

Life's November 29 issue appeared on newsstands on November 25, three days after Kennedy's death, one day after Jack Ruby gunned down Lee Harvey

Oswald, and the day of Kennedy's funeral. Since Zapruder's was the only direct footage of Kennedy's assassination, acquiring it gave *Life* a huge advantage over other media outlets. They had the exclusive on the assassination's only close-up image. Yet, despite the recency of the event and the importance of the footage, *Life* did not go the route of "news." Instead, as the magazine's cover indicated in a portrait of Kennedy's face surrounded in black, the magazine was more interested in offering a memorial text than a news report.[19] Even as televisions broadcasted the somber and dark funeral of Kennedy, *Life* put its shrouded issue on American newsstands. Aesthetically, the issue is much nearer to the spirit of the funeral coverage than to that of the breaking news that propelled newspaper presses so frantically across the nation in the days after Kennedy's death.

The thirty-one frames of *Zapruder* were presented in four pages. The four-page spread was situated amid a fourteen-page section that narrated pictographically and typographically the events of November 22, spanning from the president's arrival at Dallas's Love Field to the transport of his body back to Washington, D.C. In the *Zapruder* spread, the arrangement of images, captions, and black or white space was such that the editorial hand was conspicuous.[20] *Life* did not offer a simple sequence of frames in uniform size, suggesting the neutral hand of objectivity. Rather, it offered an oblong, stylized, and hypotaxic visual presentation complemented by an imposing narrative enclosed in captions. The *Zapruder* pages began on page 3 of this larger spread. Thus there was little prologue. What prologue there was, however, consisted of two images and a blurb of text that together set the theme and established the dominant figure for the pages that followed. The theme was the violent movement from control to chaos, and the figure was that of Jacqueline Kennedy.

The first image was the most picturesque in the entire fourteen-page section (fig. 5): a full-page, full-color photograph of Mrs. Kennedy standing beside her husband at Love Field, bearing a dozen roses and a wide smile. It was Mrs. Kennedy, not the president, that the photograph foregrounded: she is pink-suited, he is dark-suited; she is front and center, he is off-center, and the right side of his body is cut off—he thus frames her. Together, they greet what seems to be a jubilant crowd. On the facing page, however, Mrs. Kennedy's roses are strewn in black-and-white across the otherwise empty rear seat of the presidential convertible. Side by side, these two images enact a violent movement between extremes: from color to black-and-white, from roses clutched to roses strewn, from buoyancy to vacancy. The theme here was one of movement from composure and control to chaos and confusion. And Jacqueline Kennedy was the central object in this movement.

FIGURE 5. The Kennedys disembarking at Love Field in *Life*.

The tale that was emerging here, which would become far more explicit in the pages that followed, was complex. As Lubin argues, the story contained something of the classical tragedy—we have a great fall, the specter of fate, and the evacuation of hope.[21] However, in the figure of Jacqueline Kennedy there was another tale, one that superimposes modern resonances and ideologies over those that are more antique. It is a tale that echoes Max Horkheimer and Theodor Adorno's curious notion of "sublime love."[22] They use this phrase to describe the gendering of a counterpart to the hyper-rationality of modernity. Indeed, as I discussed in chapter 2, sublimity is historically associated with what Kant named as *Achtung*—fear, reverence, awe, or respect. *Achtung* is a masculine trope, suggesting a standing-at-attention that is associated with military decorum. The brave soldier, in fact, represents one of Kant's most vivid examples of sublime "disinterestedness."

> For what is that which is, even to the savage, an object of the greatest admiration? It is a man who shrinks from nothing, who fears nothing, and therefore does not yield to danger, but rather goes to face it vigorously with the most complete deliberation. Even in the most highly civilized state this peculiar veneration for the soldier remains, though only under the condition that he exhibit all the virtues of peace, gentleness, compassion, and even a becoming care for his own person; because even by these it is recognized that his mind is unsubdued by danger.[23]

Love, on the other hand, is personal, desiring, and, as Kant would say, *interested* in its object. What is sublime, then, about love? And yet, as others have noted, the sublime is also about excess, and is often assumed to be a form of irrationality.[24] As Christine Battersby has argued, if we were to engage in a genealogy of the sublime, we would find that, especially in eighteenth-century Anglo culture, "emotion, strong imagination, wildness, and powerful sexual appetite—characteristics previously despised and associated with females— were revalued when located in the bodies of elite males."[25] Madness, the primitive, and instinct—though still "feminine" characteristics—came to be lauded as long as they were expressed within a masculine economy that privileged dominion, power, and control. "Sublime love" in this economy is not a strict oxymoron, but rather an expression of the gendering of tropes of chaos and control.

Horkheimer and Adorno's short description of sublime love, written circa 1944 during their Californian exile and with the cultural industry in view, echoed, complicated, and remystified Kant's homage to the soldier, and anticipated Jacqueline Kennedy's appearance in *Life*:

> Woman herself, on behalf of all exploited nature, gained admission to a male-dominated world, but only in broken form. In her spontaneous submission she reflects for her vanquisher the glory of his victory, substituting devotion for defeat, nobility of soul for despair, and a loving breast for a ravished heart. At the price of radical disengagement from action and of withdrawal into the charmed circle, nature receives homage from the lord of creation. Art, custom, and sublime love are masks in which nature reappears transformed into her own antithesis. Through these masks she acquires the gift of speech; out of her distortion emerges her essence. Beauty is the serpent that exhibits a wound in which a thorn was once embedded.[26]

Woman here is caught up in the violent movement from coherence to incoherence and order to disorder that characterizes the sublime. Contra the sublime soldier, who merely faces catastrophe, she bears catastrophe upon her very form. She does not cast off violence and replace it with nobility. Rather, she assumes upon herself both the violence and nobility of sublimity. The transition in *Life*'s prologue from the image of Love Field to the empty, disheveled limousine so framed Mrs. Kennedy's vanquishing. The conqueror, however, was not the assassin, but the heavy editorial hand that, in managing Jacqueline Kennedy's fragmentation, managed a public implicitly judged to be "not ready" for the disclosure of the president's violent death in any form other than a hyper-stylized one. Indeed, the thirty-one frames of *Zapruder* that *Life* extracted and disclosed managed not merely Jacqueline Kennedy but a mass public as well.

The degree to which *Life* sought to control the presentation of the Zapruder film is suggested by two omissions in the November 29 spread. First, despite the widespread publicity that a Dallas man named Abraham Zapruder had filmed the assassination, *Life* did not acknowledge Zapruder in the issue, or even that the images were derived from a motion-picture film. Instead, the caption accompanying the photos began, "On these and the following two pages is a remarkable and exclusive series of pictures which show, for the first time and in tragic detail, the fate which befell our President."[27] Second, *Life* printed the frames in black-and-white. One of the first viewers of the film, Phil Chamberlain, a production supervisor at the Kodak plant in Dallas that processed the film, was struck by the film's vivid color and "needle-sharp" resolution.[28] In the *Life* issue, however, the film's frames are not only stripped of their color, but appear grainy and muted when contrasted with other photos in the spread. These omissions—the latter, especially—may be explainable according to the fortunes of production (the unavailability of a color lab, for example). However, the significance of the omissions lay not in the reasons for them, but in the staging of the film as if there were no omissions. *Life* sought and achieved a controlled presentation free of apologies or explanations.

Jacqueline Kennedy's story in that issue of *Life*, as I have noted, began vivid and whole. The full-page color shot of the presidential couple at Love Field was captioned, "Now in the sunny freshness of a Texas morning, with roses in her arms and a luminous smile on her lips, Jacqueline Kennedy still had one hour to share the buoyant surge of life with the man at her side."[29] These references to and images of "life" here in *Life* are strong but strictly measured into "one hour." And even this hour, the caption suggested, is heavily laden with the ironies and tragedies of being coupled to iconic presidential exposure: "Vibrant with confidence, crinkle-eyed with an all-embracing smile, John F. Kennedy swept his wife with him into the exuberance of the throng at Dallas Love Field. This was an act in which Jack Kennedy was superbly human. . . . For him this was all fun as well as politics. For his shy wife, surmounting the grief of her infant son's recent death, this mingling demanded a grace and gallantry she soon would need again."[30] Crinkle-eyed "Jack" comes as freely into the narrative as he will depart from it. He is "superbly human" only because he is supremely iconic, bidding us to look at him but also through him and beyond him to that higher reality of which he is an embodiment. Jacqueline, on the other hand, appears already in cracked form, like a fallen icon put back on the shelf unrepaired. Wounded by her son's death and hindered by her own lack of confidence, she must surmount her private ruptures in order to meet her public fate.

These character sketches of the presidential couple, which immediately preceded the storyboard-like presentation of *Zapruder* (figs. 6 and 7), are set underneath the bold heading, "THE ASSASSINATION OF PRESIDENT KENNEDY."[31] Hence, the death of Mrs. Kennedy's son, we surmise, is but preparatory work for greater maternal grief. The Mrs. Kennedy of Love Field seems to have been only partially stripped of her of innocence and naïveté through becoming a mother of a dead male. Her smile, the roses, the pink Chanel suit, and the pillbox hat signify a woman still blithely incorporated into publicity. On Love Field, romance and pageantry are momentarily as real for her as the deaths from which she comes and to which she goes. She alone is oblivious to the absurdity of her publicity, for the readers of *Life* possess not only a foreknowledge of her fate, but glaring signs of it in the headline and in the black-and-white photo of the empty limousine set opposite her image. Mrs. Kennedy, the pages insisted, decidedly lacks such understanding. In the magazine's layout, she was positioned in such a way that if she had eyes to see across the fold to the facing page, she would envision her destiny. But she has no such vision.

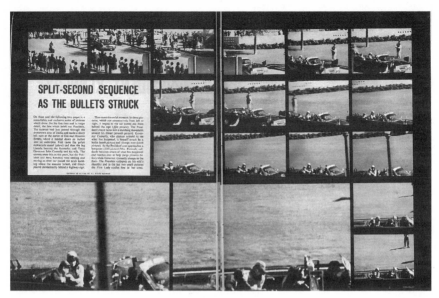

FIGURE 6A AND 6B. The first two-page spread of *Life's* frames from the Zapruder film. The layout runs left to right, across the two-page spread.

Upon a turn of the page, a headline announced a "Split-Second Sequence" of the president's assassination. However, the sequence was of a very different order than *Zapruder* in motion. Indeed, the arrangement lacked an intuitive order. The eighteen images on the facing pages (fig. 6a/6b) have to be laboriously fit together into a sequence. The frames initially run left-to-right, and then downward, just as with lines in a book, but then assume a different order in the last four frames, which run along the bottom of the facing pages and show Jacqueline Kennedy reaching toward her husband. To navigate the sequence of these frames well, a reader must refer to the blocked-off caption. The text of the caption reads, for example, "First came the police motorcycle escort [above] and then the big Lincoln."[32] Visually, without the caption, the last four frames draw immediate attention because they disrupt the linear flow of the layout and because the fourth- and third-to-last images are disproportionately larger than the rest. They feature Jacqueline Kennedy frozen in a half-turn toward her wounded husband. (The caption states, "Mrs. Kennedy suddenly becomes aware of what has happened and reaches over to help."[33]) The final two images resume the size of the other, smaller frames on the page, but are stacked strangely on top of each other, and placed together to the right of the enlarged third-to-last image. These last two images show the president falling toward the bosom of his wife. The caption reads, "The President collapses on his wife's shoulder and in the last two small pictures the First Lady cradles him in her arms."[34] Stacked, as these two frames were, one on top of the other, they looked quite like a colon, and did indeed anticipate what follows.

A colon precedes an explanation or a list. The second two-page spread of *Zapruder* images (fig. 7) explained via a list of images Jacqueline Kennedy's own collapse in light of her husband's. The first image—that is, if we read the images as a paragraph, left to right, top to bottom—has the slain president at the breast of his wife (fig. 7a). This shot reenacted the image evoked in the prologue of a mother cradling a dead child. As such, it represented a second and more perfect maternal loss, as well as the moment when Mrs. Kennedy is finally let in on what the audience knew from the start. As if to accentuate this moment, the second and the third images on the page seem to almost be identical to the first.

But then we arrive at the fourth image. Here, her love is made sublime, and her image fragmented. In the fourth image it becomes apparent that, in a certain sense, Jacqueline Kennedy has not been cradling her husband at all; rather, she has been pushing him away from her breast, turning from him to climb out of the car. "Jackie," the caption's title announces, "Crawled for Help." The mother is a child. The caption reads,

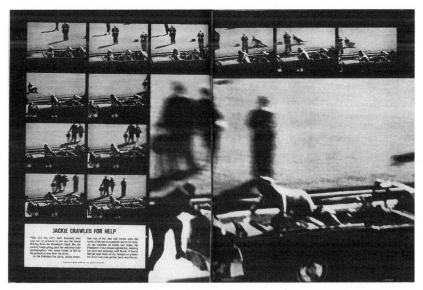

FIGURE 7A AND 7B. The second two-page spread of *Life's* frames from the Zapruder film, continuing the sequence begun in Figure 6.

"Oh, no!, Oh, no!," Mrs. Kennedy cries (*top row of pictures*) as she sees the blood flowing from the President's head. But the convoy keeps going, past the onlookers and photographers who stand frozen or fall to the ground as they hear the shots. As the President lies dying, Jackie scrambles out of her seat and crawls onto the trunk of the car in a pathetic search for help. As she crouches on hands and knees, the President's head presses against her, staining her skirt and stockings with blood. A Secret Service man leaps on the bumper to protect the First Lady and get her back into the car.[35]

The caption and its image break Jacqueline. Her cries are ineffective; "the convoy keeps going." And her flight is ineffective; it is her scrambling, in fact, which produces the prominent bloodstained skirt, featured a few pages later. In the manner of the classical tragedy that functions as the substratum of *Life*'s tale, the magazine makes this mark something like a punishment for her flight.

It is here, too, that the narrative itself is most ruthlessly controlling. "Jackie's" rejection of the destroyed head of the president and her impulse to flee are characterized as "pathetic." She is helpless, an infant or an animal. Her crouching "on hands and knees" dirties her. She is shown to have behaved carelessly as the "Secret Service man" jumps to protect her, not from the bullets, but from her own excessive impulses. Visually, the largest picture in the sequence—more than twice the size of the large pictures on the previous pages—is of Jackie crawling onto the trunk, where she is being met and restrained by the Secret Service agent.

This rendering of Jacqueline Kennedy's transgressions and regressions enacts what Horkheimer and Adorno call a "myth of enlightenment," in which both iconoclasm and sublimity participate. The dramatic action of the *Life* text places the meaning of Kennedy's death in a dialectic of gender. Jacqueline Kennedy is Woman, momentarily open to another with a sacrificial, motherly love beyond comprehension. However, her rapid devolution into an animal-like infancy calls for the strong hand of Man, seen in the Secret Service agent. When love fails, natural flight, instinctive terror, and primal panic take over. These latter chaoses, the narrative suggests, need the deft and definitive control of the hand of Man. When the image breaks, a higher, stronger power is revealed.

That the narrative itself exercised the same sort of masculine power extended the implications of this myth of enlightenment into the consciousness of the Cold War. For in 1963, Mrs. Kennedy was not the only figure coupled to presidential exposure—this was the fate of all the subjects of Cold War presidential publicity. And, of course, panic-stricken terror characterized not only Woman but also the threat of the masses. In the late 1950s and early 1960s, mass society was renewed as a subject of elite discourse. Books like C. Wright Mills's *The Power Elite* (1956), William Kornhauser's *The Politics of Mass Society* (1959), and Edmund Stillman and William Pfaff's *The Politics of Hysteria* (1964) each worried over mass society. On the other hand, Edward Shils's "The Theory of Mass Society" (1962) argued, contra Kornhauser and Mills, that mass society offered opportunities for increased political participation. A special issue of *Deadelus* in 1960, entitled "Mass Culture and Mass Media," drew together mass media professionals and academics to debate the merits of mass society for political and cultural life.[36]

Amidst such controversies about the prospects of the masses, Elias Canetti's 1962 English edition of his esteemed study of group psychology, *Crowds and Power*, introduced an archetypal outline of the dilemma of mass society. The book opened with an account of the fear of being touched—Canetti argues that such fear is an extension of a more primal fear of the sudden intrusion of the unknown. "There is nothing that man fears more than the touch of the unknown. He wants to *see* what is reaching toward him, and to be able to recognize or at least classify it. Man always tends to avoid physical contact with anything strange. In the dark, the fear of an unexpected touch can mount to panic. Even clothes give insufficient security: it is easy to tear them and pierce through to the naked, smooth, defenseless flesh of the victim."[37]

Canetti's opening meditation concluded by positing that "it is only in a crowd that man can become free of this fear of being touched."[38] *En masse* one grows used to being touched by the unknown—to not seeing the invisible hands that structure or otherwise steer one's movements. The hand, Canetti later notes, is the tool of "seizing and incorporating."[39] It is therefore, he notes, economic: "The essence of trading is the giving of one object in exchange for another."[40] It is mechanical: "There is a separate destructiveness of the hand, not immediately connected with prey and killing. It is of a purely mechanical nature and mechanical inventions are extensions of it."[41] It is martial: "A branch which broke off in the hand was the origin of the *stick*. Enemies could be fended off with a stick."[42] Finally, the hand is the primal means of communication: "*Words* and *objects* are . . . the emanations and products of a single unified experience: *representation by means of the hand*."[43] And communication gives rise to culture and politics.

Life's tale was an economic, mechanical, and martial, but it was not political. The invisible editorial hand fabricated according to an economic logic of surplus, depression, and stabilization, according to a mechanical logic of invention and dominion, and according to a military logic of threat, power, and control. It did not, however, invoke a political logic of contingency, dialogue, and practical judgment. As a figure of sublime love who moves violently between a composed decorum and an animal-like chaos, the Jacqueline Kennedy of *Life* ratified managerial force: she was the warrant for the incorporation of the controlling hand into the rhetorical production of the assassination. Expressing far more than a nation's grief—what we always assume Jackie signifies—she stood in for the subject of assassination publicity and displayed the exigency for invisible hands to overcome the destruction of the image.

The Warren Commission *Report*

The effect of *Life*'s presentation of *Zapruder* depended on a critical omission, that of the frames that depicted the impact of the bullet on the head of President Kennedy. For if these frames had been included, the centrality of Jacqueline would be challenged, the tale of sublime love compromised, the story of the fragmentation of Woman and the overcoming hand of Man itself ruined. *Life*'s photo spread was wrapped around this omission: for even as the effect of its presentation depended on the reader's ability to see what Jacqueline Kennedy could not—her fate—this focus on her fate over his is reached via an editorial vision that sees what the film, as a film, did not present. As a motion picture consisting of 486 frames run in split-second sequence, *Zapruder* is fragmented, but it is decidedly not a stark narrative about the dissolution of Jacqueline Kennedy and the need for controlling hands. Such a re-presentation of the film depended on strategic gaps in disclosure. It is all the more than critical, then, that in the next major public representation of *Zapruder*, the Warren Commission's *Report*, lacunae would come to dominate the discussion.

In the ten months between *Life*'s *Zapruder* and that of the Warren Commission *Report*, the Kennedy assassination became a worldwide spectacle that also held out the potential of becoming a similarly scaled scandal. Oswald's televised claim to be but a "patsy," his untimely death at the hands of another obscure Dallas businessman (Jack Ruby), and the already apparent gaps within the assassination story itself combined with the growing consciousness of the dark and dangerous underbelly of America's Cold War to throw into question all that Kennedy had seemingly stood for: confidence in the power of government, hope in America's adventures abroad, and a credence in the image of America. In ten short months, such liberal faith in representation—political and aesthetic—gave way to a diffuse and popularized hermeneutics of suspicion. Lacunae, omissions, gaps—that is, what was *unseen*—became central texts in this newly emergent culture of suspicion, not the least in reactions to the Warren Commission *Report* itself.

Lee Harvey Oswald was gunned down before he could be brought to a jury. Thus, the trial of the Kennedy assassination would not appear in a formal, juridical state. Instead, President Lyndon Johnson appointed the Warren Commission, whose members included not only Chief Justice Earl Warren, but also Richard Russell, a powerful Southern Senator from Georgia, Gerald Ford, who would later succeed Richard Nixon as president, and Allen Dulles, the influential former head of the CIA during Eisenhower's tenure and a collaborator with *Life*'s C. D. Jackson in the covert Cold War of the 1950s. The commission's *Report*, published in September 1964, less than a year after Kennedy's death, confirmed what the Dallas police had claimed: Oswald acted alone in killing the president. However, as is well known, the commission's conclusion was met with deep skepticism, further investigations, and a host of accusations.

But, again, what is too often overlooked is that the *Report* itself emerged from the climate it is often accused of creating—a climate Max Holland has described as one of "boundless and utter disbelief."[44] In fact, the Warren Commission explicitly presented its findings as a corrective to this rhetorical climate. Of the day of and day after Kennedy's death, it stated, "The events of these two days were witnessed with shock and disbelief by a Nation grieving the loss of its young leader. Throughout the world, reports on these events were disseminated in massive detail. Theories and speculations mounted regarding the assassination."[45] The *Report* promised that it would, on the contrary, "appraise this tragedy by the light of reason and the standard of fairness," so as "to present to the American people an objective report of the facts relating to the assassination."[46] It thus looked for a public interested in empirical facts, tethered to calculations, and, as it suggested later, capable of beholding the "substantial light" of investigative reason.[47] In this regard it offered itself not only as a counter-rhetoric to the mass-mediated and mass-disseminated assassination rhetorics of 1963 and 1964, but as a counter-sublime.

Indeed, relative to the drama of *Life*'s 1963 presentation of *Zapruder*, the film appeared rather unspectacularly in the *Report*. Its main function was to establish the "assassination."[48] The *Report* stated, "Examination of the Zapruder motion picture camera by the FBI established that 18.3 pictures or frames were taken each second, and therefore, the timing of certain events could be calculated by allowing 1/18.3 seconds for the action depicted from one frame to the next. The films and slides made from individual frames were viewed by Governor and Mrs. Connally, the Governor's doctors, the autopsy surgeons, and the Army wounds ballistics scientists in order to apply the knowledge of each to determine the precise course of events."[49] The film was thus presented as a measuring instrument in a forensic investigation. The Warren Commission numbered each frame of the film, allotted each frame a time factor of 1/18.3 seconds, and then used the film to denote temporal points in the assassination sequence. For example, in discussing the second shot fired upon the president, the *Report* stated, "From the timing evidenced by the Zapruder films [*sic*], there was an interval of from 4.8 to 5.6 seconds between the shot which struck President Kennedy's neck (between frames 210 and 225) and the shot which struck his head at frame 313."[50] Measuring instruments, however, are only as good as their capacity to bring objects into conformity with a priori categories. The Warren Commission, in fact, did not find *Zapruder* to be quite as accommodating to casting substantial empirical light as they had hoped or promised. The film resisted objective penetration in one section especially—when from frame 193 to 225 it presents the image of the backside of the Stemmons Freeway sign. Somewhere behind the sign, of course, is President Kennedy. And there, at some*time*, Kennedy was first shot, in the neck.

The lacuna is a sign, but not an image. The lacuna is premised on the possibility, if not the presence, of knowledge—the gap or erasure it signifies is a gap or erasure of something. Syntactically, the lacuna works as a genitive of possession, suggesting ownership or possession. However, the possessor is unknown, and thus the lacuna becomes an object of dispute. To what does this lacuna belong? Put in a scientific frame, then, the syntax of the lacuna leads to probabilistic reasoning. Aesthetically, however, the lacuna is a space—a vacancy or void. It is impenetrable only because it is endlessly penetrable. Put in a rhetorical frame, then, it leads to mystery and may be filled with magnified meanings.

Indeed, in its invocation of the scientific frame, the Warren Commission *Report* determined to make the lacuna in *Zapruder* a matter of probability. However, it opened up mystery, for in the *Report* the film functioned far more than as a register of time. It functioned as a register of certainty, and certainty is an end so high that the failure to reach it plunges knowledge into depths. The commission members used *Zapruder* to construct a strong claim of certainty—they knew, they insisted, to 1/18.3 of a second exactly when the president was shot in the head. However, because the Stemmons Freeway sign stood in the way, they could not reach the same degree of certainty with respect to the shot to the president's neck. Here they presented themselves as resigned to probability. Thus, placed between certainty and probability, the thirty-two-frame lacuna, less than two seconds long, became much more than an object of dispute; it was magnified into a vast space of meanings about American government in the Cold War.

This was compounded by a second, more literal lacuna in the *Report*, layered on top of that gap the film itself offered in its view of the back of Stemmons Freeway sign. In volume 18 of the unabridged edition of the *Report*, the commission reproduced what was presented as the entirety of *Zapruder* frame by frame. However, critics soon discovered that frames 208 to 211 were missing—these frames depicted the back of the Stemmons Freeway sign. The *Report* neither acknowledged nor explained the missing frames. In the context of the film's use as a scientific measuring instrument, their omission invited accusation not only of error, but of distortion, manipulation, cover-up, and conspiracy.

So the credible image of government itself began to fracture as, under the pressure of a criterion of indisputability, minutiae and gaps were amplified and made the centerpiece of a plethora of counter-rhetorics to the Warren Commission's own counter-rhetoric. At issue, in part, was the poverty of what Habermas referred to as the "administrative production of meaning." Thus William Manchester, author of *Death of a President*, identified in 1993 a basic problem of the Kennedy assassination "aesthetic": "If you put the murdered President of the United States on one side of a scale and that wretched waif Oswald on the other side, it doesn't balance. You want to add something weightier to Oswald. It would invest the President's death with meaning, endowing him with martyrdom. He would have died for something."[51] However, the amplification of minutiae and gaps meant that the aesthetics of the Kennedy assassination extended further than the question of proportionality between the magnitude of the event and the size of the assassin. The dominant aesthetic became not only one of proportionality but of magnification in the microscopic sense. The commission's report brought the spectatorial awe of the laboratory microscope to assassination discourse. It made scale the central problem of rhetoric about Kennedy's death, scale that no image and no institution could legitimately represent.

In this regard, Thomas B. Farrell has argued that "magnitude" is basic not only to aesthetics but to ethics and politics, as it is in and through magnitude that certain things come to "matter" relative to other things. He further notes that "magnification" has two senses: amplifying or making something bigger through expansion, and amplifying or making something bigger through zooming in, as with a microscope. For Farrell, rhetoric and, by extension, politics, operate between "the microbe and the gargantuan."[52] The Warren Commission *Report* unwittingly pushed public discourse about the Kennedy assassination to the outer limits of this continuum between the microbe and the gargantuan, both of which can be sublime, to a point where rhetoric and politics no longer seemed able to operate effectively.

In November 1966, two years after the *Report* was published, this problem came into view as *Life* published new frames of *Zapruder*, this time in color and accompanied by a lengthy article featuring Governor Connally's doubts about the findings of the Warren Commission. Significantly, whereas the 1963 issue featured a portrait of President Kennedy on the cover, the cover of the 1966 issue was solid black, except for a single color frame of the Zapruder film and text that included in block letters, "A Matter of Reasonable Doubt." Now the Warren Commission was on trial. Blackness as a backdrop to a judicially phrased declaration of suspicion highlighted the irony: on the one hand, there is a form of light present, an aspiration toward the truth about the matter, a belief that reason may yet arrange the facts into an indisputable order and reveal with needle-sharp clarity the cause and meaning of Kennedy's murder. On the other, this enterprise is set against blackness, the antithesis of light, which absorbs and nullifies the orienting and illuminating texture of the world of appearances. The stark interplay of light and darkness on *Life*'s 1966 cover set seeing and not seeing not in opposition to each other, but as ironically interdependent. Truth and light emerge only out of deep obscurity and darkness. By 1966, insight into the assassination depended upon such a fundamentally ironic stance. Tropes of light and darkness, color and black-and-white, and clarity and obscurity intermingled to produce startling revelations of corruption, conspiracy, and cover-up. *Zapruder* emerged in this rhetorical climate as an icon of such irony and interplay. It became an image that promised to represent and reveal, yet all the while it was made empty in the eyes of American spectators, a mere image. Indeed, after the Warren Commission *Report*, seeing *Zapruder* became chiefly seeing what was not.

What was it, then, that came to be seen and not seen in *Zapruder*? Something of the answer to this question became apparent more than eleven years after Kennedy's assassination, when *Zapruder* was shown for the first time on national television on *Good Night America* and almost thirty years later when the film was cut into Oliver Stone's *JFK*. In both instances, we see forms of rational subjectivity put in play against dark backdrops of conspiracy and corruption. Political subjects are magnified and seen only as the social institutions that they depend on are rendered obscure, incomprehensible, and even obsolete.

Good Night America

Though by 1975 thousands of people in the United States and elsewhere had viewed bootlegged copies of Abraham Zapruder's film, *Good Night America* was the first to present it to a television audience. ABC television decided to show the film even though its copyright was still owned by Time, Inc. At the conclusion of the episode, in his commentary, the show's host, Geraldo Rivera, called for "an intensive official investigation."[53] In effect, his call was heeded. Spurred on by the presentation of *Zapruder* on the show, in 1976 a House of Representatives Select Committee renewed investigation into the assassination.[54] The House committee was the culmination of years of challenges to the Warren Commission's findings, mostly by independent investigators, historians, or media personalities. The catalyst for *Good Night America*'s showing of *Zapruder* was one such figure. Robert Groden was an optical technician turned assassination researcher who had obtained a copy of the film in 1969 after New Orleans prosecutor Jim Garrison surreptitiously distributed copies of a subpoenaed version of film to contacts. Groden used his experience in the film laboratory to work on enhancing *Zapruder*'s visual quality, producing, in historian David Wrone's words, "a film version with devastating visual impact."[55] His enhanced version set him on his way to becoming one of the most prominent assassination conspiracy theorists in the United States. With respect to publicity, his big break came three months before the *Good Night America* show, in January of 1975, when the Assassination Information Bureau's "Politics of Conspiracy Conference" in Boston invited him to discuss the film. The night before the conference was to begin, Groden participated in a press conference where he showed the film. News coverage of the press conference led to huge turnouts at the convention the following day. One of the people who turned out was Dick Gregory, a well-known comedian and civil-rights activist. Upon seeing the film, Gregory joined Groden to promote more showings. Within a short time, Rivera invited Groden and Gregory to appear on *Good Night America* with the film.

Gregory's entrance into the story of the Zapruder film is significant, for it indicates a possible, and indeed sometimes actual, political alliance between civil-rights activists of the 1960s and 70s and white activists on the political left energized by Vietnam and Watergate. Here, the Zapruder film, not unlike the scenes in newspapers of whites spitting on Elizabeth Eckford in 1957, might have represented the brokenness of the American Cold War political system. It might have served as an index, indeed an icon, of what Peter Dale Scott calls "deep politics"—"all those political practices and arrangements, deliberate or not, which are usually repressed rather than acknowledged" and which, like the body of Kennedy, produce a "victimized body politic."[56] But this was not the conclusion of *Good Night America*. Rather, the show offered the brokenness of the president's body, and indeed that of the political system, as an occasion to experience a "higher" form of American subjectivity, one that could stand up to the brokenness of American Cold War politics by transcending them in the experience of the self.

Good Night America's March 6, 1975 episode presented the Zapruder film as conclusive evidence not only that the Warren Commission was wrong, but also that a conspiracy was behind Kennedy's assassination. The show's third guest, Ralph Schoeneman, argued along with Groden and Gregory that the CIA coordinated Kennedy's murder. His claim rested in part on documents he claimed to have, but even more on his assertion that virtually everyone connected to the assassination was also connected to the CIA. "The Central Intelligence Agency," he said, "particularly counter intelligence, constantly appears in the lives of these disparate people, they are all connected to it." Rivera, in turn, warned viewers that in the aftermath of the Pentagon Papers and Watergate, it seemed more probable that the FBI and CIA were engaging in illegal activities against American citizens. These institutions, which Rivera described as "so solid in American history and the fabric of American society," were threatening the future of the country.

In this claim, Schoeneman and his company were in step not only with an increasingly skeptical political left but with a larger worry in America about Cold War institutions—one that stemmed from the political right as well. In 1971, Nixon put an end to the Bretton Woods regime by breaking from the gold standard and instituting in its place a free-floating exchange system, ending a particular form of Cold War American institutional hegemony and beginning, in the eyes of many, the neoliberal economic regime. Vietnam and Watergate, meanwhile, were seen on both the left and right as signifying the cancerous condition of the Cold War American state, one that threatened to metastasize to bring about America's death unless overcome through acts of moral transcendence. What was most significant about *Good Night America's* showing of *Zapruder* in this regard was its construction of an American self that could stand up to such malignant institutional infiltration and corruption. This self was simultaneously authentic and expressive, sublime and ridiculous. Under the pressure of fragment, gaps, vacancies, and ironies of government, an American self was made that could make encounters with the destruction of images and the breakdown of institutions mere occasions for the feeling of its own power to transcend such political and symbolic disorders.

Traditionally, one of the contraries of the sublime has been the ridiculous. Kant, for example, argued in *Critique of Judgment* that the ridiculous arises when a subject pretends to actually see and comprehend positively that which is sublimely beyond sensibility and representation. The sublime is a pure negative mode of presentation; the ridiculous is a faux positive mode. Within an iconoclastic regime, the iconic is always ridiculous, for it pretends a capacity to represent what cannot be seen. For Kant, the boundaries between the sublime and the ridiculous are so clear that he can describe the ridiculous as "least of all compatible with the sublime."[57] Nevertheless, however firm their division may be under an Enlightenment order, they are difficult to neatly segregate under the pressures of neoliberal ironies, where the instability of institutions is the rule rather than the exception, as social and economic pressures are beyond representation even as political institutions are held in reserve for emergency functions. Before such an unstable order, the self performs an act that is neither positive nor negative, as pure negativity is translated subjectively as pure positivity. The self that emerges from this pure positivity is empty but authentic; authentic because of its interminable ability for expressivity. Consequently, it defiantly refuses its own reduction to representation. Its prolific and promiscuous expressivity places it beyond representation. It is sublime. And yet its pure positivity makes it ridiculous too.

This interplay was evident in *Good Night America*'s showing of *Zapruder*, beginning with Rivera's disclaimer that preceded the presentation, which became a short discourse on the peculiar ethics of television spectatorship:

> It's become very chic among television producers to put a disclaimer at the head of any film: "The film you are about to see might be shocking, it might be horrifying, you might not want your kids to watch it." And I think that the unfortunate net effect of that is to make more people watch it. Well, I'm telling you right straight out that if you are at all sensitive, if you are at all queasy, then don't watch this film. Just put on the late-night movie because this is very heavy.[58]

Rivera's riff on the genre of disclaimer featured the gossamer feel of generic custom itself. He announced that formality is fashionable (it is "very chic" to disclaim) but suggested that because formality is external and imposed, it is suspect. Rivera suspected that it may even be counterproductive to offer formal warnings against spectating. People, he suggests, take proscriptions as prescriptions. Rules are made to be broken. Thus, having called into question the convention of the disclaimer, Rivera proceeded to assert a self, himself, "right straight out" as an authentic voice quite distinct from conventional voices. He presented himself quite like a conscience, which supposedly arises from without the strictures of convention to guide the spectator. He directed the spectator to choose and act according to the unformalizable rhythms of feeling: "If you are at all sensitive, if you are at all queasy, then don't watch this film." In fact, Rivera reminded his audience, there are other affective channels to travel down, ones that are more familiar. There are late-night movies, for example. In any case, the message is, only watch the Zapruder film if it is your self-possessed choice. Be true to the truth within you.

Rivera's call to authenticity in his discourse on the disclaimer enacted a motif that was repeated during the subsequent showing of the Zapruder film. The motif had to do with the presentation and construction of the self. The pattern was this: the self is placed in contradistinction to institutionality (in the broadest sense of external convention, form, and rule) and therein called to feel and express and thus construct its selfsame self. If we ask upon what grounds spectatorial subjectivity rests, it is this capacity to express and thus construct the elusive selfsame self.

As the film was shown, Groden argued that it demonstrated conclusively the incredibility of the Warren Commission account. He stated during the display of the mortal shot on Kennedy, "Now the Warren Commission said that all the shots were fired from behind by Lee Harvey Oswald, a lone as-sassin, firing at the president. And as you can see clearly, the head is thrown violently backward, completely consistent with a shot from the front." From Groden's perspective, the commission's failure to account for the obvious, for what is clearly and plainly evident to any rationally minded spectator, casts deep suspicion on the commission's motives. *Zapruder* indicts the commis-sion and reveals, as Rivera did with the genre of disclaimer, the artificiality and inauthenticity of an institutional order. This in turn opens a space for a supra-institutional ground to emerge from which to grasp reality, to see the truth, and to engage in a form of judgment.

Good Night America (re)produced such a ground.[59] It was purely affective, yet referred itself to a truth. The ground, we might say, was the pure feeling of truth. The incessant talk of Groden and Rivera during the showing generated it. The modern "prism of the self," as Jean Bethke Elshtain suggested in 1995, finds a source of its own construction in talk, that is, through the free exhibi-tion of subjectivity. "Indeed, we now like to talk endlessly about the self," she writes. Through talk, we can refer the self back to the self.[60] Charles Taylor has described this particular mode of self-construction as "expressivism."[61] He argues that along with the decline of externalization, that is, external or-ders as the source of selfhood, the subject turned toward self-expression to "make" the self. However, as Taylor vigorously argues, the self is not therefore merely narcissistic. It operates according to the moral ideal of authenticity, an ideal that presupposes the existence of a type of truth, the truth of autonomy, the truth of natural rights, the truth of personal dignity, and so forth.[62] It is, above all, the truth that is within us, the truth of the selfsame self, and it is heard in the voice within. On *Good Night America*, the Zapruder film summoned this truth, as Groden's and Rivera's incessant talk brought the truth of the selfsame self to life.

As the show begins, Groden talks. He had spliced onto the front of the Zapruder film external footage that showed the presidential motorcade before its turn onto Elm Street, where the Zapruder film begins. With each brief strip of prefatory and anticipatory footage, Groden states, "This is commercial footage"; "This is a film taken by Mary Muchmore that leads into the Zapruder film; it's for time continuity"; "This is from Orville Nix's film; . . . this is originally 8mm footage." Groden's speech here is deliberate and technical. He speaks very much as the technician he advertises himself to be. He continues:

GRODEN: Now this is the Zapruder film.
RIVERA: Okay, so the cars are coming along now into Dealey plaza.
GRODEN: Right, these are the lead motorcycles in the motorcade.
RIVERA: Alright now with the President and Mrs. Kennedy is also Governor Connally?
GRODEN: Right. Now before he goes behind the sign, the President is waving to the crowd; when he comes out from behind the sign he is shot, and then Governor Connally is shot.[63]

Here, the function of the talk is expressive, though it may not seem so. If we read it as it appears, as denotative and descriptive, we would have to presume that either the audience is unfamiliar with the event, so that basic details need to be explained, or that the film is cryptic, even incomprehensible, and that therefore it must be spoken for. Yet, both of these presumptions are unwarranted. Massive public attention had already been given to the assassination, and most audience members would be quite familiar with the event. Furthermore, the film is far from cryptic in its visual depictions. The talk, then, functions expressively to makes selves. The talk proceeds:

RIVERA: He's already been hit?
GRODEN: He's already been hit.
RIVERA: And now?
GRODEN: At the bottom of the screen, the headshot [*in-studio crowd gasps*].
RIVERA: That's the shot that blew off his head. It's the most horrifying thing I've ever seen in the movies.[64]

Rivera's words here, "It's the most horrifying thing I've ever seen in the movies," indicate that in the expressivism of the self, reality is transfigured. In his disclaimer, Rivera's strong move toward the authentic led him to move away from the security of external points of reference and toward the interiority of feeling. Here, the apparent gaff of equating the Zapruder film with "the movies" can pass freely through his lips because the question at hand is not external reality, but a quality of feeling. As Susan Sontag observes, the phrase "It seemed like a movie" is often invoked in common speech in order to try to explain how real something is subjectively.[65] Movies, in this sense, are not forms of representation, but the loci of forms of experience. Rivera's pure subjectivity speaks when he exclaims, "It's the most horrifying thing I've ever seen in the movies." Groden's voice is quite different. He seems to be an unfeeling subject and thus appears as Rivera's alter ego, the voice of reason. Groden shows no signs of being moved by the Zapruder film's devastating display of violence. His scientific voice works to unhinge the Warren Commission's supposed fact-based findings.

The showing of the Zapruder film ends with a replay of the headshot. Groden and Rivera continue their dialogue:

GRODEN: Now the Warren Commission said that all the shots were fired from behind by Lee Harvey Oswald, a lone assassin, firing at the president, and as you can see clearly, the head is thrown violently backwards [*here the Zapruder film ends*], completely consistent with a shot from the front.

RIVERA: Right. [*They begin to reshow a section of the film.*]

GRODEN: Now this is an extreme blow up of just the President from the film; coming out from behind the sign, he's shot.

RIVERA: He's hit!

GRODEN: He's hit here.

DICK GREGORY: From the front, too.

GRODEN: From the front. Now, Jackie doesn't realize what's happened yet; she goes to his aid.

RIVERA: And now . . . [*headshot strikes the president; the crowd gasps*] he's hit.

GRODEN: The violent backward motion, totally consistent with 80 percent of the witnesses who said the shot came from the grassy knoll in front and to the right.

GREGORY: It is interesting to note how many people are running toward where most folks thought the shots come from [*they now show Orville Nix's film of the immediate aftermath of Kennedy's shooting on Dealey Plaza*].

GRODEN: The head goes backwards in the Nix film from the other side of the street [*the Nix film shows a distant shot of Kennedy's headshot from the opposite vantage point*].

RIVERA: Oh God, that's awful. That's the most upsetting thing I've ever seen; we'll talk about it in a minute.

On the heels of the most upsetting thing Rivera has ever seen, *Good Night America* cut to a commercial break. This time, Rivera offered no disclaimer or warning. Spectators were suddenly given no choice. *Good Night America* had given its audience their moments for authentic self-willed spectatorship and moments for the pure experience of the truth. Now, with the cut to the commercial, they took them away.

If *Good Night America*'s display of the Zapruder film had a profound effect on public perceptions of the Kennedy assassination, culminating in the formation of the House of Representatives Select Committee to investigate the assassination in 1976, this is not without its own irony. Given the basic motif of the *Good Night America* episode—the motif of authentic expressivism—it is ironic, but not surprising, that the matter ended up back in the very institutional structures that were made suspect. It is not surprising either that the House Committee did so little to mitigate the cottage industry of conspiracy theories that Groden represented. *Good Night America* suggests that what characterizes these theories, at least as they are articulated in the popular media, is not a judicial desire for justice, but the making of selves.[66]

Alluding to Kant's discussion of the sublime and the ridiculous, Kenneth Burke argues that each represents the pivot of "equipment for living." He states, "Some vastness of magnitude, power, or distance, disproportionate to ourselves, is 'sublime.' We recognize it with awe. We find it dangerous in its fascination. And we equip ourselves to confront it by piety. . . . The ridiculous, on the contrary, equips us by impiety, as we refuse to allow the threat its authority."[67] *Good Night America* evinced piety and impiety simultaneously. The expression of awe at the horror of Kennedy's mortal wound and at the threat of the CIA-led conspiracy behind it also refused the threat its authority, for the threat becomes the occasion for a new sort of self-fashioning. Each figure on *Good Night America*'s set represented this new kind of self-making, shaped as public figures from the fiber of exposé, expressivism, and entertainment. Moreover, the dialectic between Groden and Rivera, between pure truth and pure experience respectively, systematically excluded a tension-filled dialectic between subject and object. The space between subject and object is empty. Subject and object are each all in all. The transference between the sublime and ridiculous shows the ironic stance of the self that confronts a system it already has refused. Such a self finds in the corrupt institution a source of its own making and a sense of piety. Yet, in disclaiming institutionality, the conspiracy discourse refuses to acknowledge as a genuine threat the institutions that are being confronted. The institution qua institution is determined to be ridiculous, a mere token, its threat thus refused.

JFK

Oliver Stone's *JFK*, released in 1991 on the heels of the Persian Gulf War, pursues this logic a step further by abandoning the object altogether as a necessary, albeit provisional and fleeting, site upon which the subject can project its superiority. Stone's freeness with the evidence surrounding Kennedy's death has been widely noted. Many critics have claimed that the cause of this freeness lay in Stone's commitment to "revisionist" history. Martin Medhurst presents a sophisticated version of this claim:

> On the one hand the film functions as "revisionist history" as it winnows, selects, adapts, and constructs the story of the assassination plot. Such an approach to history is clearly informed by the view . . . that history is created, not discovered ready-made. History is a rhetorical construction of the historian or historical filmmaker. On the other hand, however, the film features an epistemological position holding that there is only one truth and that it is absolute and unchanging. . . . Thus a basic contradiction appears between Stone's theory of history, which is relativistic, and his theory of truth, at least as those theories take on a concrete expression within the cinematic world.[68]

Yet, the contradiction Medhurst stresses in *JFK* is resolved in the film through Stone's portrayal of a particular political vision. The film itself suggests that its freeness with the facts is neither an expression of creative license or of a philosophical commitment to revisionist history, but the expression of a form of political being.

JFK argues that the conspiratorial efforts of the CIA, the FBI, the military, and anti-Castro ideologues were responsible for the violent death of Kennedy. That death, as the film's long and complex opening montage contends, represented the loss of American idealism and the demise of democratic hope. "Kennedy," we are told by the narrator during the montage, "is the symbol of the new freedom of the 1960s signifying change and upheaval to the American public."[69] His death, consequently, is the symbol of the ominous triumph of the military-industrial complex, the presence of which is announced at the beginning of the montage with clips from Eisenhower's farewell speech. The idealistic cast of the opening montage is the first major indication to viewers that Stone would offer much more than an analysis of facts. He seems from the start of the film to be much more interested in presenting an exposé of motives and, as I consider below, exploring the meaning of political being under the governance of a militarized, bureaucratic nation-state. Mr. X, a military operative turned mysterious informer, tells Garrison, "The organizing principle of any society, Mr. Garrison, is for war."[70] Society is motivated by states of emergency, and thus perpetuates violence. In *JFK*, Stone carries this logic out by suggesting that the political self, therefore, must be able to find a source for its own authentic being in emergency violence. In an apparent contradiction, the coercive state becomes the occasion for the realization of a free self.

The shape of *JFK*'s political vision is indicated at the penultimate moment of the film's opening montage, which presents footage from *Zapruder* that leads up to, but does not include, the graphic scene of a bullet entering Kennedy's head. In place of the frames depicting the headshot, we get a 2.5-second lacuna—a black screen with no sound. This lacuna is dramatically ended by the sound of a gun being cocked, then of a gunshot, then another, then another, accompanied by a cut to a view of the Texas School Book Depository, where birds are shown scattering from the roof at the sound of the shots. The film then cuts to a CBS television special bulletin announcement, before returning to a clip from the Zapruder film that shows the scene of Jacqueline Kennedy climbing out from the back seat of the limousine. Because the lacuna, in its blackness and silence, is the most conspicuous frame of the montage, it asks to be interrogated for meaning. It represents the most critical point of the montage, and the montage, as other critics have argued, presents in compact form the entire message that drives the film. As one critic states, "The montage is the message in *JFK*."[71] Thus a void sits at the center of the film.

However, lacunae, as we have seen, can present serious challenges to interpreters of texts. They represent an empirical limit that constrains the act of interpretation. Yet, lacunae are significant in this way only if one is dependent upon an object, image, or model without for understanding. Stone's placement of a lacuna at the center of the montage suggests what *JFK* goes on to confirm, that what is objectively without is in fact tangential to understanding. He is a true iconoclast. Whether we see the president's headshot or a black screen is incidental to the message of the film. The most effective way to make this point is to impose the latter where we expect the former.

As many critics have noted, *JFK* pursues the truth about Kennedy's assassination in a way that magnifies themes of spiritual angst, national identity, and political subjectivity. Stone's protagonist, Jim Garrison, as Medhurst argues, engages in a Platonic quest. This quest is indicated not merely by his pursuit of the Truth, but by his increasing skepticism about the world of appearances, about what is given. Medhurst writes,

> The dialectical pairs of sight/blindness, appearance/truth, and interior/exterior point to the central mechanism by which Garrison—and through him

the audience—come to knowledge. To be able to "see" is to come to know the truth. But such knowledge is a function of mind, not of physical sight. It is produced internally as the result of cognitive operations that do not depend upon simple one-to-one correspondence between events, objects, and people as they exist in the world of sensory impressions. Indeed the world of the senses is explicitly rejected as a source of knowledge when Garrison tells his investigators, "We're through the looking glass here, people—white is black and black is white." The world experienced by the senses is not to be trusted.[72]

What, then, is the meaning of citizenship when the world experienced by the senses is suspect? Throughout the film, we find Garrison posing in different ways this basic question, and suggesting an answer.

The most important answer comes in one of the final scenes of the film, when Garrison offers his closing arguments in his prosecution of Clay Shaw for participating in a conspiracy to murder the president. Stone's Garrison declares, "We've all become Hamlets in our country, children of a slain father-leader whose killers still possess the throne. The ghost of John F. Kennedy confronts us with the secret murder at the heart of the American dream. He forces on us the appalling questions: Of what is our Constitution made? What is our citizenship, and more, our lives, worth?"[73] Hamlet is a figure possessed by a ghost and by the secrets of conspiracy. Hamlet is motivated by fear, love, anger, and loyalty, all of which refer themselves to a specter. Garrison, likewise, is motivated by such spiritual affections. This is evident at the genesis of his quest. The first time the audience meets Garrison, he is alone in his New Orleans law office when he is interrupted by his assistant, Lou. Lou tells him that the president has just been shot. "Oh no! How bad?" Garrison asks. "No word yet. But they think it's in the head," Lou replies. "Come on," Garrison responds. "Napoleon's has a TV set." From the office, the film cuts to Napoleon's, where Garrison is pictured watching CBS news. The news anchor reports, "Apparently three bullets were found. Governor Connally also appeared to be hit. The President was rushed by Secret Service to Parkland Memorial Hospital four miles from Dealey Plaza. We are told a bullet entered the base of the throat and came out of the backside, but there is no confirmation, blood transfusions are being given, a priest has administered the last rights." To this news, Garrison replies, "There's still a chance, dammit! Come on, Jack—pull through."[74] The exclamation "Jack" reverberates with intimacy. It is a term of endearment. In calling out to Jack, Garrison leaps across the boundaries of spectatorship and political association, and lands in the sphere of the private and personal. Garrison thus becomes a "private" investigator in public office, the state agent deeply suspicious of the state, the iconoclast within.

JFK uses the subplot of Garrison's domestic life to support the private and personal character of his purportedly public quest. As the narrative progresses, the more possessed Garrison is by the truth of the assassination conspiracy, the more estranged he grows from his wife, Liz. In one scene, Garrison arrives home late on Easter Sunday night, having missed the family's holiday celebration. Liz exclaims, "You know what I think, I think you care more about John Kennedy than about your own family!" So the couple grows more divorced, until—in what, to modify Stanley Cavell's term, might be called a dark comedy of remarriage—they are reconciled to each other on the evening of Robert Kennedy's murder.[75] Liz is sleeping upstairs. Garrison witnesses the murder on television, shocked. He goes upstairs, wakes her, and tells Liz the news. "They've killed him, honey. They won." She replies in alarm, "Both brothers! You were right. It hasn't ended." Liz then embraces Garrison and they begin to make love—this is the only time the couple makes love in the film. In this way, the movements of Garrison's marriage and "remarriage" are organized and reorganized around Garrison's quest. His physical encounter with his wife signals the consummation of the spiritual union he has been seeking with her as they join together as co-witnesses of the specter of conspiracy. This consummation is reenacted in the courtroom a few scenes later, just as Garrison is preparing to show the jury *Zapruder* for the first time. At this pivotal point in the lengthy trial, Liz walks through the rear doors of the courtroom; it is the first time she has appeared in court to support her husband. Garrison gives her a long, knowing look, and then starts the projector.

We see in Stone's Garrison just how much we all would be like Hamlets if we were to become the sort of citizens Stone imagines through *JFK*. Specters and ghosts compel political action in *JFK*. Political association consists of the tender and personal union of co-possession. Just as the world experienced by the senses is rendered suspect, so *JFK* makes bodies and the space between bodies, together with the space between life and death, tangential to authentic political being. Political subjects can leap over such limitations by grabbing hold of the ethereal cords of affection. Just how Platonic Stone's political vision is is indicated by the reorganization of eros around the quest. Garrison's progression follows the trajectory of Plato's eros, as described by Diotima, the philosopher of love in Plato's *Symposium*. As Diotima describes the erotic, ecstatic ascent from boy-loving to the love of Beauty unspoiled and unchanged, she states,

> When a man has been thus far tutored in the lore of love, passing from view to view of beautiful things, in the right and regular ascent, suddenly he will have revealed to him, as he draws to the close of his dealings in love, a wondrous

vision, beautiful in its nature.... Existing ever in singularity of form independent by itself, while all the multitude of beautiful things partake of it in such
wise that, though all of them are coming to be and perishing, it grows neither
greater nor less, and is affected by nothing.[76]

This classical account of eros would richly inform theologies of the icon.
Through them worshippers would pass from view to view, culminating in a
wondrous vision of the ideal. But Plato's theory need only be radicalized to
become a vindication of iconoclasm. For if Being is to be "affected by nothing," why not expose the sensible world as a mere rung on the ladder and
make a direct transcendental leap into the ideal? Indeed, the political ideal of
JFK is to be possessed by such a wondrous vision as to be "affected by nothing," that is nothing in the concrete, visible, objective world. Stone's political vision presupposes that concrete, particular political bodies are there to
be overcome. Political space is for him disembodied, affective, and singular.
Garrison's political being matures and grows only as he renders more and
more suspect the world of appearances. News media, governmental agencies, judges, juries, and even some of Garrison's own assistants are rendered
incredible because they have not yet grasped that "white is black and black is
white." In this topsy-turvy political world, the sheer givenness of the world
is not only subject to this ironic gaze, it is subjected to destruction. The lacuna we are presented with in the opening montage is not innocent. It is the
manifest product of cutting and splicing. Here, Stone takes Epstein's theory
of film art one step further. If film is inherently illusory, stringing together a
chain of fragments into a perceived continuousness, and thus dependent on
a "purely interior phenomenon" for its coherence, Stone cuts the Zapruder
film further, disrupting the illusion, and imposes in its place a blackness from
which the viewer is to construct a concept of citizenship. Thus, in contradistinction to Diotima's vision, Garrison's vision is forebodingly dark, as dark
as the lacuna in the montage. Just before Garrison and Liz make love on the
night of their newfound spiritual union, Garrison states, "For the first time,
I'm scared."

The political vision Garrison represents is frightening indeed, for to
achieve its affect, it depends upon a violent act, the destruction of the image,
and likewise on the ubiquity of the emergency violence of the state. In order
for Garrison to be possessed by an authentic political being and to realize
profound political affections, he must witness on the television the transformation of John Kennedy into a ghost beyond such violence. The "Jack" Garrison calls out to through televisual time and space is an ephemeral Jack. In the
same manner, Garrison and Liz's spiritual union is achieved in the aftermath

of Garrison's viewing of Robert Kennedy's murder, and their reenactment of that union in the courtroom comes just before the projection of the Zapruder film. Garrison's political bonds are thus consistently formed through observing the destruction of images. Thus, for all its allusions to Platonic idealism, Stone's *JFK* is far darker than the Platonic vision. The sort of subjectivity it produces is premised neither on the fleetingness of the objective world, nor on the objective world's violent demotion to the level of a mere token; rather, visibility itself is destroyed. Blindness is the only legitimate mode of insight.

Conclusion

It is true, as has often been noted, that John F. Kennedy's popularity as president was suffering as he began his fateful trip to Dallas. Nevertheless, he was still the president of the United States in the high age of Cold War image management begun by *Sputnik* some six years earlier. The open convertible was an echo of an open society, the presidential couple an index of American domestic contentment, the motorcade a reflection of American mobility, and the gunshots an attack on the entire symbolic system—as was Abraham Zapruder's hasty decision to sell the contents of his late-model camera to the most aggressive corporate bidder. No amount of state "ideology planning," to invoke Habermas again, could overcome that attack on its image; no governmental meaning management could manage to make assassination violence meaningful if the only live record of the event would be commodified before it could ever be politicized.[77]

Indeed, the career of the Zapruder film began ominously for the state. While *Life*'s tale featured the state's hand reaching out, almost literally, to contain the assassination violence, this was *Life*'s tale, not that of the state. It is as if *Life*, under the wily management of the cold warrior C. D. Jackson, knew there could be no administrative production of meaning; therefore Time-Life, Inc. would take on the function of meaning making. To be sure, *Life*'s tale would be managerial, anticipating the Warren Commission's *Report*. Yet, the more fundamental politics of its rhetorical form were apparent: in reaching, the state could only overreach. The state's failure would be as inevitable as its failure to adequately manage and regulate the transforming global economy.

Good Night America and *JFK* appeared in a later age of Cold War image management. Their stories were symptomatic of the profundity of the motivation crisis that the failure of the state, however inevitable, had produced. For, as Habermas suggested but two years before *Good Night America*'s *Zapruder* exposé, advanced capitalism was not only placing insurmountable pressures on the state but on more resilient forms of material culture as well.

Good Night America and *JFK* each asserted the incapacity of material culture to adequately account for political meaning. They were in turn symptomatic of a broader iconoclastic culture that had emerged, one that reduces all institutions to mere tokens or idols.

Whether in *Life*, the Warren Commission *Report*, the television exposé, or the Hollywood conspiratorial blockbuster, the initial failure of the state to acquire and manage Abraham Zapruder's film meant that the most important and monumental images in America would be images of the destruction of the image. To be sure, political identities and social authorities would still be materialized, but the most powerful statements would be presented in ideal terms. With *Zapruder*, the destruction of the image would become a unique and singular occasion for the expression of national feeling. Thus Frederic Jameson wrote of President Kennedy's death in 1991, the same year *JFK* was released,

> Yet this inaugural event . . . gave what we call a Utopian glimpse into some collective communicational "festival" whose ultimate logic and promise is incompatible with our modes of production. The sixties, often taken as the moment of a paradigm shift toward the linguistic and the communicational, can also be said to begin with this death, not because of its loss or the dynamics of collective grief, but because it was the occasion (like May 1968 later on) for the shock of a communicational explosion, which could have no further consequences within this system but which scars the mind with the briefly glimpsed experience of radical difference, to which collective amnesia aimlessly returns in its later forgetfulness, imagining itself to be brooding over trauma where it is in fact seeking to produce a new idea of Utopia.[78]

Indeed, it is precisely this new idea of Utopia, this new sublime, which was expressed in *JFK*. There we had the presentation of a freedom and autonomy so radical that it rendered the political, together with meaning, a merely interior and indeed spiritual phenomenon. The classical liberal political contest between the citizen and the state was transfigured in the blockbuster product of an iconoclastic culture into an ontological opposition between the private American citizen and the ubiquitously violent American Cold War state.

Here was a dark version of neoliberal discourse. As Alasdair MacIntyre has noted, "Those who persistently attack bureaucracy effectively reinforce the notion that it is in terms of a relationship to bureaucracy that the self has to define itself."[79] In an important sense, neoliberalism is as bound to the state for its definition as the state is bound to managing profit maximization. In its optimistic comedic form, the state steps in like a *deus ex machina* to resolve the tensions of the plot and reconcile free subjects to free markets. In its dark comedic form, the state is just as integral to the resolution of the plot, but now it is itself the problem to be overcome through the redefinition of selves. These two modes of neoliberal discourse, one dark and the other light, are ironically interdependent, for it is only against the backdrop of darkness that light gains its luminance. The 1960s and 1970s in America were in many respects an era of dark neoliberal comedies; in the 1980s, however, the darkness of the state was transformed into the light of "America." There, in the age of Reagan, a neoliberal discourse came to the fore that imagined, in a manner far more effective than any weak state ideology planning, a third way, a Utopian alternative where state and cultural institutions alike are idols, and all other images, like brands, are mere tokens.

4

Challenger

It is not that the Zapruder film created the iconoclastic appetite. It's that it rationalized it in a Cold War political culture that was, in a crucial geopolitical context, premised on the preeminence of the image. In the Eisenhower years in particular, ideology production and image management were not only means of buttressing the state's legitimacy as it weighed corporate interests against more general public interests; they had as well the form of strategic maneuvers in a confrontation with global communisms. Thus it was taken as axiomatic by every cold warrior, even those most hardened by *Realpolitik*, that the security of the United States depended on the production of images.

Consider the motivating image of the high age of Cold War image management, *Sputnik*, which appeared in 1957, only weeks after images of Little Rock, to once again disrupt the image of America. Wanting to create an alert and prepared citizenry, the Eisenhower administration worked in 1953 toward introducing Americans to the new, catastrophic potential of a nuclear age through a program called "Operation Candor" that would include speeches, brochures, press articles, traveling exhibitions, and films. But the administration would soon conclude that candor could backfire, stirring anxieties among citizens, even panic, rather than fostering an alert, soldierly sobriety.[1] Indeed, before the end of his tenure as president, Eisenhower would find that it did not take mushroom clouds to cause Americans to panic, but only a little speck in the sky. *Sputnik I* signaled to Americans the prospect of their own horrible destruction, producing an alarmed, if not exactly alert, citizenry. The great American disaster of the 1950s, the "breaking news" which both shocked and awed the nation, was a little Soviet bug-like device. *Life* wrote, "Let us not pretend that *Sputnik* is anything but a defeat."[2] Likewise, Senator Lyndon

Baines Johnson proclaimed that *Sputnik* "demonstrates beyond question that
the Soviet Union has the propulsive force to hurl a missile from one continent
to another."[3] Johnson opened Senate hearings on *Sputnik* with the solemn declaration, "We meet today in the atmosphere of another Pearl Harbor."[4] Who
would have thought, as one legislative assistant commented at the time, that
"before the end of the year [1957], the United States would suffer a Pearl Harbor in the Cold War"?[5] Of course, *Sputnik* was a vision of what was not—or at
least not yet. As US leaders well knew, it was one thing to launch a satellite and
quite another to target an intercontinental missile. *Sputnik* was but a projection. Yet, if in 1957 the legitimacy of the United States as a world leader rested
on the premise that the American liberal economic style was superior to the
Soviet command-and-control system, and on the corresponding technological premise that the United States possessed more sophisticated weaponry
than the USSR, then *Sputnik* wrecked both premises.[6] America was destroyed
by that speck in the sky.

The Zapruder film would model a means of surviving the precariousness
of the image. It suggested that if meaning could not be found in the administrative production of the image, it might be found in the destruction of the
image. In the preceding chapter, I considered a form of American subjectivity that emerged against the stark and obscure backdrop of assassination
violence, a dark civic piety that took shape before violent movement, trou-
bling lacunae, and exposés of vast, institutional conspiracy. This subjectivity,
however, could give way to a proportionately stark objectivity. Iconoclasm
is not just the assertion of a will against an image; it is an announcement
of an objective, immaterial presence—a Law. It entails, in a pseudo-Platonic
manner, a claim about Being. It declares, in radical Protestant fashion, that
the material of culture is an illegitimate home for the transcendent. It finds
in the broken image, in romantic fashion, a transcendental sign. It asserts,
in neoliberal manner, the presence of an ordering, meaning-making agency
beyond material institutions.

In this chapter, I look at the second great American iconoclasm of the
Cold War era proper, the *Challenger* disaster. Here I consider the appearance of a radical object in the fiery fragments of an image. That this object,
America, appeared not in the image but in the interpretation of the broken
image is consistent with the iconoclastic tradition and its cultural, political,
and indeed civic religious legacies. That the image, broken by disaster, contained a female school teacher meant a transformation in the rhetorical logic
of the Zapruder film: here the ordinary citizen was taken from behind the
camera and put in front of it, where, like Jacqueline Kennedy, she was met

with the managerial hand, but now only to be sacrificed to it. Moreover, that this image was not just broken but consumed by fire might even suggest a purification of the rites of ideology production and image management.

Such purification was the distinct achievement of the Reagan presidency in the Cold War. Whereas Eisenhower at times wanted the image, and wanted it iconic, only to find it the source of repeated legitimation crises, Reagan seems to have understood from the start that images of America, like B-movie actors, were but tokens, and that the smoothest channel for ideology production was the discourse of transcendence. Thus, his "*Challenger* Address," a consummate text in the rhetoric of the modern American presidency, pit "America" *against* the image. Indeed, for all the well-known staging of the Reagan presidency, it was possessed by a tokenism that, far from having a trivializing effect, was premised on the incapacity of institutions—be they primarily economic, political, or cultural—to contain the nation. The nation, like outer space itself, was uncontainable.

New Frontiers

In 1893, at the World's Columbian Exposition, Frederick Jackson Turner famously argued that "American social development has been continually beginning over again on the frontier."[7] As Turner explained, "Behind institutions, behind constitutional forms and modifications, lie the vital forces that call these organs into life and shape them to meet changing conditions. The peculiarity of American institutions is the fact that they have been compelled to adapt themselves to the changes of an expanding people—to the changes involved in crossing a continent, in winning a wilderness, and in developing at each area of this progress out of the primitive economic and political conditions of the frontier into the complexity of city life."[8] Turner thus Americanized the classical liberal theory of the origins of institutions: if institutions reflect social arrangements and aspirations, he argued that the social arrangements and aspirations of Americans (in contrast to Europeans) had been bound to the frontier, "the outer edge of the wave—the meeting point between savagery and civilization."[9]

Much of the subsequent century made Turner's thesis seem prophetic as well as retrospective. Though he meant to announce the closing of the frontier, Turner forecasted the ways in which social life in twentieth-century America would continue to be reborn upon the frontier. But these latter-day frontiers would not be found only amid "the colonization of the Great West."[10] Rather, they were located abroad, across oceans, where Americans

would fight the savageries of totalitarianisms in the world wars, and communist expansionism in Korea, Vietnam, and the missile silos of that Great West.

However in the early 1970s, some eighty years after Turner's address, the
terrestrial frontier before America did indeed close, and the relatively short-
lived "American Century" came to an end.[11] Détente meant that foreign fields
of battle were no longer Americanized frontiers but simply localities on a
complex geopolitical map. Henceforth, as Nixon would signal in his so-called
"silent majority" speech of 1969, America would disassociate its aspirations
from its institutional commitments: "In the previous administration, we Americanized the war in Vietnam. In this administration, we are Vietnamizing the
search for peace."[12] That is to say, America was retreating from the frontier,
pulling out, evacuating. Indeed, Nixon would cut America loose from a series
of Americanizations: not only from the war in Vietnam, but also from the
tense, tit-for-tat engagements with the Soviets and the Chinese and from the
US commitments made at Bretton Woods in 1944 (above all, the commitment to back dollars overseas with gold, that great material treasure of the
Great West).

This last decision, made in 1971, would be the most permanent. By 1980,
Vietnam was a morose memory, and Cold War tensions had returned, but
monetary policy in the United States, and globally, was firmly on the far side
of a point-of-no-return. Money was now free from matter. The Federal Reserve had within its ethereal grasp a free-floating system. There was no longer
any territorial treasure by which to guarantee the good fortune of the nations. This transformation was not only systemic; it was rhetorical. It her-
alded the end of the old form of empire premised on territory and treasure
and the advent of the new empire of finance. While American presidents of
the 1970s—Nixon, Ford, and Carter—having retreated from the Americanizations of decades prior, spoke regularly in a minor key, Nixon's monetary
revolution nevertheless suggested a symbolic logic that could produce a new
image of America, one free from material deposits altogether—be they territorial, commoditized, or iconic.

Such a free-floating symbolic logic was not strictly the domain of economics, and it was certainly not a simple reflex of economic outcomes. Indeed,
while there were severe economic pressures and contradictions in the early
1970s that motivated the dissolution of the liberal Bretton Woods system, a
condition of its legitimacy, if not its possibility, was the capacity to imagine
a free-floating symbolic system in the first place. The needed imaginary was,
in a certain sense, as old as liberalism itself—we can think of Locke's description of money, riches, and treasure as possessing but "Phantastical imaginary

value; Nature has put no such upon them."[13] But this fantastical quality was, for Locke and later liberals, a problem as much as a fact, and thus conceits like geographical boundaries and gold standards were developed to give the currency of nations the semblance of the real. At-homeness in a free-floating world, it was assumed, can be hard-won through territorial incursions and the mining of treasure.

Still, there were two other Cold War frontiers in the 1970s that resembled the new free-floating symbolic system of the Federal Reserve: science and outer space. After *Sputnik*, Americans quickly found out that outer space was no ordinary frontier—not with chimps, airtight capsules, space suits, rockets, and control panels filling magazine pages and television screens. More fundamentally, space lacked anything like geography. Its fundamental logic was scalar. Once out of the terrestrial orbit, its navigation could be as free-floating as the post-gold-standard monetary system. Whatever targets might be set, they could not be justified geographically, other than in a wish to transcend geography. Destinations would instead be determined by the interanimating calculi of national security and symbolic economy. In this regard, outer space was not a frontier at all; it was, like the power of science of America's Cold War, an endless frontier, a sublime space of free-floating exploration.[14]

Indeed, in America's science-packed space program, something like the inverse of Turner's thesis was shown. Rather than institutions arising out of social developments derived from the experience of the frontier, the new space frontier arose from social developments that came on the heels of decisive institutional failures—most immediately, the failure of the Eisenhower administration to beat the Soviets into orbit, but more fundamentally, the failure of governments and political institutions worldwide to adequately manage the global behemoths of military and economic modernizations. For the Eisenhower administration, *Sputnik* was a decisive defeat, but only because it had invested so much institutional capital in the image. Eisenhower had determined that ideology planning would be front and center in the conflict with the Soviets. Therefore, virtually anything could be subject to the long photographic exposure of the Cold War, even that speck in the sky. *Sputnik* was an image disaster, anticipating the inevitable end of an American Century premised on ideological and symbolic factors. Indeed, in the wake of the *Sputnik* disaster, Karl G. Harr, one of Eisenhower's cold warriors, could only vent, "We cannot permit an image to exist that is the end of the U.S. Golden Age."[15] It was, of course, too late.

Yet the shock of *Sputnik* might have been prevented had the Eisenhower administration not been so preoccupied with managing the image. They felt it was not enough simply to be the first to get an object into space. Rather, as

Nelson Rockefeller, who had succeeded C. D. Jackson as Eisenhower's psychological warfare chief, told the National Security Council in 1955, the image of America's efforts in space had to be "under auspices that are least vulnerable to effective criticism."[16] For the Eisenhower administration, this would mean a modest space program sanctioned by the supposedly boundary-free aspirations of science and technology. The United States would not be content merely to launch a ball with a "beep" (as *Sputnik* would later be characterized by US officials). Their symbolic satellites would have instrumentation, and their sendoff would be reserved for the high ceremonial occasion of the International Geophysical Year (I.G.Y.), a global cooperative venture among scientists from sixty-six countries, including the United States and the USSR, intended to survey from above Earth and its atmosphere. The United States would thereby free itself of charges of mere tokenism or, worse, warmongering.[17]

All this image massaging, however, ended up working against US Cold War interests. When in the mid-1950s the Army confirmed that it could launch a satellite as early as the winter of 1957 (some six months before the I.G.Y. was to begin), the plan was shot down out of fear of compromising the United States's "strong moral position internationally."[18] America would wait for the opportune moment, which was never to come. The Soviets beat them to it. And in yet another irony, when the Soviets, as part of I.G.Y., launched *Sputnik* in October 1957, the United States would accuse its adversary of warmongering, precisely the intention an I.G.Y. launch was intended to subvert for the United States.

In hindsight, therefore, it seems odd that *Sputnik* would begin the high age of Cold War symbolism in the United States. It seems that it should have signaled instead its qualification, if not its defeat. For *Sputnik* showed just how difficult it is to keep the image from effective criticism. Indeed, this is the democratic virtue of the image, if not its geopolitical advantage. Nevertheless, the lesson was not learned, and it would not be until the decade of *Zapruder*. Instead, in 1958 Eisenhower formed the National Aeronautics and Space Administration (NASA) out of the ruins of an America destroyed by *Sputnik*. As Joseph Trento writes, "Had it not been for national humiliation [at *Sputnik*] there would have been no American space program"[19]—at least not as we now know it. From *Sputnik* onward, all the major decisions about the nature and fate of the US space program were even more preoccupied by the public relations impetus than they had been before.

This impetus was manifested most clearly in the decision of the Kennedy administration to send humans into space. As Kennedy's defense secretary Robert McNamara and NASA chief James Webb argued in a top-secret memo in 1961,

It is man, not merely machines, in space that captures the imagination of the world. All large-scale projects require the mobilization of resources on a national scale. They require the development and successful application of the most advanced technologies. Dramatic achievements in space, therefore, symbolize the technological power and organizing capacity of a nation. It is for reasons such as these that major achievements in space contribute to national prestige.... Major successes, such as orbiting a man as the Soviets have just done, lend national prestige even though the scientific, commercial or military value of the undertaking may, by ordinary standards, be marginal or economically unjustified.[20]

We see here again that reversal of Turner's liberal theory of institutional development: the institution ("large-scale projects") is made to stand behind and give rise to a vital imaginary force, man in space. To be sure, throughout the *Mercury*, *Gemini*, and *Apollo* programs, image economies would compete with, and often trump, engineering valuations in decision making. The priority of the *human* image was not merely a screen meant to hide from view the real material forces driving the space program. Rather, it was the culmination of the Cold War wager that the fate of nations could rest on the image. As Kennedy told Congress in 1961 when proposing the moon landing, "We take an additional risk by making it [manned flight to the moon] in full view of the world, but as shown by the feat of astronaut Shepard, this very risk enhances our stature when we are successful."[21]

Indeed, after Kennedy's speech the human image was the centerpiece of America's space program, and no party insisted on this more than the *Apollo* astronauts themselves. They bought into the primacy of the human image (their own, of course) from their press conferences right down to the technical processes of their moon landings. As historian David Mindell has explored, engineers designed the *Apollo* spacecraft to land on the moon automatically, through a then quite sophisticated, tried-and-tested computing system. Nevertheless, in every moon landing the commander shut off the automatic function after entering the lunar orbit and instead brought the ship down manually, to their own peril and the chagrin of NASA's engineers.[22] Yet, no one denied that *Apollo*'s commanders here operated in accord with the symbolism of their enterprise. As Mindell writes, "In creating that symbolism, the Kennedy administration drew on imagery of exploration, individualism, and geographical conquest to sell Apollo to the press and to Congress. Kennedy seized on the most powerful mythology in American history, the frontier narrative, and reopened it by aiming for the moon. Within this framing, the endeavor had all the elements of a classic frontier adventure: an unknown, but conquerable geography full of lurking dangers, even villainous antagonists—the competing Soviets."[23] "Most important," Mindell continues, "the frontier narrative called upon heroic pioneers."[24] While the manual landings increased the risks of moon flights, they minimized crucial rhetorical risks, making the astronauts invulnerable to criticisms of being the subjects of "mere machines," mere token passengers (just monkeys!) in an automatic adventure.

To be sure, Kennedy's advisors were right: the symbolic payoff of the manned Apollo program was immense. The astronaut, in the words of one history of the program, became a "strange new breed of man, . . . something larger than ordinary human life, with gallantry and nerve beyond the common experience."[25] Their space exploits reintroduced not only extraordinary figures into a public imaginary (last seen in World War II), but also a vigorous vocabulary of deterritorialized national and technological pioneering. Indeed, under the pressure of space publicity of the 1960s, the frontier was pushed to the point of disintegration before the boundlessness of space. The 1967 "Treaty on Principles Governing, Including the Moon and Other Celestial Bodies," developed by the United Nations Committee on the Peaceful Uses of Outer Space, prohibited claims by nations to territory in outer space. Space was herein conceived as exempt from boundaries, limits, and regions. It was the same sort of new frontier that Vannevar Bush had presented in his acclaimed *Science, the Endless Frontier* (1945).[26] Indeed, in the 1960s, scientists and engineers were recruited to work for space-race contractors like American Bosch Arma, Marquardt, and Douglas in advertisements that evoked the fusion of the scientific and celestial endless frontiers.[27] Both science and space offered ways of conceiving of professional conscription into state-corporate activities that kept the human at the center of a boundless script.

As a space of publicity, this meant that this new frontier became the object of some the most spectacular national claims ever made. "It will not be one man going to the moon," Kennedy told Congress in 1961, "if we make this judgment affirmatively, it will be an entire nation."[28] And when in 1969 American astronauts finally stepped onto the moon, American flag in hand, Neil Armstrong announced the giant leap not of a nation, but of "mankind." On earth, President Nixon was far more hyperbolic, claiming for America "the greatest week in the history of the world since the Creation."[29] America was no longer an image; it was an archetype, as boundless as outer space.

Yet, it was neither Kennedy nor Nixon who most fully understood and exploited the potential of the imagination of space to launch America into a primeval boundlessness. Rather, this was the accomplishment of Ronald Reagan—largely because Reagan understood, almost intuitively it seems, the underlying logic of free-floating symbols. As Reagan's speeches show, he was familiar with the archetype, and not merely as it stood behind the image, but as it stood over it, above it, beyond it. Thus, even as Reagan oversaw a decline in the US space program in general, and its destruction in *Challenger*, he intensified its significance. In this regard, his *Challenger* speech was profoundly iconoclastic, twice destroying the image—first in a violence to the image-centric view of space exploration inherited from Kennedy, and second, and more profoundly, in an insistence on the impossibility of any image adequate to America.

Sublime Spaces

When Ronald Reagan assumed the office of the presidency, the regulatory institutions of government were already under attack. As Sheila Jasanoff writes of the 1970s, "The perception that regulators were permitting political considerations to corrupt the integrity of their scientific analyses spread across the entire political spectrum."[30] The attacks against regulatory institutions like the Environmental Protection Agency and the Occupational Safety and Health Administration were, in a certain respect, inevitable. The whole idea of government regulatory institutions based solely on objective judgments and free from all political interest was a house of cards. But under Reagan, the problem of political influence was not presented in terms of corrupting special interests; rather, it was presented in terms of economic performance. As Jasanoff writes, "the Reagan administration identified government regulation as the prime impediment to technological innovation and as an important contributor to America's flagging performance in the world economy."[31] Regulation foreclosed the infinite possibilities of economy; it made the market something other than free; it prematurely and unnecessarily determined an indeterminate field of economic action. If regulatory institutions had been created to help navigate the tricky terrain of *social* risks and rewards, the Reagan administration saw such navigational efforts as the unwarranted intrusion of social and political spheres into the economic sphere, arbitrarily constricting the free movement of the latter.

Nevertheless, the market had to be navigated in some way. If government institutions would not regulate, then how would the national economy steer its way forward? Here, perhaps in ways as yet unrecognized, speech played a vital role in Reagan's leadership. Indeed, his public speeches can be read as an ongoing demonstration of how to navigate free-floating spaces, above all a free economy. Just as navigation apart from ground control is a major problem for the space vessel, so too interpreting a symbolic system loosed from any regular relationship to empirical measures can be profoundly disorienting. Thus, like a navigator at one of Earth's poles, where north and south lose their significance, Reagan turned toward forms of rhetorical triangulation to locate his ideological points. Finding two accepted positions, he drew a fraction from them to locate his rhetorical concern. Consider as an example the first lines of his first inaugural: "To a few of us here today, this is a solemn and most momentous occasion; and yet, in the history of our Nation, it is a commonplace occurrence. The orderly transfer of authority as called for in the Constitution routinely takes place as it has for almost two centuries, and few of us stop to think how unique we really are. In the eyes of many in the world, this every-four-year ceremony we accept as normal is nothing less than a miracle."[32] The rhetorical object of concern, America's constitutional uniqueness with respect to the transfer of powers, is located not by historical comparison and contrast, nor by centering on the particular brilliance of the constitution itself, but by marking two starlike points, the normal and the miraculous, and then finding America's uniqueness from their measurement. For Reagan, here as elsewhere, interpretative horizons—those accepted positions by which we confront the novel—consist not of historically contingent vantage points, but generally accepted abstractions evacuated of any particular historical texture.

Here empirical measures are not abandoned. They remain, but only to serve a token function; they offer objects to be surveyed rather than studied; they are approached as stimuli in processes of association rather than as icons to look at and through; rather than denoting, they are subjected to a "language of connotation."[33] Consider Reagan's first inaugural again, as he surveyed the sacred geography of Washington from where he stood on the West Front of the Capitol:

> Standing here, one faces a magnificent vista, opening up on this city's special beauty and history. At the end of this open mall are those shrines to the giants on whose shoulders we stand. Directly in front of me, the monument to a monumental man: George Washington, father of our country, a man of humility who came to greatness reluctantly. He led America out of revolutionary victory into infant nationhood. Off to one side, the stately memorial to Thomas Jefferson. The Declaration of Independence flames with his eloquence. And then beyond the Reflecting Pool, the dignified columns of the Lincoln Memorial. Whoever would understand in his heart the meaning of America will find it in the life of Abraham Lincoln. Beyond those monuments to heroism is the Potomac River, and on the far shore the sloping hills of Arlington National Cemetery with its row on row of simple white markers bearing crosses or Stars of David. They add up to only a tiny fraction of the price that has been paid for our freedom.[34]

These were the words of a symbolic surveyor. Another pass-through would produce another set of associations. And a third survey, yet another. For Reagan, as for an advertiser, images are not denotative, but "fragments in flight," to use Jameson's fine phrase, plotted points in the play of connotation.[35]

In fact, as Reagan spoke these lines that inaugural day, the television cameras turned away from him (an unprecedented gesture in the age of televised inaugural addresses), first to a zoom shot of the Mall at the center of which stood the Washington Memorial; then a cut to medium long-shot of the Jefferson Memorial; then a jump to the Lincoln Memorial; then a switch to a full-shot of Lincoln's statue; and then finally, in a kind of cinematic flight, a leap to an image of rows of white tombstones at Arlington. With each new scene, the cameras showed their power to defy on-the-ground spatial logics, hopping as they did across the D.C. historyscape, turning a variegated if continuous terrain into a seamless "flow."[36] Here, the flow hid the cuts it made into the D.C. landscape; the gaps were themselves discarded, useless as they were to both the television camera's visual technology and Reagan's oratorical imagination. Indeed, it was as if only the magic of video editing could keep pace with Reagan's capacity to rapidly and nimbly hop through symbolic spaces.

Scholars like Michael Rogin and Daniel Rodgers have argued that Reagan's rhetoric as well as his vision were profoundly cinematic. Rogin has argued that Reagan "found out who he was through the roles he played on film," leading to a political career, and indeed a political culture, conditioned by "the conflation of movies and reality."[37] So too, Rodgers argues, Reagan's speeches were possessed by a "film-making imagination;" they "worked on cinematic rather than sermonic principles."[38] Importantly, Rodgers argues, Reagan was not the subject of his cinematic gaze. Rather, he was its *medium*, its channel, its means. Reagan "effortlessly blended his self into his story of America"—he was one with America's gaze.[39] As such, he accomplished "a remarkable re-imagining of the presidential role," less a figurehead than, like Geraldo Rivera, a program host.[40] Rodgers notes that this meant a "relinquishing of overt authority" as president. At the same time, this anti-authoritative posture was consistent with the culture of television, which in many respects gave up the cinematic hero to relatively fast and cheap video production processes featuring anchors, hosts, or celebrities rather than Hollywood-style screen stars. "Reagan," Rogin writes, "suggests not the producer self who makes things happen but the celebrity who shows them off."[41] Whether we locate Reagan's persona cinematically or televisually, it is apparent that it meant as well the adoption of a new form of presidential (anti-)authority—the (anti-)authority to determine the character and structure not of America's (hi)story, but of America's gaze. If the authority of the cinematic star is iconic, we might say that the host's is homiletic—it entails the power to see the story rather than write or enact it.

In Reagan's view, the story typically had the form of the pan, or at least a form of the pan that mimics what Jameson described as "pastiche"—a "vast collection of images, a multitudinous photographic simulacrum."[42] Guided by a spatial rather than a temporal logic, this pan in fact attacked the latter, reducing time to a flat space. Reagan thus swung like a camera on a free-floating axis, not to offer a comprehensive view of the landscape, but to suggest an inestimable vastness, out of reach of the imagination. Every view moved, but still every view offered in its moving but a fraction of what might be seen had the camera cared to linger. For Reagan, every vista was a magnificent vista, every space sublime. But the effect of this aesthetic proclivity was to contain, and indeed remake, the authority of the camera's subjects. Reagan made all things small. Even the monuments of Arlington were but "a tiny fraction" of the price of freedom. Thus Reagan's gaze upon the landscape of Washington in his first inaugural had the startling effect of rendering it supplementary, simple, and slight—a mere visual interlude in an airy sketch of grander vistas.

This aesthetic logic was both new and familiar by the early 1980s. Raymond Williams had suggested its familiarity already in the 1970s in the "flow" of television.[43] Still, in 1981 it was new to the institution of the presidency. Modern presidents may have been uncomfortable with their own iconicity (e.g., Eisenhower, Nixon, and Carter), but they still fashioned it. Reagan, however, destroyed it. He was not so much uncomfortable with presidential iconicity as opposed to it: for him, as Rodgers writes, the rhetorical task of the presidency was "blending his self and his story-telling voice into the fabric of everyday dreams and aspirations, by dissolving the distance between people and president."[44] The goal, in cinematic terms, was not to locate a subject but to offer a panorama, blending all subjects into a magnificent scene. This, of course, was by 1981 a familiar view: it was in the imagination of outer space; it was the scenic form of conspiracy theories; and it was offered in theories of deregulated capital and markets. Indeed, each scene called for hermeneutics of belief in vast possibilities, transcendent economies, and unrepresentable identities.

Thus, Reagan could take up in his first inaugural address the theme of cost and crisis he associated with Arlington to energize economic discourse. "These United States," he asserted, "are confronted with an economic affliction of great proportions." Such afflictions necessitated, he argued later in the speech, "our best effort, and our willingness to believe in ourselves and to believe in our capacity to perform great deeds; to believe that together with God's help we can and will resolve the problems which now confront us."[45] For Reagan, it was not figures that were heroic, but belief itself. Heroism was not an object, but a subjective state, a kind of attitude in motion. As such, Reagan's eye for the miraculous and normal alike was aimed at seeing beyond the form of the manifest appearance to a supersensible realm where the miraculous is ordinary, and the ordinary is miraculous. Constantly triangulating, Reagan defied images to be sufficiently orienting.

Consequently, throughout his presidency, he was fundamentally concerned with the great deeds of American imagination and memory. In this way, in his farewell address some eight years after that first inaugural, Reagan warned not against a military-industrial complex or even a Cold War enemy, but against forgetting the dimensions of American magnitude. "If we forget what we did, we won't know who we are. I'm warning of an eradication of the American memory that could result, ultimately, in an erosion of the American spirit."[46] *Identity*, Reagan insisted, was the root source of a belief that can look beyond the world of appearances. Thus, as James Jasinski has argued, the "rhetorical coherence and force" of Reagan's presidential discourse depended upon his ability to manipulate antithesis and oxymoron.[47] Antithesis sets up polarities (as we see in Reagan's polarization between the "Evil Empire" and American benevolence); oxymoron complicates antithesis by making "paradoxical and/or contradictory prescriptions" the basis of a political program.[48] Reagan's navigation of antitheses and oxymorons had the effect not only of discrediting the world of appearances (appearances, for Reagan, were not indexes of realities, but tokens of possibility), but also of driving home the primacy of identity. "Americanness" for Reagan consisted of the peculiar capacity to *believe* in spite of manifest appearances. American identity was for Reagan at home in the oxymoronic.

The sublime, of course, is also antithetical and oxymoronic. It sets up an antithesis between large and small and then posits a program wherein this stable polarity is disrupted by the absolute scale of the *beyond*, the total, and the transcendent. Thus, as Kant emphasized, "The *sublime is that in comparison with which everything else is small*."[49] The sublime turns sight toward absolute space and measures all else accordingly. That we cannot measure absolute space is no matter; we can think it, perhaps feel it, and certainly believe in it, for the destination of the sublime is the supersensible. That is where it transports us, and there all we thought we knew about navigation no longer applies. Thus, in a speech to NASA employees two and a half years prior to the *Challenger* disaster, Reagan characterized those who opposed space exploration as "doubting Thomases" and "dreary souls." Their problem, he argued, was essentially subjective. "With their pessimism, America could have never gotten off the ground. And with your space shuttle, we have again and again. And I'm convinced your success confirms a vision that we share: an America unafraid, reaching into space with courage and leadership, will be an America unsurpassed. We have it within our power to create a bounty of new jobs, technologies, and medical breakthroughs surpassing anything we've ever dreamed before or imagined."[50] The greatest of the great deeds of the American imagination would be to reach its own limits and come to believe in that which is beyond its representational power—to think, as Kant wrote, what we cannot envision.[51]

This is to say, on the one hand, that no image is too grand: when Reagan delivered an address at the Johnson Space Flight Center to mark NASA's return to space flight after the *Challenger* disaster, he spoke without irony of America's mission "to colonize this galaxy."[52] On the other hand, however, no image is suitable to America's destination, no imagination adequately strong, no gaze sufficiently comprehensive, no sight reliably orienting. The pan is the means by which to register this paradox, because it substitutes a rhetoric of motion for a rhetoric of the object. Indeed, the pan doubles the power of the cinematic: not only is the camera possessed by film-in-motion (or tape), but the camera itself moves. Movement within movement. Always movement. Only movement. Hence, in a final oxymoron, time is reintroduced as *topos*, as space: space is time, being is becoming, history is the future, actuality is possibility.

Manifest Destruction

Nowhere was the capacity of Reagan's rhetoric to make things small through movement more evident than in the *Challenger* address. In their study of Reagan's rhetoric, Kurt Ritter and David Henry present the *Challenger* speech as the epitome of his presidential discourse. "In many ways the *Challenger* speech included the most salient features of Reagan's rhetoric: unself-conscious references to God, emphasis on heroes, appeals to values of freedom and progress, and Reagan's fitting presentational manner."[53] More fundamentally still, the *Challenger* address concerned the limits of the American imagination. Its words acted, in turn, to produce an America that, to quote the famous last line of the speech (itself a quote of a John Gillespie Magee Jr. poem), "slipped the surly bonds of Earth," and hence an American spectatorial subject that was infinitesimally small.

The *Challenger* address is readily called a eulogy.[54] In one respect, the speech fulfilled the central generic obligation of the eulogy: it offered comfort and memorialized the victims of the accident. Indeed, *comfort* is a key word that has circulated through academic and popular writings about the speech. As columnist Anthony Lewis wrote days after the accident, "People waited: Not for an answer . . . but for words of consolation. They came, with rare grace, from President Reagan."[55] Thus the speech was very careful to draw attention to the astronauts who lost their lives, listing each by name. However, the rhetorical action of the *Challenger* speech was more manifold than the notion of a eulogy would suggest. The speech was an argument. Through a series of central claims and a complementary positioning of speaker and audience, Reagan argued that the *Challenger* disaster was but a small, token-like event in the vast historyscape of America.

Minimizing the ultimate significance of the disaster was a chief concern in the Reagan Whitehouse in the immediate aftermath of January 26, 1986. In a strict instrumental sense, a key purpose of the *Challenger* speech was to tell American and world publics that the space program would go on.[56] At stake were two political commitments. The first, still lingering from the days of Eisenhower, was the image of US technological superiority in the context of the Cold War. As Cold War rhetoric became, for a time at least, more strident under the Reagan administration, space regained a great deal of the rhetorical energy it had in the 1950s and 1960s as a field upon which the symbolic war with the USSR was fought. For example, Reagan's push in 1982–83 for the invention of a missile defense system bloomed into a symbolic extravaganza of American born satellites, space ships, laser beams, and sublunar explosions— this even though Reagan's famous "Star Wars" speech never once actually used the phrase itself, and Reagan himself never argued in it that the missile defense system must be based in space. Nevertheless, images of the system disseminated in the media always pictured space as its locus—it was as if a boundless realm was needed to satisfactorily stage such a fantastic idea. But even for the more grounded, in the 1980s it was axiomatic that any real advances in armaments would reach into space. Space constituted the new frontier of military strategy.

More particular to Reagan, however, was a second political commitment, the reinvention of America's relation to outer space along the lines of a neo-liberal economic approach. Of course, the superiority of liberal economics was also integral to the US position in the Cold War. However, under Reagan, *commercialization* became a watchword in the space program. In Reagan's first term, Kennedy's vision of the New Frontier underwent a transformation: space-as-frontier became as much about commercial exploitation as daring explorations. In a 1983 essay, George Keyworth, Reagan's science advisor, expressed the ideal, if not the reality, of the Reagan administration's use of space. He wrote of Kennedy with admiration: "With astute political timing, he capitalized on three of the traditional strengths of the US citizenry—its pioneering spirit, its technological expertise, and it competitiveness—to promote a renewed sense of national unity."[57] Keyworth argued that space afforded the United States a great opportunity for scientific, military, and political advancement. However, corporate and economic terms dominated his portrayal of the future of space. "How can the United States fashion a space program that addresses today's national aspirations and needs?" he asked.[58] He provided his own answer: "Like an evolving company, the US space program has options for both horizontal and vertical expansion. . . . I would characterize the evolution of commercial launch services as a kind of vertical expansion. Conversely, horizontal expansion would require revolutionary new ventures in space exploration. These would be the kind of initiatives that open new frontiers, develop new technologies, or recapture the sense of national unity that *Apollo* did."[59] The proposal was crafted in the new neoliberal language of economic common sense, offering corporate models and the logic of efficient capital as means of retaining in spirit and symbol what in fact the program was designed to destroy—namely, the era of "big government" adventures in science and technology. Yet this required that the economic motive here would have to redraw the portrait of space that Kennedy had painted. Specifically, as with every mass settlement of a frontier, the perception of *risk* would have to be managed. Some risk, to be sure, was not only tolerable but desirable—it would sustain the spirit of economic adventurism. Still, catastrophic risk made the newly economized program vulnerable to criticism, not of the Cold War sort that Eisenhower's advisors once worried a premature satellite launch would invite, but rather of the "big government" sort that would challenge the commercialization of space.

Thus, the Reagan administration's vision of a space program premised upon the expansion of semi-privatized ventures and the development of new technologies called for, in an important respect, the domestication of space, inasmuch as it required this management of perceptions of risk. In order for space to become an economic frontier, it had to undergo a certain familiarization, be made more commonplace. It had, that is, to adopt something of the tenor of the commonsensical that was so well managed in neoliberal discourse. A vision of a vast and hostile frontier had to be repainted to house the private. NASA's so-called Teacher in Space Program was in keeping with this revision. Drawing on an age-old American means of the domesticating the frontier, it put a New England woman, Christa McAuliffe, on the space shuttle *Challenger*. Space travel, as the publicity around her flight claimed, was now safe.

Although the *Challenger* disaster represented serious flaws in the organizational decision-making processes at NASA and thus compromised NASA's institutional status, it was not so much the fact of the explosion as it was its highly visible and widely disseminated presentation that transformed it into a late Cold War crisis. This visibility was the consequence of the intense efforts NASA made to publicize the *Challenger* space voyage, and the Teacher in Space program was at the core of this campaign. Indeed, while in a more or less literal sense, the camera's pan followed the ascent of the spacecraft into the sky, in a truer sense the spacecraft followed the arc of the camera's pan. Across the nation and elsewhere around the globe, people watched the live televisual presentation of the *Challenger* launch and celebrated the transportation of the first civilian into space. It was time for America to move, to move into new economic frontiers, the infinite frontiers of space. In classrooms in the United States teachers not only showed the live coverage of the launch on television, but integrated this showing with a NASA-prepared supplementary curriculum. The high point of the *Challenger* voyage was to be Christa McAullife's "lesson from space," where the television camera would collapse the gulf between the heavens and Earth in the moving image of a New England woman in orbit. Americans would get, however, a very different lesson, a lesson in the iconoclastic imagination of America.

Making All Things Small

In one respect, the *Challenger* explosion represented a significant ideology crisis for the Reagan administration. The space shuttle's visible and tragic demise would quash the hopes of those in the Reagan administration who sought a much more privatized space program, and NASA would take years to recover (if it ever did). However, the ideology infused within the talk of the privatization of space—the neoliberal economic ideology of expansion, technological revolution, venture, and growth—did not wait to be reinstituted. Reagan's *Challenger* speech argued that America is and will interminably be the instantiation of that ideology. It does so by invoking what can be approached as three structures of the sublime: a revelatory structure, a positional structure, and an eventful structure. With regard to the revelatory structure, the speech posits that the manifest experience of disaster is inherent in the logic of freedom, and hence that disaster is but an occasion for spectators to see "the way freedom is." With regard to the positional structure, the *Challenger* speech carefully positions speaker and audience in a radically incommensurate relationship and makes a critical claim about the meaning of the space shuttle disaster—"It's all part of the process of exploration and discovery"—within the context of that relationship. With respect to the eventful structure of the sublime, the speech amplifies the extraordinary quality of the disaster by placing it within a series of extraordinary co-incidents that construct a transcendent order.

Relative to the *Challenger* speech that would come that evening, President Reagan's initial comments to the press after learning of the disaster were unexceptional. Yet they are important, for they would be transformed by Peggy Noonan, the speechwriter for the *Challenger* address, into the themes that pervade the speech. Noonan has published notes of an impromptu press conference Reagan held with network news anchors just after the space shuttle disaster. The notes reveal a Reagan preoccupied with the event's visibility and traumatic potential, but still limited to clichés:

Q: Who brought the news to you?

A: We were all sitting there preparing for your questions when the Vice President and Admiral Poindexter came in and said they had received a flash that the space shuttle had exploded—we then went to see the TV and saw the replay—it was just a very traumatic experience.

Q: Do you take comfort in the fact that we have not lost as many as the Soviets?

A: We all have pride in that, but it doesn't lessen our grief.

Q: What do you say to the children to help them understand?

A: Pioneers have always given their lives on the frontier. The problem is that it's more of a shock to all as we see it happening, not just hear about something miles away—but we must make it clear that life goes on.[60]

These relatively nondescript comments formed the basis for the *Challenger* speech. Visibility, the Soviets, trauma, children, and the commonplace character of the loss of life in pioneering ventures are major themes in the address. The former two are especially pertinent to Reagan's claims about the meaning of the experience of witnessing the disastrous destruction of an image. Indeed, the *Challenger* address navigates the nebulous experience of shock in America.

Even as it eulogized the seven victims of the *Challenger* disaster, the address functioned as a vigorous apologia for American-style publicity. The visibility of the event was taken up in the speech as a locus for a judgment about America. Visibility functioned doubly, as both an inventional source in an argument for the uniqueness and superiority of the American way and as a warrant for Reagan's political policy. "I've always had great faith in and respect for our space program, and what happened today does nothing to diminish it. We don't hide our space program. We don't keep secrets and cover things up. We do it all up front and in public. That's the way freedom is, and we wouldn't change it for a minute."[61] In contradistinction to Reagan's impromptu press conference comments, which present the *Challenger* explosion as an abnormal occurrence that problematically shocks the public, his address that evening framed the shocking and manifest character of the disaster as a normal product of political freedom. Publicized disasters, Reagan argued, have a direct ideological function—that is, through their visibility we are reminded of "the way of freedom is." Thus, Reagan went on to insist that the space shuttle program would continue. "We'll continue our quest in space. There will be more shuttle flights and more shuttle crews and yes, more volunteers, more civilians, more teachers in space. Nothing ends here; our hopes and journeys continue."[62] From an argument for the importance of visibility, he moved seamlessly to promise liberal economic progress in space exploration, complete with volunteers, civilians, and teachers.

This rhetorical movement was navigated via notions of publicity, freedom, and progress, a route implicitly put in contradistinction to the Soviet system. Though the speech never mentions the Soviets by name, it implicitly differentiated the American way from Soviet ways. America does things "up front and in public," an idea derived from the civic republican ideals of openness, common goods, civic virtue, and public access, and these republican ideals flow fluidly into the liberal economic promise of progress centered on civilian enterprises. Reagan's appeal to American openness, freedom, and advancement distinguishes "us" from "them." More profoundly, however, in arguing implicitly that the sight of a national disaster is actually the site of a distinct form of American freedom, Reagan makes traumatic visions of the destruction of icons a normative American experience. Here we are met again with the logic of *Good Night America* and *JFK*—the most powerful way to experience America is in the destruction of its iconic images—but now in the optimistic, comedic frame.

But this reading goes too far, and does not yet go far enough. It assumes that a heavy ideological impetus underlies the speech and fails to reckon with its intense pragmatic design. Noonan's account of the speech's preparation emphasizes the administration's concern that the speech should make clear that the space program would continue, and she identifies the lines beginning with "We'll continue our quest in space" as the place in the speech where she meant to do this.[63] Hence, a more pragmatic reading of these lines would stress how the visibility of the *Challenger* disaster clearly put the reputation of space program on the line and how Reagan wanted to argue that, despite the traumatic scene on the television screen, the space program would continue. Reagan's appeal to "freedom" in this pragmatic context becomes a savvy means by which to resuscitate the status quo in light of a major public relations challenge.

However, within neoliberal discourse, we need not side with either an ideological or pragmatic reading. What both readings share is a revelatory logic wherein the explosive and traumatic sight of the *Challenger* disaster is incorporated into the logic of the speech only to be overridden by a purportedly rationally driven insistence that nothing ultimately will change. Even *Challenger's* sudden and shocking destruction is made to reveal what the original construction of the flight was intended to prove in the first place: American technological and ideological supremacy and the promise of a neoliberal economic relation to the galaxy. Thus, the ecstatic, disorienting, and painful experience of the national disaster marks not a turning point, but confirms the degree to which an American neoliberal economic progressivism can overcome and incorporate its own traumas and disruptions.

In fact, the *Challenger* address undermines the premise behind the general commitment to openness and visibility that it purports to celebrate. The nature of the premise was evident in Rousseau's description of Geneva as "a State, in which all the individuals being well known to one another, neither the secret machinations of vice, nor the modesty of virtue should be able to escape the notice and judgment of the public."[64] As far back as Aristotle, visibility has been tied to the practice of deliberative judgment. It is not merely that to be noticed is to be judged, but that to judge, one must be able to "get hold of" things.[65] Reagan's neoliberal premise, however, is different. A manifest disaster is the occasion for the reification rather than the reconsideration of status quo policy. Breakdowns in the system are overridden by ideological, administrative, and ultimately economic imperatives. Manifest disaster is subsumed by enforced manifest destinies. Under such imperatives and destinies, both the American subject and American catastrophes grow increasingly small. It is significant then that smallness figures into Reagan's *Challenger* address at critical moments. It is not only that Reagan's speech minimizes the significance of the *Challenger* explosion for US policy and thus renders the event and the publics who witnessed it insignificant; the speech positions Reagan and his audience in a way that intensifies this effect.

By now it should be clear that characterizations of the *Challenger* address as a eulogy need to be complicated and qualified by the obvious attempts in the speech to define both the implications and meaning of the disaster in light of an American neoliberal economic ideology. With respect to the implications of the event, I have argued that Reagan uses notions of visibility and freedom in implicit contradistinction to Soviet secrecy and command-and-control to argue that the *Challenger* disaster should have no significant institutional or policy implications. To use a cliché—but a very appropriate one for Reagan's America—the show must go on. Here we see something of a neoliberal truism. However, with respect to the meaning of the *Challenger* disaster, even apt clichés will not suffice. Reagan represents this meaning as the absolute space of America. We see it put forth in the interaction between assertions and arrangement in the speech.

There are four main assertions in the speech. It is helpful to single them out so that the general argument about the meaning of the *Challenger* disaster can be highlighted. In sequential order, the four assertions are these:

1. "This is truly a national loss."
2. "We're still pioneers."
3. "It's all part of the process of exploration and discovery."
4. "Nothing ends here; our hopes and our journeys continue."[66]

Even lifted from their contexts in the speech, these four statements are quite meaningful. The first statement characterizes the scope of the disaster and the nature of the event; the second, the identity of America and the nature of national agency. It is the third statement that sets the scene for the disaster—the process of exploration and discovery. And this scene leads to the conclusive fourth statement: "Our hopes and our journeys continue." If these four statements are read together, the argument is that the national loss of *Challenger* is but a mere part of the ongoing process of exploration in which the pioneering nation America partakes. It is a tight, circular argument that insists that America must continue to pioneer because it must. Thus, as we have already seen, even national disasters do not pose a significant challenge to the nation, for they *cannot*. America moves on after disaster because movement is what America is. In dialectic-like fashion, the process of expansion subsumes and incorporates its own momentary disruptions and deconstructions. Reagan thus provides a perspective on national loss that is longitudinal, drawing upon myths of American pioneering and the process of manifest destiny. He asks his audience to look ahead to America's expansive future and behind to other incidents of national loss and to find in this temporal vision a warrant for accommodating the *Challenger* disaster into the fluid outward movements of America.

If we read these assertions in their speech context, we find that context and arrangement reinforce this circular argument. The scope and nature of the accident as a "national loss" comes at the beginning of the speech and on the heels of Reagan's claim that he and Nancy are "pained to the core by the tragedy" and they "share this pain with all the people of our country." This introduction makes the particular national character of the *Challenger* loss derivative of the common experience of the president and the people—the shared pain of the people, of which the president is but a part, makes the disaster a national one. The scope and nature of the disaster are thus laid out in emotive terms. The second assertion, "We're still pioneers" comes several paragraphs later in the speech. In between the first and second assertions, Reagan recalls the previous deaths of three astronauts in a flash fire in 1967, describes the courage of the shuttle crew, lists their names, addresses their families, and commends their service. Then he states, "We've grown used to wonders in this century. It's hard to dazzle us. But for twenty-five years the United States space program has been doing just that. We've grown used to the idea of space, and perhaps we forget that we've only just begun. We're still pioneers. They, the members of the *Challenger* crew, were pioneers."[67] In defining the identity of America and the nature of national agency here, Reagan defies the historic logic of the figure of the pioneer. Historically, pioneering figures grant the American people their pioneering identity; through identifying with the pioneer, America becomes a pioneering nation. Here, however, in characteristic fashion, Reagan posits the pioneering identity of America first—"We're still pioneers"—and then that of the astronauts, suggesting the identities of the latter are derived from the former. Though wonders have grown commonplace, Reagan insists that America remains at its essence pioneering. Figures like the *Challenger* astronauts derive their pioneering identity from this essential aspect of America. Thus, together in their respective contexts, these first two assertions concentrate on the meaning of the particular *national* character of disaster. That the president and the people indistinctly share the emotive aspects of disaster, and that tragedies like the *Challenger* disaster are derived from the risks inherent in America's pioneering essence, make the space shuttle explosion national in scope. However, this argument is potentially problematic, for if traumatic and shocking collective experiences and great risks are essential to American nationhood, is not this form of nationhood itself put in sharp question? At this existential level, Reagan created rather than pacified a crisis in national identity.

It is at this point that his third assertion intervened to resituate not the content of these claims about the traumas of national identity but the intersubjective context in which they were ultimately made: "And I want to say something to the school children of America who were watching the live coverage of the shuttle's takeoff. I know it is hard to understand, but sometimes very painful things like this happen. It's all part of the process of exploration and discovery. It's all part of taking a chance and expanding man's horizons. The future doesn't belong to the fainthearted; it belongs to the brave. The

Challenger crew was pulling us into the future, and we'll continue to follow them."[68] Here Reagan named and responded to the angst his speech had produced; he described the profound difficulty of understanding why traumatic and shocking experiences and deep risks are essential to national experience and nationhood itself, and then answered the question raised by asserting, "It's all part of the process of exploration and discovery." And this comes in an address to *children*. Reagan thus positions his audience as children before he answers them. Here the child (the purported addressee), the hero (the *Challenger* crew), and the paternalistic host (Reagan) are figured in terms of scale. Faced with the evident trauma and danger of national existence, Reagan turns to forms of minimization and amplification to sustain the myth of progress and process. The amplified astronaut hero pulls and leads; "we" follow, all now reduced to children.

All, that is, except Reagan. The *I* of the speech is able to separate itself from the "we" through a persistent and powerful presence. Throughout, the speech is infused with the intimate and personal speaking voice of the *I*.

> Ladies and gentlemen I'd planned to speak to you tonight to report on the state of the union, but the events of earlier today have led me to change those plans.
>
> Nancy and I are pained to the core by the tragedy of the shuttle *Challenger*.
>
> And I want to say something to the school children of America who were watching the live coverage of the shuttle's takeoff. I know it's hard to understand, but sometimes painful things like this happen.
>
> I've always had great faith in and respect for our space program.
>
> I want to add that I wish I could talk to every man and woman who works for NASA or who worked on this mission and tell them: "Your dedication and professionalism have moved and impressed us for decades. And we know of your anguish. We share it."[69]

But this is not an iconic *I*, no matter what conservatives and neoconservatives have made of Reagan since. Rather, it is the *I* of a television host, who merely channels the spirit of the occasion. Reagan's repeated invocations of *I* effectively subsume and govern the pain of the shuttle disaster. The process of exploration itself, which subsumes and governs American existence and America's future, is articulated in a voice that mediates between children and heroes, subject and object. This powerful *I* helps solidify the myth of process and progress by humanizing it through the heavy infusion of his hostlike persona. As Noonan wrote of the *Challenger* episode, "Reagan embodied; he became the nation holding you, he was the nation hugging you back, and there was nothing phony about it, nothing careless."[70] His voice articulates the tragic dimension of exploration in a vocabulary of personal pain and thus suggests a piety commensurate to the destruction of the image and violence to the imagination. It is, indeed, political piety that is at stake in Reagan's speech. However, it is kept from being a *question* in the hostlike figure of Reagan, who claims for himself, as his own, the multiple affective and political dimensions of the *Challenger* disaster.

Reagan's mediation of national disaster is the key to his rhetorical sublimation of the affective and political power of the destruction of an icon into a narrative of American progress. The efforts by his administration not simply to maintain the status quo but to articulate an affective response for the American spectator suggest that, for them, that spectator was a risk. Reagan's speech itself characterizes the United States space program as a series of "wonders" that "dazzle." But he worries that Americans have "grown used to the idea of space," having developed a certain immunity to its symbolic power, and thus to the prospect of its spectacular neoliberal privatization. In short, like Kant's sublime, the risk of the American spectators is that they might stand either too close to the disaster or too far away; both stances would result in a certain affective dissonance that would undermine the potential for incorporating the catastrophe into a narrative of American destiny. Just as in his first inaugural address, the *Challenger* speech attempts to bring the American spectator to see America *with* Reagan. But what exactly is it that Reagan sees in America from the median?

From the start, Reagan identifies the space shuttle disaster as a national tragedy. I have shown how Reagan's appeal to the "national" in the opening of the speech is constructed around the emotive dimensions of the *Challenger* loss. More pragmatically, we could also say that it is national by virtue of its object, the US space program, and by virtue of its consequences, the US reputation. However, in the first words of the speech, Reagan introduces a much more spectacular sense of the national than any of these senses: national timing. "Ladies and gentlemen," the speech begins, "I'd planned to speak to you tonight to report on the state of the union, but the events of earlier today have led me to change those plans." Indeed, January 28, 1986, was originally designed by the Reagan administration to be a day for national celebration before the *Challenger* explosion transformed it into a day of national disaster. The space shuttle liftoff had been coordinated so as to coincide with the State of the Union address.

Thus the first words of Reagan's *Challenger* speech are complex, for the *Challenger* accident appears in them as just that—an accident. This accident unpredictably forced Reagan to change plans, to give a eulogy rather than a State of the Union speech. His speech consequently appears as unplanned, undetermined, and unique. However, the coincidence of the *Challenger* event and the scheduled date of the State of the Union address had not been an accident. The Reagan administration had been engaged in a piece of political timing. Weather permitting, the shuttle's takeoff would coincide with the president's planned speech to Congress. The shuttle's fate, for sure, was an accident; however, the coincidence of that event with the planned State of the Union address cannot be said to be entirely an accident.

Rhetorically speaking, this coincidence would be largely insignificant had not Reagan seized upon the idea of the "co-incident" itself as a primary strategy for constructing America as an object to see in the speech. When we ask what it is that Reagan sees from the median, it is an extraordinary image of American destiny. His version of destiny is predicated upon the presence of a transcendent and powerful order: fate, providence, gods or a God. It rests upon a certain orchestration of incidents into co-incidents. It makes coincidence transcendentally meaningful. The particulars of time conspire to manifest or disclose some higher meaning. Reagan's speech orchestrates incidents into co-incidents and so constructs an image of American destiny strongly allied to the pioneering identity of the America he puts forth.

The first such orchestration comes in the opening lines of the speech, where he ties the *Challenger* disaster to the planned State of the Union address. But six sentences later, Reagan orchestrates a second co-incident, recalling the three *Apollo 1* astronauts who were killed aboard ship at Cape Kennedy on January 27, 1967. He states, "Nineteen years ago, almost to the day, we lost three astronauts in a terrible accident on the ground." Hence, the speech opens with references to two co-incidents with the *Challenger* loss. And it closes with a third. In the final section of the speech, Reagan states, "There's a coincidence today. On this day 390 years ago, the great explorer Sir Francis Drake died aboard ship off the coast of Panama. In his lifetime the great frontiers were the oceans, and a historian later said, 'He lived by the sea, died on it, and was buried in it.' Well, today we can say of the *Challenger* crew: Their dedication was, like Drake's, complete."[71] Thus, that which is argued in the speech—that destruction is part of the process of pioneering—is confirmed by a distinctive historical structure constructed in the speech. Audiences are brought to see in the *Challenger* disaster a national loss formed and fitted to a larger historic rhythm. The "process of exploration and discovery" becomes a template *for* exploration and discovery: destruction is progressive. *Challenger's* loss, in this template, becomes *Challenger's* fate. The event thus becomes both ordinary and extraordinary, as it is normalized as part of a normative process of pioneering and discloses a transcendent pattern.

The emergence of this extraordinary aspect of the catastrophe is at the core of the meaning the speech gives to the *Challenger* disaster. Reagan has argued that destruction is part of the process of discovery. However, the transfiguring and transformative power of the speech does not and cannot rely on such a statement as mere platitude. Nor can it rely fully on his host-like persona, for the persona, as a mediator, must be in relation to another order in order to derive its power. Nor even can it fully rely on the genre of the frontier myth embedded in the pioneering metaphors of the speech, for the frontier can turn barren. It is only as these features of the speech are put in relation to the extraordinary co-incidents of the *Challenger* disaster that platitude, persona, and myth assert a transcendent picture of American destiny. When Reagan states, in addressing the children, "I know it is hard to understand," he outlines a form of subjectivity that the entire speech works to generate: a subjectivity realized beyond understanding and before America as transcendental object. Reagan acknowledges and identifies the tracings of providence, but does not proffer an understanding or interpretation of them beyond their suggestion of the ineffable manifest destiny of America. He operates neither as a zealous believer who claims a kind of holistic knowledge of the designs of God, nor as a radical skeptic who refuses such claims altogether. Reagan, rather, operates in the middle space of general but incomplete knowledge: he presents his audience with the mystery of the order of America. He is large enough to incorporate the collective feeling of America but too small to understand the specifics of America's course. He can, as with Kant's sublime, think and feel the *total*, but not represent it.

Conclusion

A flag-bearing obelisk stands at attention on a vast plain, pointed upward, ready for launch. The countdown drums, spectators wait, cameras roll. First a rumble, then a glow, then an eruption of fire and smoke. Lift off. Hands clap, eyes follow, and cameras pivot. Power becomes propulsion; propulsion, speed. The ship finds an arc, the arc a sky, the sky a limit, and beyond the limit space—dark, dramatic, and hidden to the naked eye. The ship follows the arc, its success marked in verbal gestures sent through radio waves and into television signals. The sky becomes bigger, the ship smaller. The plume follows, the ship now a point cutting into the blue. The sky seems to open up before it. Then the smoke suddenly becomes a cloud, hiding the point. Then flames. Then the arc twists; a coagulation of fire and smoke; a disaster. The applause stops. The eyes question. The cameras follow an icon of an iconoclasm.

The president speaks, and the story is told of explorers, adventures, dangers, and disasters. He begins eulogistically, by naming the *"Challenger* seven" and describing their desires, courage, and determination. But this eulogy, as it turns out, is but an establishing shot, setting the scene for a grander national story of daring and dreaming: "We've only just begun. We're still pioneers;" "It's all part of the process of exploration and discovery;" "We'll continue our quest in space. There will be more shuttle flights and more shuttle crews, and yes more volunteers, more civilians, more teachers in space. Nothing ends here. Our hopes and our journeys continue."[72] The presidential camera not only rolls, it flows, confidently consuming the future. And this future, America, is seen in the destruction of the image.

An icon of an iconoclasm. A paradox? An impossibility? Doesn't iconoclasm negate the iconic? Doesn't it deny the conditions of legitimate representation, including its own? Isn't iconoclasm, as I argued in chapter 2, an attack on the logic and rhetoric of iconic representation as such? How, then, could an image of the destruction of an image be made representative, be made iconic?

Rather than seeking to resolve this paradox, I want to note its presence and consider its rhetorical and political possibilities and impossibilities. Let's start with Christa McAuliffe, very much the subject of the state-corporate cameras that turned toward the *Challenger* adventure in 1986. There was communicated in the choice of this civilian subject both an economy of vision and a vision of economy. The volunteer teacher-in-space program was a component of the Reagan administration's larger quest to privatize space, to make it, like so much else in the neoliberal frame, the subject of a free-floating, self-propelling register of individual enterprise and venture capital. In McAuliffe, we were not to see duty and sacrifice, those old republican virtues, but opportunity and choice. Thus the relationship between the citizen and the state was in an important sense reversed, relative to that which Abraham Zapruder assumed in November 1963. Rather than the citizen making the symbol of the state the subject of his cinematic desires, here state-corporate cameras eagerly sought a civilian subject. The civilian was brought out from behind the camera to stand before it, even as the state and its uneasy allies took their place behind the camera. But in becoming the subject rather than the operator of state-corporate cameras, McAuliffe was twice destroyed: once in the violence done to her body in the fiery demise of *Challenger* and again, more profoundly, in her reduction to a mere token before the object America. "There will be more shuttle flights and more shuttle crews," Reagan assured his audience, "and yes more volunteers, more civilians, more teachers in space." Christa McAuliffe, though named by Reagan, was, like the white tombs at Arlington, but a subject of connotation, a small figure within a vast American historyscape.

Robert Hariman and John Louis Lucaites have argued that in the iconic images of the *Challenger* explosion, we are met with "an ambivalence [that] mirrors the anxiety of living in the machine age."[73] The technological subjugation of nature is, as they note, a great gamble, "modernity's gamble," and the spectacular destruction of human machines reminds us of this.[74] But there is in such events as well an equally profound anxiety concerning the artificial status of political culture, one that mirrors anxieties about the artificiality of movies, television, and other forms of mass media. From modernity's perspective, all images are in a sense technologies: they are *made*. From late modernity's perspective, they are made to be managed, manipulated, and conflated with what was once called reality, to the point where the latter loses its purchase. As such, images are both *merely* made, and hence inadequate to legitimate meaning, and *manipulatively* made, and hence incapable of being legitimate. Thus they may become authentically meaningful only in their destruction.

Indeed, in the iconoclastic rhetoric before *Challenger*, the image was not twice but rather thrice destroyed: first, in the destruction of the *Challenger* vessel itself, then in Reagan's artful rejection of its significance, and finally in Reagan's denial of his own iconic authority. For if, as Rogin writes, "Reagan confuses the world depicted in the movies with the world outside it," then it is equally true that Reagan denied the significance of this confusion—not because he would revel in postmodern simulacra and the like, but rather because artificiality, even his own artificiality, was relegated to a token status before the sublime object of America.[75]

Here too we are met with the neoliberal imaginary: the artificial is inadequate to meaning. This is to say that the relationship of the economic laws that drive neoliberal progress is negative; its law is not institutionalized; it is de-institutionalized. It is liberated from the strictures of the artificial. It is not free to move; rather, it is *freed* to move. Neoliberalism is in this way reactionary, or as it might be, revolutionary. It is constructed as a political project in relation to older, outdated models, which means that *neo*liberalism refers to an object to be overcome, an order to be destroyed. Hence, its oxymoronic organizing image: the icon of iconoclasm. In the neoliberal imaginary, an objectivity appears that denies the truth-capacities of artificial institutions other than in the image of their destruction.

Neoliberalism's ascendency came on the heels of two such dialectically related images. *Zapruder*—that tragic image of the destruction of a liberal icon—was a materialization and transformation of *Sputnik*. In *Sputnik*, America—that great liberal icon propagated, and sometimes quite literally projected, across the globe—was destroyed. The speck in the sky was a missile bearing a nuclear warhead headed straight for the iconic continent of North America, where it would wreak ruin. Thus the flight into outer space, as Hannah Arendt eloquently wrote within a year of *Sputnik*, was a flight from Earth: "for although Christians have spoken of the earth as a vale of tears and philosophers have looked upon their body as a prison of mind or soul, nobody in the history of mankind has ever conceived of the earth as a prison for men's bodies or shown such eagerness to go literally from here to the moon."[76] *Sputnik* was received in America as an icon of iconoclasm, signaling an odd triumph over an Earth-bound human condition and an entryway into new forms of deregulated movement: the human traveling the cosmos, capital roving the globe, America panning through a historyscape of tokens.

The oxymoronic logic of Reagan's *Challenger* speech is that a magnificent, disastrous event is really not a consequential or substantive event at all. Against the sublime historyscape of America, it is rendered small. Just as the crew of *Challenger*, to quote the famous last line of the speech, "'slipped the surly bonds of Earth' to 'touch the face of God,'" so the *Challenger* disaster itself slips away into the pure spirit that is America. This oxymoronic logic also can be called an irony, for it calls upon the American spectator to see what is not: to see in and through a politically motivated technocratic orchestration a neoliberal American destiny; to see in and through an American president a transcendent order; to see in and through a national catastrophe a sign of American freedom, progress, and supremacy. In Reagan, however, oxymoron is more apt than irony. For while Reagan's rhetoric is full of deregulated movements in perspective, it lacks the wink and knowing nod that a Kennedy-like ironic discourse possesses. In other words, it lacks the full distance irony requires to be effective.

What Reagan's discourse of disaster mastered more effectively than any of its antecedents is the sublime movement between smallness and largeness, chaos and control, icon and iconoclasm. Reagan was a master at standing in the median spot and orchestrating the sublime by picturing the magnificent vistas of America. In this space, the relationship between the ideological and the idealistic was broken, as disaster became a means of ideology production. Thus, when on September 11, 2001, the United States was met with another iconoclasm, this politics of form was not only in place, it was a kind of rhetorical institution in its own right, a form that could be readily summoned by state officials, media personalities, civilians, and foreign terrorists alike to turn the destruction of the image into a condensed and intensified moment in which to see America.

5

9/11

It was the end, a seemingly natural culmination of this decades-old discipline in the American imagination of catastrophe. It was a *Sputnik*-like moment in American history, stimulating national anxieties, reviving patriotic pieties, and even the rebirth of a credence in strong, centralized governmental adventures. Like the Kennedy assassination, it not only came suddenly, unexpectedly on a bright fall day, it came in images that would inform its narratives and regulate its memories. As with *Challenger*, those images would be replayed relentlessly on television sets in schools, homes, and offices scattered within the complex network of broadcasting. September 11 was in these ways not only a culmination; it was a synthesis, an integration of a cumulative history in the content of a form.

Yet it was in other respects a novelty. To begin with, a new national security anxiety was recognizable, a product of developing, state-managed, digitally based, global surveillance and intelligence operations. Hence September 11 introduced a new form of state regret intimately tied to the possibility of preemption. In the opening of Stephen Spielberg's 2002 *Minority Report*, we were met with a police apparatus for which information is so perfect as to be predictive, disclosing still future criminal acts in graphic form to a police operations center before they happen, and thus allowing the police to preempt the crime. Though the film's production began before September 2001, when it appeared in theaters in 2002 it did so as a counterfantasy, for September 11 was everywhere presented as a miscarriage in national intelligence—not with regard to information per se, but with regard to the failure to "connect the dots," outline the terrorist plot, and thus to preempt it. Here was an anxiety about *vision*, which has long sought to bring the future within its field through the medium of the image (thus seers, prophets, diviners, and such).

At the turn of the millennium, states and their contractors had already chan-neled this anxiety into an appetite for limitless information and the means of mining, processing, and visualizing it, as the cybernetic networks of state security sought not only spatial mastery, but a temporal one as well. Septem-ber 11 proved that the future remained fuzzy, if frustratingly so.

September 11 was integrated as well into a still young, global, twenty-four-hour television news network. The infrastructure as well as the appetite of this information complex meant new interanimations among multinational corporate, state, civilian, and activist agencies in the production of the me-dia event. Beyond video's flow, September 11's production was characterized by an unbroken but unstable fluidity, a rough integration of proliferating still and moving images, street views, studio sets, sounds, voices, captions, and crawls. It was an acutely disorienting production when measured against television's management of the Kennedy assassination and the *Challenger* di-saster. Far more than these events, the scale, source, and character of the in-formation flow appeared ad hoc and deregulated, leaving the nature of the disaster itself unclear. Here Americans were met, arguably for the first time, with a media situation that was thoroughly networked and globalized (as the nation had been for some time!), one wherein the image of America was not a reactive concern of cold warriors but integral to the event itself. The situation was disorienting.

More than the sheer result of a new networked globalism, however, this disorientation was a product of America's post–Cold War, postmodern, post-monumental political culture. While September 11 entailed a synchro-nized, iconoclastic assault on monuments of a global empire, it was not an attack on a monumental American political culture, for that culture too had slipped away in the age of *Challenger*. Thus, the symbolic logic of the at-tacker's targets—the World Trade Center, the Pentagon, and apparently the White House—needed explanation to American audiences. Its surprise was not only in its sudden synchronicity but in the very appearance of America as a monumental empire, so visible to millions upon millions living outside the borders of the United States, but curiously invisible to the empire's citizens. It was as if the end of the Cold War and the triumph of capitalism over-and-against all other "isms" had brought about not so much a "new monumental-ity," as postmodernism had portended, but rather a post-iconoclastic age, one where not only the logic of icons but the logic of their destruction had been forgotten.[1]

An entire American public therefore had to be reeducated in iconography. Rudy Giuliani, speaking before the United Nations General Assembly several weeks after September 11, resurrected the iconic logic. "This was not just an

attack on the City of New York or on the United States of America," he told
the United Nations. "It was an attack on the very idea of a free, inclusive, and
civil society. It was a direct assault on the founding principles of the United
Nations itself." As if channeling Truman, he called out, "Now is the time in the
words of your charter, the United Nations Charter, 'to unite our strength to
maintain international peace and security.'"[2] Giuliani's speech was as much
about reclaiming lost iconic and institutional logics for the American people
as about garnering U.N. support. Indeed, not only the United Nations but a
cluster of 1940s-era institutions and icons reappeared in the star-spangled
American political imaginary post–September 11: Washington's World War II
memorial, still under construction, assumed a new public poignancy; memories of Pearl Harbor were resuscitated; tributes to "the greatest generation"
written; and the giants of early Cold War strategy recalled. For the iconoclasm of September 11 was not intuitively self-evident; the case had to be
made in revivals of myth and memory that reminded Americans, in the first
place, what an *icon* was.

Nevertheless, there was in Giuliani's speech a discourse of transcendence
that was truer to the iconoclastic logic he seemed to abhor than to the iconic
one he seemed to be resuscitating. This was a discourse of America consistent with Bellah's account of American civil religion, but far more manifestly
global in scope. So Giuliani told his audience, "Americans are not of one race
or one religion. Americans emerged from all of your nations. We're defined as
Americans by our beliefs, not by our ethnic origins, our race or our religion.
Our belief in religious freedom, political freedom, economic freedom, that's
what makes an American. Our belief in democracy, the rule of law, and respect for human life, that's how you become an American."[3] The refrain was
familiar enough. But Giuliani took its logic one step further, finding America
not only in a creed but in a globally dispersed spirit: "Each of your nations,
I'm certain, has contributed citizens to the United States and to New York. I
believe I can take every one of you someplace in New York City, and you can
find someone from your country, someone from your village or town, that
speaks your language and practices your religion. In each of your lands, there
are many who are Americans in spirit by virtue of their commitment to our
shared principles."[4] Yet, what does it mean to be American "in spirit"? Far
from a peculiar interest of a New York mayor before a United Nations assembly, this question preoccupied American public discourse in the aftermath of
September 11. America suddenly formed strange solidarities with the forgotten nations of the world. It would look for allies in the most obscure places.
Azerbaijan, Bahrain, Bangladesh, Bulgaria, Congo, Cyprus, Estonia, Kyrgyz-
stan, Lithuania, Montenegro, Oman, Slovakia, Slovenia, Sudan, Tajikistan,

Turkmenistan, and Uzbekistan were among the "coalition partners . . . fighting against [the] evil of terrorism," as a Pentagon press sheet put it, in the 2001–02 US-led assault against Afghanistan known as Operation Enduring Freedom.[5] Romania, El Salvador, Moldova, Tonga, Singapore, Macedonia, and Mongolia were among the "multi-national force" summoned for the 2003 Operation Iraqi Freedom. "We are supported," President Bush said upon the attack on Afghanistan "by the collective will of the world."[6] Yet this will was startlingly univocal—"Either you are with us, or you are with the terrorists," Bush told the world in an address to Congress a week after September 11, infamously organizing power into two first principles in endless war.[7] Indeed, this was not a discourse of an "imagined community," replete with malls, monuments, and markers, and thus "imagined as both inherently limited and sovereign."[8] No, this was a discourse of the sublime, of the infinite, of transcendence, accessible not in image and icon but only by faith in unseen principles.

For in it the world, as one widely read book maintained in 2005, was "flat."[9] The elevation of forgotten nations like Oman and Tonga to the status of allies was itself an implicit repudiation of the iconic logic of an earlier age of Great Powers. Here—in an era subsequent to both Great Wars and the Cold War wars of national liberation—the flags of the United Nations were as undifferentiated nodes scattered across a global map. And this map was not only flat, it was unequivocal and flexible, like the ideal digital database, and thus maximally efficient with respect to the exigencies of a power that would, and in limited respects could, rearrange the world order at will. Thus, correlated with this map was a *perspective*, a "subject position," a point-of-view, one typified by the strange solidarity of a neoliberal order. It is this solidarity that I explore in this chapter through a consideration of CNN's live production (in the United States) of the September 11 attacks, to which I will refer as *9/11*.

Why a discrete text like CNN's September 11 coverage? What about the vast proliferation of texts that September 11 generated? CNN's coverage, I argue, represented both the culmination of television and the beginning of the age of computer-based "new media." It thus participated in a media logic that has been called "remediation," but in a different form than typically described. *Remediation* typically refers to the way in which new technologies adopt the styles and logics of older ones.[10] But in CNN's *9/11* we see the reverse: an old technology, television, adopting the style and logic of the new computing and web-based technologies. Thus, on the one hand, *9/11* recalled JFK's assassination, which critics ranging from Frederic Jameson to Barbie Zelizer have seen as television's founding moment.[11] On the other hand, *9/11* functioned less as a "prodigious . . . display of synchronicity," television's great achievement, than as an *interface of "information,"* as with a computer interface.[12] It is not only that time here was reduced to space, it is that the presumption of full information rendered the image at once a new sort of icon—in the sense of a means of visual navigation, as with a computer desktop icon—and a fragment, a necessarily partial and incomplete representation. Thus, in focusing on CNN's 9/11 rather than surveying a portion of the vast textual field left by September 11, I intend to consider the logic of the interface out of the typical technological context of the digital computer.

Terror and Triumph

CNN's live coverage of the September 11 attacks was no more or less produced than the tributes to its victims that would follow in the months and years after. It did offer, however, a distinctive window into the American iconoclastic imagination, for in it the specifics of the day's events—the journalistic whos, whats, wheres, whens, and hows—were in short supply, buried as they were within restricted-access state and private databases. Therefore, it would seem that imagination not only would have to make proximate and intimate the horrible spectacle on the screen, but would have to fill in voids, gaps, lacunae, and such. Indeed, as we noted in the debates around *Zapruder* decades before, we once again saw vacancies rhetorically activated and filled with magnified meanings. But here that imagination was additive rather than supplementary, productive of the voids rather than responsive to them.

To begin with, 9/11 worked tirelessly to define and delimit the scope and significance of the event, pushing at the boundaries not only of the catastrophe but of the existence of the nation. The most prominent issue on CNN was not *what* happened, but *how big* it was (a rhetorical gesture that not long ago would have drawn the notice of Freudians everywhere). CNN's anchors Aaron Brown in New York (fig. 8) and Judy Woodruff in Washington, D.C., with their guests, repeatedly tried to describe the scale of the event: "enormous," "massive," "extraordinary," "phenomenal," "horrific."[13] In the late morning, about two hours after the first tower collapsed, Woodruff declared, "Clearly, the United States has never experienced anything of this magnitude." Similarly, Mayor Giuliani stated on CNN, "It's one of the most heinous acts certainly in world history." Former US Ambassador to the United Nations Richard Holbrooke told Brown, "This is the most skillful, murderous attack ever." In a recap of the day's events during the one o'clock hour, Brown invoked the language of magnification to characterize the day's events: "What has happened is not simply a series of moments, but something much larger." This emphasis on magnitude and expansion was, to be sure, enabled by a lack of relevant information,

BREAKING NEWS
TWO PLANES CRASH INTO TOWERS
OF WORLD TRADE CENTER
CNN
LIVE
9:37a ET

FIGURE 8. CNN's Aaron Brown reporting live from New York on September 11, 2001, shortly before the first tower collapses.

but here the gaps in information seemed as much a projection onto the events as an attempt to interpret them. Faced with unknowns, apocalyptic fantasies ran wild. For example, in their speculations about the number of casualties, CNN reported that "untold numbers" had been injured or had died. Beneath the repeated video footage of the towers collapsing, CNN's crawl announced, "10,000 emergency personnel scrambled to Trade Center fires, [towers] eventually collapsed.... More than 150,000 people visit the Trade Center on an average day." One survivor interviewed on the street said, "I believe tens of thousands of people are dead." "We are in the middle of an extraordinary catastrophe," Brown declared near the noon hour. The United States faced "chaos."

Imaginary bedlam infiltrated the coverage: CNN reported, all falsely, that the Washington Mall was on fire, that the Capitol was just about to be attacked, that a car bomb had exploded at the State Department, that a helicopter had crashed next to the Pentagon, and that the United States may have begun bombing Afghanistan (the "dots," one presumes, having been instantly connected not only by US intelligence agencies, but by the news media). Such fantastic embellishments extended to the coverage's presentation of the significance of the attack. Though the footer on the television screen read "America Under Attack," the attacks were framed as being not only against America but as against the "free world" and "civilization" more generally. As Israeli Foreign Minister

Shimon Peres said in his interview with Brown, "It was not only an attack on America but an attack on civilization." On one occasion, Brown expressed a note of caution about the language of magnitude that he and others used so liberally. "There is no point in allowing this thing to seem worse than it is; it is already horrendous, and we don't need to make it worse by misstating numbers, and we want you to keep that in mind." However, although the crisis was very bad, CNN did make it worse than it was, not simply by misstating numbers, but by representing a situation that was, to use a phrase repeated throughout the day, "beyond imagination."

Still, the official imagination was well within reach. During the two o'clock hour Brown interviewed George Shultz, who had been US secretary of state under Reagan:

BROWN: We mentioned a moment ago, there were 50,000 people who come to work each day at the World Trade Center. There are literally tens of thousands more who come into the city, each of them affected. But the effect of this, we suspect, is much broader than that, that it will affect everyone in the country. Former Secretary of State George Schultz, to say American life [has] been changed forever seems a bit farther than I want to go, but has American life been changed today?

SCHULTZ: American life will pick up. We have to look to our security, obviously, and be careful about it. But we're not going to allow these terrible people to change our way of life. They just aren't going to be able to do it. We'll defend ourselves adequately, we will find out who they are. We will get rid of them, and we'll learn how to preempt these attacks. But we're not going to change our way of life because of these people. I reject that entirely.[14]

There was in this exchange more than another instance of rhetorical magnification; there was a clear construal of America at a border situation, and Brown's question seemed to want to lead Schultz to probe what philosopher Tsang Lap-cheun refers to as the bottom-limit of the sublime, the borders of a nonexistence (here an existence in the status quo).[15] Brown's question was both expansive and deep. Formally, it started with the smallest number—50,000—and then took two steps outward, through "tens of thousands more" to "everyone in the country." But its tone probed depths. Brown asked Schultz to articulate the ways American life might fundamentally be changed with intonations that suggest decline. Schultz, however, insisted that it would not be changed. He promised adequate defense, due justice, decisive triumph, and even preemption. In this way, Schultz invoked a rhetoric of the top-limit of the sublime, emphasizing the nation's inevitable victory and ability to transcend historical contingencies themselves.

This short, highly formulaic exchange typified a rhetorical movement repeated throughout CNN's coverage that day. The movement was between two polar ends, cataclysmic fall and imminent, ultimate triumph. For Americans, watching CNN's coverage was, on the one hand, to watch the spectacular, massive, and tragic denouement of America. On the other hand, however, in the comments of officials representing the US government, it was to watch America elevated like a phoenix to new, military-won heights. Neither vision, though, pictured a future in which unpredictable political process would be in play. Indeed, the constant probing of the bottom-limit and top-limit (we might label this a bipolar rhetoric, rather than Jameson's "schizophrenic") represented the significance of the day's events as falling well outside of political arts of possibility, contingency, and relative indeterminacy.[16] Here we were confronted, however, not with the onward march of history, assumed to have ended with the Cold War triumph of capitalism; rather, here history was a game to be mastered. For there was no Hegelian "world spirit" cunningly working through great works and great men to guarantee a progressive future. Instead, official interviewees offered the cunning of state power as sufficient reason for the surety of America's future.

Thus, the ubiquity of *war*. War appeared in CNN's broadcast as the bridge from the extremes of national apocalypse to that of triumphant nationalism. It was the means of converting a tragic discourse into a polemical one. The word *war* itself was used some twenty times per hour in the first twelve hours of the coverage—on average every three minutes.[17] Most of these uses were condensed in the comments of state officials or their proxies. For example, in an interview with CNN's Wolf Blitzer in the early afternoon, Senator John McCain announced, "This is obviously an act of war that has been committed on the United States of America." US Representative Curt Weldon said, "We're at war. We're absolutely at war." (Earlier, just after the first tower collapsed, Tom Brokaw announced on NBC, "There's been a declaration of war by terrorists.") A drastic example of the use of *war* came in the ten o'clock hour, when Brown asked correspondent John King to describe what the government's national security apparatus was doing. King described the White House situation room, where, he said, "a President or a Vice President can direct a war, can direct a full scale world war. . . . The White House situation room is prepared just for a situation like this." A subtler example of the way war filled the reportage of the terrorist attacks was seen in its more metaphorical use. For example, in a mid-morning interview with Howard Safer, the former New York City police commissioner, Brown asked,

"Mr. Safer, what do you see?" Scenes of destruction played on the television screen as Safer replied, "I see something that is unimaginable." Brown asked, "Does the [city's emergency] plan cover the scope of what appears to have happened here?" "No," Safer continued, "nobody ever would contemplate that we would lose the two World Trade Centers and in this manner." Brown then asked Safer to describe what was happening at the scene of the towers' collapse. Safer answered, "It's like a war zone, and you have to logistically treat it like a war zone." Here and elsewhere, war was a way of apprehending the disaster. It functioned not only as a central logistical symbol to bring order to the day's events; at important moments in CNN's coverage, war was a means of overcoming tragedy—indeed, of bringing a kind of comedic resolution to the story.

Amid all this talk of war, a particular story of war and its inevitable, triumphant end filled the coverage. Congressmen and former congressmen, ambassadors and former ambassadors, security experts, retired generals, and international leaders all promised an American triumph over its enemies. They spoke of military-led victory and ultimately revitalization, rebuilding, and retaliation. Thus, there were persistent references to Pearl Harbor. Brown frequently asked official guests for "historical perspective" (as if only the stewards of the state could have such a perspective), and here they would reply, as Senator Lyndon Johnson had done in describing the magnitude of *Sputnik*, with "Pearl Harbor." For example, James Kallstrom, former assistant director of the FBI, claimed that the terrorist attacks were "everything that Pearl Harbor was and more." Senator Christopher Dodd claimed that the attack "rivals if not exceeds" Pearl Harbor. Anchors, dignitaries, and a few survivors interviewed on the streets of New York City each recalled Pearl Harbor. No doubt, Pearl Harbor was, in a certain sense, a fitting historical analogy—like September 11, it was a surprise attack with devastating consequences. However, embedded in an official discourse, as almost all of the references were, Pearl Harbor meant something more than another surprise attack on America: it entailed an outline of a vertical movement from America at its bottom-limit (America attacked unexpectedly and vulnerably exposed) to the country at its top-limit (imminent and heroic victory over the enemy).[18] Here was an arc of triumph that was purely formal in appearance, and we would soon learn that this ideal form was not a Clausewitzian image of "absolute war," constructed as a theoretical point of reference for the practical judgment of real wars.[19] Rather, it was an agenda, both martial and economic. Militarily, we would see it carried out in the early days of the wars in Afghanistan and Iraq, both of which were approached in strategy and rhetoric in terms of near-immediate and certainly inevitable victory. Economically, we would see it heeded in the presumption of limitless resources for such adventures—*scarcity* and *sacrifice* were left out of the political-economic lexicon of the War on Terror. In offering a vision of an American triumph loosed from Clausewitzian limits and frictions, this discourse was one of transcendence, directly challenging the most fundamental premise of an iconic culture: *material is meaningful.*

Indeed, to back away from 9/11 briefly, we can here consider a more general distinction between iconic and iconoclastic cultures with respect to the destruction of images. Within an iconic political culture, the destruction of images has a radical force, and is met with a legislative, dogmatic, and ideological response aimed at preserving the integrity of the image as a locus of true representation. In the *descent* of law in the wake of the destruction of images, iconic cultures reestablish the mundane. Here we can think not only of the history of icons within the Byzantine Empire, but also of the general assumption within European culture more broadly that the preservation of the relics of the past is integral to the constitution of European identity and society. Within an iconoclastic political culture, on the other hand, the destruction of images does not have such constitutive consequences. Iconoclastic cultures are not first and foremost destructive cultures; rather, they are cultures wherein destruction can be at most penultimate, a kind of prelude to something greater, more superior, more profound. An iconoclastic culture moves vertically, so that spirit prevails over matter.[20]

There were, to be sure, counter-rhetorics on CNN that day. There was the rhetoric of the perpetrators themselves, which efficiently exploited the medium to spectacular ends. This rhetoric was neither iconic nor iconoclastic, but what might be termed "iconic(clastic)," for in destroying the image, the attackers sought to destroy what those images *represented*, rather than *representation* itself. There were as well occasional unofficial, vernacular voices of witnesses or survivors.[21] These voices uniformly probed the bottom-limit of the disaster, none of them adopting the official, top-limit rhetoric that was heard in the voice of Schultz and other dignitaries. Yet, neither did these voices invoke a rhetoric that mirrored the apocalyptic imagery that CNN ran throughout the day. Rather, their voices hovered in the depths of despair, but in a way that sought to make sense of the events and to make do. Illustrative is Brown's phone interview during the one o'clock hour with William Rodriguez, a Trade Center maintenance worker, who spoke with a thick Latino accent:

BROWN: Tell me what happened.
RODRIGUEZ: I was in the basement, which is the support floor for the maintenance company, and we hear like a big rumble. Not like an impact, like a rumble, like moving furniture in a massive way. And all of sudden we

hear another rumble, and a guy comes running, running into our office, and all of skin was off his body. All of the skin. We went crazy, we started screaming, we told him to get out. We took everybody out of the office outside to the loading dock area. Then I went back in, and when I went back in I saw people—I heard people that were stuck on the elevator, on a freight elevator because all of the elevators went down. And water was going in, and they were probably getting drowned. And we get a couple of pipes and opened the elevator and we got the people out. I went back up and saw one of the officers from the Port Authority Police, I been working there for twenty years so I knew him very well. My routine on the World Trade Center is in charge of the staircase, and since there was no elevator service, I have the master keys for all the staircase doors. So, I went up with the police officer and a group of firemen. As we went up, there was a lot of people coming up, and while we got up, it was very difficult to get up.

BROWN: Mr. Rodriguez, how much time has taken—has elapsed here in this, as you recount the events? Did it seem like hours, minutes, seconds?

RODRIGUEZ: No, it wasn't hours.

BROWN: What did it seem like?

RODRIGUEZ: Well there was a big time, like a gap. There was a gap of time. I won't be able to tell you if it was 15 or 20 minutes.

BROWN: Okay.

RODRIGUEZ: But there was a gap of time. We heard, while we were on the thirty-third floor, I'm sorry on the twenty-third floor, because we stopped there with the fire department because their equipment was very heavy, and they were breathing very hard. They took a break because they couldn't continue going up. So they wanted to take a break. And we had a person on a wheelchair that we were going to bring down on a gurney, and a lady that was having problems with a heart attack, and some other guy that was bleeding hard. And we went a couple of floors up. While they were putting the person in the gurney, got up to the thirty-ninth floor, and we heard on the radio that the sixty-fifth floor collapsed. It collapsed.

BROWN: Mr. Rodriguez, let me stop you there at the sixty-fifth floor, and let me add you are a lucky man, it seems like, today. Thank you for joining us.[22]

Rodriguez's disoriented narrative of his experience was characterized by the absence of the heroic. The elevator rescue and his cooperation with the firemen were narrated as haphazard incidents where Rodriguez tried to help out. His story did not evoke in the least the transcendence of all limitations and contradictions, as heard in official voices. Rather, it pronounced those limitations: screaming at the sight of a skinless man, struggling up the stairs with weary firemen, hearing on the radio of floors collapsing. Rodriguez's voice, however, did not therefore prophesy imminent global catastrophe. His voice is best characterized as traumatized, confused, and perplexed. But such voices were the sole province of the person-on-the-street in CNN's coverage, and thus were managed. While apocalyptic or triumphant images saturated the coverage and possessed the voices of officials and news anchors, the intense perplexity and confusion of September 11 was restricted to unofficial voices.

In these ways, CNN offered an official story of an America beyond limits. Limits of a kind, to be sure, were presented: the bottom-limit of apocalyptic nonexistence and the top-limit of imminent and ultimate American triumph. But to see "America Under Attack" on CNN was to be introduced to an economy where even such extreme limits would be denied their purchase. It was not only to get caught up in a violent movement between extremes, but to be transported into a world of indeterminate power, one where history and cunning blended into an inexhaustible field of action. Here we were met with a familiar theological form, but without all the pieties of theological formalism. Indeed, the form was made acute not by a formality (as in Kennedy's inaugural address, for example) but by its "live" and hence seemingly informal character. CNN performed in an impromptu manner. The coverage was characterized by interruption, unpredictability, and nonlinear eruptions. In this way, the very form of the coverage replicated its apocalyptic subject matter. Yet, as the interaction between Brown and Schultz typified, the coverage was also bound to a strong formalism. Official voices spoke in patterns of polemic and denial—polemic not only against enemies, but against the iconic(clastic) logic of the acts of the enemies; denial not only of America's decline, but of the possibility of a decline.

Image, Interface, and Information

To see events unfold live on television on September 11, 2001, was to witness an extreme national situation narrated incongruously yet hierarchically in vernacular, official, and oppositional rhetorics. And yet to see the events unfold that day was also to have replayed, ad nauseam, moving images of the towers' collapse. Two truisms immediately arise: the iconic(clastic) image was a rhetoric of protest against the institutional and indeed symbolic legitimacy of the West for a variety of audiences worldwide (including the perpetrators who organized the operation from afar); on the other hand, for the many who identified with the victims of the attack as Americans, it was a visceral, spectacular assault on a monument of an imagined community. Still, there was a third, less axiomatic function of the image of the towers' collapse: it, together with the host of visual information broadcast that day, was an organizing image, an interface, a "graphic design" whereby interaction with the global networks that so violently erupted that day was both facilitated and consolidated.

For one way in which the events of September 11, 2001, appeared in public differently than those on November 22, 1963, or January 28, 1986, was with regard to the assumptions of information. From a state perspective, September 11 was a full-information event, and the state's discourse of polemic and denial can be read as deriving from this presumption of full information. The images did not in fact tell the full story, for they could not. Forensically, they falsely concentrated perception on a small set of spectacular events when in fact these events were but "hot points" within a global network of "terror." Hence, the forensic argument implied an assumption about the ontology of images: they were but "dots," so to speak, within a vast database of state knowledge.

Here we can again turn to the operational logic of technologies of representation, as we did with Zapruder's home-movie camera and the television cameras of the 1980s—for the gaps were here too in at least one respect a product of a technology, but that of networked information rather than the filmic shutter or televisual flow. The use of the camera for information is as old as the camera itself, but in World War II and its aftermath, filmic information was incorporated into bureaucratic networks of command and control, where it was processed, interpreted, and used selectively as intelligence or scientific evidence.[23] If photographic technology has been a technology of control, these bureaucratic networks sought to acquire the image in order to control. The development of digital networks grew out of these bureaucratic networks. But the digital is not mainly a matter of acquisition but of input: the first principle of its network is not to grab and capture eagerly, as with the camera, but to passively receive and then process. Such processing is ideally seamless and uninterrupted, like television's flow, but even more so, as the ideal database is continuous and flat rather than ongoing and rhythmic. In this database, unlike film, there are no structural gaps. Fragments are not fragments; they are "waste." And gaps are not lacunae; they are at best products of a post-facto judgment imposed upon the database from without and have the form of a lack rather than a cut (namely, lack of input). Indeed, it is not until data is translated into an external medium—a graphic interface, human language, visual representations, and so on—that such gaps appear. Which is to say that within a digitally networked world, lacunae are not so much objects of judgment as they are products of judgment. Rather than appearing as inherent to the active cutting operations of the technology, they are external to it, *de jure* rather than *de facto* phenomena.[24]

Here we are entering a world of *design*. If there was a conspicuous "production quality" to *9/11* and the ensuing events—from the lists of "allies" discussed above to Colin Powell's presentation before the United Nations concerning Iraq's weapons of mass destruction and the Pentagon's "shock and awe" in Iraq—this was in keeping with the "language of new media," as Lev Manovich described the logic of this new global, digital network in 2001.

> The logic of new media thus corresponds to the post-industrial logic of "production on demand" and "just in time" delivery which themselves were made possible by the use of computers and computer networks in all stages of manufacturing and distribution. Here "culture industry" (the term was originally coined by Theodor Adorno in the 1930s) is actually ahead of the rest of the industry. The idea that a customer determines the exact features of her car at the showroom, the data is then transmitted to the factory, and hours later the new car is delivered, remains a dream, but in the case of computer media, it is reality. Since the same machine is used as a showroom and a factory, i.e., the same computer generates and displays media—and since the media exists [*sic*] not as a material object but as data which can be sent through the wires with the speed of light, the customized version created in response to user's input is delivered almost immediately. Thus, to continue with the same example, when you access a Web site, the server immediately assembles a customized Web page.[25]

Thus there is not only a new relation to the void (external and *de jure* rather than inherent and *de facto*), there is an ideology of abundance, and hence a refutation of the old industrial ideologies of scarcity, acquisition, and monopolistic production. The product is seen not as a product of engineering (and hence the management of scarce resources), but of consumer choice, or design, with the presumption of virtually unlimited options.

Indeed, here the image is an interface, a means of negotiating and interacting with the abundance of information. In Kennedy's death we were met with an epistemology of scarcity, an assumption that knowledge could be had, but only if it could be discovered, and its discovery was presumed difficult (recall Josiah Thompson's comment on the Kennedy assassination— "I've never remotely encountered a murder case where the more it's investigated, the less you know about what happened"). But in *9/11* we were met with an epistemology of abundance, an assumption (not even an assertion) that knowledge of the nature and scope of the event was readily available and could be had if only it could be accessed and put into a manageable design. September 11 was approached, even as it unfolded, as a full-information game; the epistemological problems presented in CNN's coverage were not ones of the ontological absence of information, but of the ontological plenitude of information, on the one hand (as the data was out there in abundance), and insufficient access via privatization, on the other (as state officials and/or proprietary interest restricted access to the data). Brown's language on CNN was in this regard telling: he said things like, "Let me throw another couple of pieces of information out, as we put this together into a straight line, if we can." Or, "There are a lot of pieces of information floating around. We need to try to button up some of this." At one point late in the morning, Brown faltered in giving an accurate chronology and declared, "You lose track of time a little bit in these situations." He thus drew attention to not so much the unknown, not even to what could not be known, but to the problems of tracking, ordering, organizing, and arranging an abundance of information. There were, to be sure, unknowns—"Whatever is happening," Brown stated, "and whoever is responsible, we have no way of knowing if it is played out yet, or if it just going on"—but here it was the unfolding "live" character of the full-information events rather than the epistemic obscurity of a forensic field that characterized the unknown. An assumption informing CNN's coverage—indicative of the postindustrial information age and of neoliberal discourse—was that sufficient information was available. The central problems of knowledge, consistent with computing and "big data," were therefore ones of access, processing, and interface.

This was a marked difference from the logic of the Cold War, which was almost always approached as a partial or incomplete information game and therefore premised on the strategy of deterrence. The full-information presumption of the War on Terror instead meant preemption. And here the image was an interface, the icon a tool for interaction with an ideally unlimited field of information. Design did not so much represent a structure as it structured a mass of information. Thus CNN persistently returned to the *scene*, to pictures and images of devastation. Anchors' verbal narratives started with pieces of information—reports and chronologies—but quickly slid into commentaries on the scenes on the screen, letting the image structure the information. For example, as Brown tried to recount the shutting down of airports across the country, his attention seamlessly turned toward the pictures being displayed of Manhattan, "The FAA has shut down every airport in the country. And to our knowledge, and we're—this is to the best of our memory, that has never happened before. We're starting to get some pictures of the scene from the ground here in Manhattan. . . . This is a live picture of the scene now." Anchor Daryn Kagan's report earlier in the day's events illustrates even more precisely the displacement of verbal narrative by the scene: "OK, once again, if you're just joining us, the breaking story that we're following out of New York City. Within the span of 18 minutes, two separate planes crashing into the World Trade Center. The rescue operations underway, it's not clear—we will show you—this is second plane, after first tower already on fire. Let the pictures tell the story. You saw it live here on CNN as it happened the plane crashed right into the side of World Trade Center, causing a huge explosion."[26] CNN's central "story," we might argue, was a visual story, told over and over again, generating a spectating subject consumed with perspectives of terror. In a certain respect, this was true. It was not the case, however, that scenes simply compensated for a lack of the type of information reporters are professionally supposed to offer (the "who, what, where, when, why, and how" of the journalistic trade). Notions of the spectacle offer an inadequate account. Rather, the image was here a means of *access*. Even as state referees (human and machine) worked tirelessly off-screen in situation rooms to amass and organize an overabundance of information, news networks produced September 11 as an information event by offering viewers a range of images through which to interface with the global, networked event. That these images were being replayed in the very same situation rooms from which global wars could be managed suggests their status as interfaces of information.

Consider even the focal moment in CNN's coverage. At the first collapse of a tower, Brown suddenly interrupted a CNN correspondent:

> Wow! Jamie, Jamie, I need you to stop for a second. There has just been a huge explosion; we can see a billowing smoke rising. And I can't—I tell you that I can't see that second tower. But there was a cascade of sparks, and fire, and now this—it looks almost like a mushroom cloud explosion. This huge billowing smoke in the second tower. This was the second of two towers hit. And—you know I cannot see behind that smoke, obviously, as you can't either. The first tower in front has not changed. And we see this extraordinary and frightening scene behind us of this second tower now just encased in smoke. What is behind it, I cannot tell you. But just look at that. That is just as frightening a scene as you'll ever see.[27]

Brown condensed into this impromptu narration the decades-long history of the American iconoclastic imagination we have been following: not just the violence to the iconic artifact, but the reference to the mushroom cloud, a profound negativity (Brown repeats the construction "I cannot" five times in this short narrative), and the expressivist impulse to turn the image of destruction into a register of experience ("But just look at that. That is just as frightening a scene as you'll ever see."). The scene was a means of accessing memory, the image an interface for retrieving, more than representing, the encoded language of late-modern American catastrophes.

Indeed, especially in their images of the towers' collapse and the chaotic aftermath, CNN approached the scene as a means of structuring not just a story, but organizing and accessing information vis-à-vis the interface. Scenes of trauma and disaster were patched together according to a logic of information. By mid-afternoon about a dozen shots of the events in New York dominated the coverage. During the noon hour, for example, CNN showed the towers collapsing more than a dozen times, the second plane crashing into the second tower about a half-dozen times, and street scenes of people fleeing the towers more than a dozen times. Footage also was replayed that hour of the silt- and rubble-covered streets, of patients being taken into a hospital on gurneys, of an elderly man collapsing on the street, of police officers taking cover in a street-side store, of firemen mounting the piles of rubble blocks away from the collapsed Towers, and of people taking cover behind and beneath automobiles to save themselves.

Amid all these images three distinct views were replayed of the tower collapses: (1) an expansive bird's-eye view (or long shot) of the towers collapsing in the Manhattan skyline; (2) street shots of a dense mass of rubble flooding down the city streets; and (3) a disorienting view of the hand-held camera in the aftermath of the collapses. Each view worked to organize information, bringing interpretations to the symbols, or—as in XML—attributes to elements: the first structured <history>, the second <experience>, and the third <existence>. The long shot framed the World Trade Center towers from afar, setting them against the Manhattan skyline. Their prominence in the horizon under the bright blue sky magnified the scale of their collapse and the vacuity of the smoke-filled space they left behind. The street shots placed the viewer in the way of the deluge of debris and dust descending down Manhattan's streets, allowing the viewer to identify with the imminent immersion of the camera in the cloud and with the imminent mortality represented by the camera's burial. Scale was magnified here by virtue of the reduction of the camera's scopic power beneath the impending avalanche. Finally, the aftershots captured by hand-held cameras, a jostled and clouded televisual view, suggested immersion by invoking the disorientation that results from having been overcome by scale.

These perspectives offered spectacular stories of death and destruction that, like many such stories, generate expansive imaginative possibilities. I do not want to minimize their narrative power. For example, near the end of the three o'clock hour, CNN showed hand-held video-camera footage shot by a medical doctor who was near the towers during their successive collapses. In a televisual scene for which the only antecedents are televisual fictions of nuclear winters, the doctor, audible but not visible to the camera he carried, ran about through the cloud of debris, his audible choking and coughing indicating his struggle to breathe, as he exclaimed, "I hope I live. I hope I live. It's coming down on me." But I do want to stress the encoded form of the stories the images accessed. The codes on which the narratives drew had been built within American entertainment industries since the middle of the twentieth century. Correspondent Jeff Greenfield, who was responsible for perspective on the day's events in CNN's live coverage, referred to Tom Clancy's fiction.

> What we see now is nothing less than the worst nightmare that one could imagine come to life, probably worse than anyone could have imagined. You may remember that Tom Clancy wrote a novel that ends with a terrorist hijacker crashing into the Capitol. The worst act of terrorism on American soil, the Oklahoma City Bombing, killed fewer than 200 people. All we know today is that tens of thousands of people work in that complex that has been destroyed, and I hate to say it this way, but this may be the day that America's luck ran out.[28]

Clancy himself would later appear as a guest in the coverage. In the days after, the press's commentaries on September 11, even as they sometimes criticized television's aesthetic excessiveness, participated in it. A piece that ran in the *Boston Globe* moved from Tom Clancy's popular fiction imaginary to the Hollywood imaginary. "The analogies to Tom Clancy novels and Hollywood movies were everywhere as the media tried to make sense out of what happened to America on Tuesday. Clancy was even a guest on CNN talking about life imitating art, while scenes right out of *Independence Day* and *Armageddon* played behind him—the whoosh of smoke and debris rushing down a city street, not to mention the bombing of US landmarks."[29] A September 12 comment in the *St. Petersburg Times* noted that "it looked eerily like a made-for-TV massacre."[30] *San Diego Union-Tribune* television critic Robert Laurence wrote on September 12, "The surrealistic images of New York crowds stampeding through rubble-strewn streets could have been taken from a horror movie. But this was all too real. 'This is of a dimension that literally dwarfs even fantasy,' CNN's Jeff Greenfield said."[31] A *Rocky Mountain News* television critic wrote, "Television had provided the unthinkable, showing the devastating live coverage of the start of a war. . . . [It was] a day, which seemed like a lifetime, of nonstop coverage of a terrorist attack far surpassing anything from Hollywood's fiction factory."[32] In these persistent appeals to Hollywood myth and spectacle, television and its critics pressed upon the aesthetic, presenting September 11 as a crisis of spectatorship. Critic Joanne Ostrow of the *Denver Post* gave succinct expression to the crisis: "We are watching death, not TV. We can't let TV become the event." Yet Ostrow admitted that we were, indeed, watching TV, and "Television can't help putting on a show."[33]

The narratives, moreover, were additive rather than supplementary—rather than filling in structural gaps, they graphically amplified the information-saturated event. Indeed, image and imagination were here forms of information, bits to be integrated into a global network of data. Here <history>, <experience>, and <existence> were elements in a field of information processing, management, and production. The image was therefore both interface and information. Indeed, in the neopositivist world of computing that has become so integral to neoliberal order—one where data and quasi-mathematical validation are the only useful (and therefore legitimate) means of knowledge production—the interface is but a form of information. The "flatness" of this order is not reflected in the structuring of the data—which can be quite hierarchical—but in the reduction of the field of knowledge to sheer data. Here the camera abandoned the mimetic logic of film (one of representation) and instead counted photons, converting light into data. Conversion took the form of *reduction*, but reduction was a means not so much of ordering the world of action, but of *positioning* it. In this reduction was an implicit process of deconstruction and, indeed, against an older liberal world of institutions and icons, an iconoclasm, a critical revelation of the inadequacy of any image for representation.

Conclusion

9/11 was thus made up of layered disorientations and reorientations. The targeted nature of the attacks assumed a vibrant monumental American political culture, when in fact that culture had been lost. Therefore, an American public had to be reoriented to the logic of icons and iconoclasms. Moreover, the unbroken but unstable flow of the wall-to-wall television coverage tended to disorient. Anchors on CNN and elsewhere struggled to "piece together" not only the day's events, but broken sequences of images and interviews that producers threw their way. Official discourses of American supremacy functioned to reorient viewers, offering as they did a metanarrative of triumph even over the severe traumas suffered by American material culture. As a full-information event tethered to global surveillance and security networks, *9/11* saturated viewers with a world of data. Indeed, *9/11* quickly left the *material* of forensic judgment (Kennedy's bullet-pierced head, *Challenger*

O-rings, and such) behind and instead turned to a discourse of "connecting the dots," where the dots were bits and pieces of surveillance and intelligence data floating in computer databanks. Here a reorientation was achieved, not only in dot-connecting, but in the iconic (indeed, iconoclastic) images themselves, which were a means of accessing and structuring the vast world of state security information.

Thus, television's spectators were brought into solidarity with state and corporate points of view, a solidarity emblematic of a neoliberal order, where the specifying (in the sense of species formation) tendencies of institutions erode under a relentless pressure to reduce society to undifferentiated generic market forces and actors. Whereas, prior to the Zapruder film, the state, Hollywood, and news agencies each independently sought iconoclastic images (sometimes, to be sure, forming strong alliances—e.g., in films of would-be nuclear destruction), through the Zapruder film, the civilian camera acquired the image, thus giving rise to new possibilities for citizenly relationships to iconoclastic national events. In *Challenger*, however, a hybrid state-corporate camera reacquired the iconoclastic image, and thus re-appropriated national trauma—a power that had been in the 1960s and 1970s in important respects stripped from the state. 9/11 was different than both of these in that these distinct operators—the state, the corporation, and the civilian—bled into one before the iconoclastic image; on September 11 the citizen, the state, and the corporation all took their respective place as one behind the camera. Many of the images of destruction shown on television that day were shot by news-media corporate cameras ready-made for the iconoclastic image, but not all—there were hundreds, perhaps thousands, of Zapruders walking the streets of New York that day, and the scenes they shot flowed into the wall-to-wall media architecture of 9/11 with little to no differentiation from their corporate counterparts (unlike the voices discussed above). So, too, as these images moved from cameras into news-network production, the state made them its own, incorporating the images into systems of surveillance and situation-room management. Here the state maintained a kind of control of the situation by incorporating the news media spectacle itself into the flat network of information-based state security operations. This complex integration of civilian witnessing, corporate media production, and state security was not the product of a strategic alliance but of the strange solidarity made possible by looking together at the iconoclastic image. As if to validate the accusation of America's attackers that in fact an Americanized West was but an undivided state-corporate-democratic Behemoth, this strange solidarity was integral to the event itself.

A postscript to the age? A culmination? A repressed memory returned? September 11 was each of these. It was in addition a chance to revive the contests of the late 1950s and early 1960s between the iconic and the iconoclastic. September 11 was in this regard a *Sputnik* moment, an image crisis that gave rise to a new institutionalism: a newly minted Department of Homeland Security, a reinvigorated Department of Defense, a reoriented FBI and CIA, the amended institutions of the Foreign Intelligence and Surveillance Act, and so on. Is there a Niebuhrian tale to be told here? Is there an irony in the ascendency of Big Government out of the ashes of September 11? Is history's revenge to be found in the fact that a flat world would produce not only such statuesque institutions as these, but a new iconography of "homeland security" (replete with uniforms and color-coded advisory systems), and indeed a new sense of the homeland possessed by a clearly demarcated border, common feeling, and a codified identity?[34]

Always there is the order and the conditions of its possibility, a duality that is itself the condition of the possibility of ideology, the false-consciousness that mitigates (but does not overcome) the contradictions of a historical order. The reinvigoration of state institutions after September 11 was congruent with the pattern of radical iconoclasms, which, faced with their own assertion of the impossibility of any legitimate representation of the ontological order that authorizes their particular form of action in the world, repeatedly end in the return of a form of emergency order—the Law in the Radical Reformation, or Reason in Kantianism (both of which, in turn, led to a distinct legalism). Thus, the institutions of emergency management stand before neoliberalism as a purer form of the condition of its own possibility. As a form of crisis capitalism, neoliberalism requires for its perpetuity the law in its absolute form to bring about by force what will not come about by nature or providence (two alternate ontological bases for other forms of capitalism). The return of the law to neoliberalism, therefore, is not an irony; it is not, in Niebuhr's phrase, an instance of another dream "cruelly refuted by history."[35] Rather, it is its oxymoronic conjunction, the political sublime.

In fact even as the law made its return, an invisible order of national security that long predated September 11 found new purpose in the War on Terror: black ops, blank spots on the map, private contractors, paralegal formulations like "enemy combatant," and a network of invisible holding cells and refugee or detainee camps.[36] Thus, two sorts of invisible orders appeared out of the ashes of September 11: the law and those hidden, secret, and private activities and institutions that the law sanctions and on which it depends. If indeed neoliberalism is premised on the power of invisible orders, as I have been arguing, then we might find in the appearance of an invisible national security state the shadows of the neoliberal state. In the next chapter, I return to the early years of America's Cold War to suggest that the neoliberal state made its first ghostly appearances in America not in the age of Reagan, but in that of Eisenhower and his New Look, which drew its impetus as well as something of its form from economy.

PART III

Economy

6

America's New Look

If there was one great fear at the 1938 Colloque Lippmann, it was the police state, that form of rule that dissolves law, property, and rights into the air of arbitrary terror and violence. And the attendees of the Colloque Lippmann had every reason to be in fear: within a matter of months, the bulk of the population of continental Europe would be living under brutal occupying powers, Nazi or Soviet, wherein the only order, if it can be called that, was violence. For the bulk of the population in the United States, however, the police state was largely an abstraction, a caricature of the living terror of others that appeared in posters, broadsheets, and political cartoons. Thus, by the time *Look* published its cartoonish version of Hayek's *The Road to Serfdom* in 1945, the police state had assumed in America the stylized form of a fascist state (though the two were not identical): men in dark collars and shoulder straps, peaked caps, and jackboots engaged in stiff-armed salutes and awed poses before the iconic image of the Führer. In Europe the fascist aesthetic was militant, animalistic, and terrifying; in the United States it was this too, but sometimes a wee bit comical as well (fig. 9).

Perhaps the comedy was corrective, for the American warfare state shared certain aesthetic traits with the fascist state. In World War II, a great leader, Franklin Delano Roosevelt, summoned millions to military sacrifice and other forms of patriotic purpose in the name of both existential threats to national survival and the destiny of a too often volkisch America. In the American warfare state, uniforms, rank insignia, military formations, machines, and men assumed a new, unprecedented cultural power in the United States. Thus, reflecting on a World War II political cartoon featuring a gargantuan FDR standing over an industrial American scene (fig. 10), James P. McDaniel notes the aesthetic ambiguity of the age, as "it seems to appropriate the imagery of

FIGURE 9. The two-headed fascist monster. A World War II poster from the US War Production Board.

FIGURE 10. Fascists as ape-like creatures bent on enslaving the world. From the *Philadelphia Record*.

Fascism for democratic purposes." Indeed, the cartoon shows a colossal FDR standing erect over a wartime industrial scene as a tyrant might stand over his dominion. Thus, as McDaniel continues, "staples of the Fascist sublime are recuperated into the democratic sublime, perhaps implying the logic that fire must be fought with fire."[1]

The remarkable popularity of *The Road to Serfdom* in the United States in the waning years of the war suggests that this aesthetic ambiguity was also a point of national anxiety. If the warfare state was but a few steps from the fascist state, the former would best be dismantled as soon as it was no longer necessary—so readers of versions of *The Road to Serfdom* in publications like

Reader's Digest and *Look* might have concluded. Even as the war was coming
to an end, Americans looked forward, often idyllically, to a return to normalcy where women would be at home, men would work plows or pull levers
rather than pump guns, and America's leaders would get back to the business
of "politics as usual."

It would not be. The warfare state, as things turned out, would be transformed into what historian Michael J. Hogan refers to as the national security
state, which emerged out of the thicket of World War II to enter the fog of
the Cold War and become a permanent feature of American life. It entailed, by
its very existence, the rebuke of traditional American isolationism and hemi-
spheric regionalism, its institutional logics presuming America's global responsibility. But the national security state was more than an institution or
set of institutions; it was an ideology, a mindset, a set of guiding assumptions
that represented "the country as a great power with an expansive military
machine and global responsibilities" and, more ominously, assumed the vulnerability of the United States to outside attack for the foreseeable future.[2]

Thus, as Hogan chronicles, even as the national security state was being
established, it was the object of profound national anxieties. Its existence
touched upon such vital issues as economic livelihood, military authority,
presidential prerogative, technological futures, and other burdens of American empire. Many of America's political debates in turn addressed its exigencies, and the biggest legislative and policy efforts of the latter half of the 1940s
were devoted to sorting out its structure: the Atomic Energy Act (1946), the
National Security Act (1947), the Truman Doctrine (1947), and the Marshall
Plan (1948). But anxieties over the national security state articulated in political arguments, policy positions, and laws were offered not only in apo-
deictic idioms but in aesthetic ones. Even when the form was not explicitly
aesthetic—for example, cover stories in *Time* and *Life*, presidential speeches,
newspaper columns, academic conferences, and perhaps especially national
security platforms—the questions were, What should America *look like* in
this new age? Was there a distinct American *style* of global leadership? How
might American policies at home and abroad affect the image of America?
And how might the very appearance of the national security state be reconciled with those democratic practices of citizenship and liberal ideals of
freedom that the nation claimed to be securing in the first place?

In this chapter, I consider such questions and anxieties about the national security state in light of a neoliberal anti-aesthetic or, better, counter-
aesthetic, with respect to the warfare state. In what is as much a typology
as a history, I consider in this chapter two policy responses to the national
security state in the first decade of the Cold War, suggesting that they en-

tailed two corresponding aesthetic responses. From 1947 to 1957, the national security state would not only be developed but would be significantly redeveloped, undergoing a major transformation in appearance, or—as I suggest—*dis*appearance. Specifically, I trace the transition in the 1950s from the Keynesian warfare state of Truman to the anti-Keynesian deterrent state of Eisenhower, attending especially to the status of economy (and economics), senses of emergency and catastrophe, and new logics of visibility and invisibility. Indeed, in the 1950s, under the auspices of President Eisenhower's New Look, the national security state retreated from both public visibility and historical contingency to become like the Law in radical Protestant iconoclasm, an invisible emergency order organized to ward off apocalyptic judgment. The consequences of this retreat are significant for our conceptions of the neoliberal national security state, which can be understood in light of the legitimation crises of the warfare state not only as the guardian of global capitalism, but also as an aesthetic answer to the liberal "tension," as it is often called, between liberty and security by means of a transfiguration in the appearance of the state.

Critics of neoliberalism have both recognized and struggled to articulate relationships between free-market economics and national security, too often suggesting or simply assuming that the latter is but the surrogate of the former, either as an enforcer of markets or as yet another means of helping corporations to expand their profit margins. In this chapter, I consider how they might be analogously related in the decades of the Cold War: both neoliberal economics and national security, after all, came to grant *economy* an ideological and ethical status, more than a merely instrumental one; both, moreover, were organized around the prospect of catastrophe; and, perhaps most importantly, both entailed a flight from public visibility and historical contingency in the name of an iconoclastic faith in lawful invisible orders. At issue here is the *appearance of the state*, both in the formal and epiphanic senses of appearance: that is, How, when, and where does the state appear, and indeed disappear?

Truman and the Warfare State

If Pearl Harbor brought a great and sudden shock to the American political and economic system, it is far more difficult to measure the shock the victorious end of World War II brought to the country, not the least because that victory was itself so full of ambiguities. On the one hand, the United States had played a major role in defeating two great powers, Germany and Japan. On the other, the nation now found itself confronting the messy business of occupation and, as events would proceed, reconstruction in both Europe and the Pacific. America, foreign policy experts were prone to say, was left to fill the "power vacuum" left by the destruction of the European-based, colonial, balance-of-power system. At the same time, possessed in the wake of Pearl Harbor by a sense of vulnerability that, it seems, could not be pacified, some decried the Soviet Union as the new nemesis of the West. In March 1946, not even a year after V-E Day, the indefatigable Winston Churchill seized President Truman's backyard, Fulton, Missouri, to claim that an "iron curtain" was falling between Eastern and Western Europe, due solely to the political avarice of the communists. Meanwhile, the publishing magnate Henry R. Luce, who had been advocating a more aggressive American foreign policy even before the war, continued to press America's obligation to secure freedom abroad for the sake of both political democracy and economic markets, against which the Soviets could only be rivals.[3] Most significantly, as things turned out, a little-known American diplomat stationed in Russia, George F. Kennan, wrote a telegram to Washington on February 22, 1946, in which he claimed that the Soviets firmly (albeit falsely) believed that they lived in an "antagonistic 'capitalist encirclement' with which in the long run there can be no permanent peaceful coexistence."[4] This meant looming trouble for the United States, or so Kennan was interpreted as saying.

In hindsight, the early alarm over the Soviets seems premature, even overwrought. In 1946, the United States was more than capable of handling any bellicosity from a Soviet state that had emerged from World War II proud but devastatingly ravaged—it had suffered somewhere in the neighborhood of twenty million deaths in World War II and had had much of its second-rate industrial base ransacked. The United States, on the contrary, had emerged from the war stronger than ever: all of Japan, the majority of Europe, islands across the seven seas, and parts of Africa were either under direct American control or subject to its significant influence; the American domestic economy had become in the course of the war the most productive not only on Earth, but in the history of Earth; the US military, which shortly before the war had not even numbered two hundred thousand, had come to number millions and was a decisive global force, patrolling the Pacific and Atlantic alike; and, perhaps most portentously, the United States held in its sole possession the atomic bomb, having dramatically shown at Hiroshima and Nagasaki its unprecedented killing power.

Still, tensions with the Soviets—which had been there throughout the war—quickly took on epochal proportions. In February of 1947, the British government secretly notified Truman that its imperial coffers had grown so light that they would have to cut off support for the governments of Greece and Turkey. They asked the United States to take over. *Greece and Turkey?* By the logic of any prior American foreign policy doctrine, these two Aegean nations would hardly merit US intervention. Yet, the Truman administration hardly blinked. The government of Greece was caught in a civil war with the Greek Communist Party, and the Truman administration assumed, wrongly, that the USSR was directly backing the communists.[5] Meanwhile, Turkey was being pressured by the Soviets to grant them rights to transit and bases in the Turkish Straits. The Truman administration interpreted Soviet intentions there as aggressively expansionist. Therefore, it became all too apparent all too quickly to Truman and his advisors that the United States must once again come to the rescue of unfamiliar foreign lands, quite apart from any Pearl Harbor–like moment. Upon receiving the British memo, despite widespread public sentiments in favor of scaling back America's overseas adventures, Truman jumped.

And so the Truman Doctrine was developed: it offered aid to Greece and Turkey on the premise that the United States was obligated "to help free peoples to maintain their free institutions and their national integrity against aggressive movements that seek to impose upon them totalitarian regimes."[6] The Truman Doctrine was incorporated into a more general policy of "containment," and containment, in turn, would help give rise to what, before long, would be known as the Cold War. In subsequent years American policymakers wrestled with precisely what it would mean to be a liberal Leviathan in this new Cold War context.[7]

For the most part, Truman and his first secretary of state, George Marshall, together with the latter's new advisor, Kennan (the first head of the newly formed Policy Planning Staff), tried to reconcile established ideas about the nation as a bulwark of "republican rectitude" with the new ideology of the national security state.[8] Truman instituted, for example, civilian control of the military and, as significantly, civilian control of atomic weaponry through the Atomic Energy Act of 1946 and the National Security Act of 1947. For much of his tenure, the president sought strict budget caps on defense spending, and—still "enamored with the citizen-soldier as a symbol of public virtue and an instrument of democratic reform and social betterment"—pushed for universal military training to supplement a would-be, small professional army with a large body of democratically minded, militarily trained citizens ready to serve in the event of a crisis.[9] Marshall and Kennan, for their part, set their sights on reconstructing Europe so as to restore something like the nineteenth-century ideal of a balance of powers to the globe. Thus, even amid the development of the Truman Doctrine and the rise of the Cold War, the Truman administration struggled to preserve in some way, shape, and form the stoic virtues of responsibility and restraint celebrated in the annals of American foreign policy as far back as Washington's Farewell Address.[10]

It was not until 1950, with the finalization of the official policy document known as National Security Council 68 (NSC 68), that the United States formally and philosophically abandoned such stoic efforts and, as a matter of perceived necessity, jumped headlong into global, neo-imperial pursuits. NSC 68 was penned under the guidance of Paul Nitze, who had replaced Kennan at the helm of the Policy Planning Staff in Dean Acheson's State Department. Whereas the Marshall-Kennan years were focused on creating world stability by reviving regional powers—above all Western Europe, but also Japan—the Acheson-Nitze years, which reached their apogee with the Korean War, would be organized around a vision of America as a necessary global hegemon. The very survival of the free world, and perhaps even humanity as a whole, was made to rest on the power of the United States to act persistently, definitively, and globally. NSC 68, while in no way causing this new foreign policy era, inscribed it in ways that authorized it intellectually and institutionally.

More importantly, NSC 68 marked the entrance of *economics* into American foreign policy as a master science.[11] Nitze's career itself exemplified this movement: in World War II, he had gone from Wall Street to Washington to work for the enormously influential but largely forgotten Strategic Bombing Survey, a government unit made up of businessmen (including Nitze, Robert Lovett, and George Ball) and economists (including John Kenneth Galbraith) that applied for the first time the statistical methods used in actuarial work and securities trading to the analysis of aerial bombardment targeting (a method widely adopted by the US military afterwards).[12] Nitze was then brought into Kennan's Policy Planning Staff from the Office of Economic Affairs in 1947 to add economic expertise to the group, an acumen that Kennan, a career diplomat, did not possess.[13]

As Nitze arrived to work with Kennan, economics was becoming for Washington liberals the most crucial aspect of postwar and Cold War policy. Despite his relative economic illiteracy, Kennan had made the economic revitalization of Europe—above all in the Marshall Plan—central to his vision for containing the Soviets through a proactive policy of strength. And economic support, of course, was at the heart of the Truman Doctrine. But economics represented more than a force in global affairs; it entailed a certain logic and moreover comprised a distinct realm of "practical" action. As Nitze himself would write in his autobiography, "The study of economics revived my interest in finding a path to understanding and influencing the real world, which I saw as something quite different from the world of either academia

or social relationships. Economics bore on the world of business and international trade, but only abstractly. Its analyses were logical but depended on
carefully defined sets of assumptions which were not self-evident and only
partially valid. In certain contexts those assumptions differed from common
sense and personal experience."[14] Economics was thus for Nitze and other
political liberals a heuristic device, a means of inquiry, understanding, and
judgment. It was, on the one hand, a means of challenging common sense. In
the late 1930s, Keynesianism, for example, had encouraged massive government deficit spending as a means of rebounding from economic depression,
a strategy mirrored by some Wall Street investment approaches but without
comparison in the commonsense world of personal finance.[15] For Nitze, like
his counterpart in the Strategic Bombing Survey, Galbraith, economics was
a means of counterintuitive reasoning drawing on statistical data and methods. But economics was not enough for these early Cold War liberals; even as
it became a master science of foreign policy, it did not represent an ethic or
a worldview, as it would for neoliberals and, as we will see, for Eisenhower.
As Nitze wrote, "Value judgments could not be derived from economics."[16]
Rather, economics was the main analytical means used to meet the demands
of necessity and, if possible, to further American values. Quite like violence,
it was an *instrument* of power.

Looking outside economics for a source of value judgments, NSC 68
kicked off its strategic analysis in creedal terms, quoting the preamble to the
Constitution: "The fundamental purpose of the United States is laid down in
the Preamble to the Constitution: '... to form a more perfect Union, establish
Justice, insure domestic Tranquility, provide for the common defence [*sic*],
promote the general Welfare, and secure the Blessings of Liberty to ourselves
and our Posterity.'" "In essence," NSC 68 explained in remarkably general
terms that would give latitude to its global agenda, "the fundamental purpose
is to assure the integrity and vitality of our free society, which is founded
upon the dignity and worth of the individual."[17] The task before policymakers, it therefore concluded, was simply to determine what "calculations of
practicality" were needed in order to see this purpose through.[18] NSC 68 thus
enumerated, counted, computed, and charted. The result was an unprecedented formal condensation of an American security agenda that worked to
undermine an old-world sense of bounded states looking for a balance, asserting instead the historical eruption of a disorderly, boundless world, one
where *forces*—above all military force—must give shape to the new world
order in the defense of *values*.

The economy would here serve military force (but it would not yet itself represent a "value"). NSC 68 is now credited with being the first official

US foreign policy statement premised on Keynesian theory, positing, as its logic did, short-term deficit spending to re-arm the nation.[19] Its advocacy of a much larger defense budget, quite likely resulting from such short-term deficit spending, was set in direct opposition to the position of then Secretary of Defense Louis Johnson, who, along with the president himself, was firmly committed to a $15 billion defense-spending cap. Truman had brought Johnson on board to help restrain military spending. Johnson and he held (as Eisenhower would too) that a sound economy and a balanced federal budget were as crucial to long-term American security as a powerful military. Moreover, they were persuaded that the latter could be achieved relatively cheaply through a strong air force in possession of a daunting atomic arsenal (again, as Eisenhower would pursue).[20] By asserting the need for large conventional forces, NSC 68 thus challenged both strategic and economic logics; while offering no precise economic figures, it suggested that some deficit spending was not only economically viable, but militarily necessary for America to survive as a great power in the near future.

Meanwhile, for strategic and moral reasons, Nitze was skeptical of calls to rely on nuclear weapons made by the air force and its political supporters. Nukes were more powerful and more economical, supporters argued, and would not require large standing armies to support them. Conventional forces, Nitze countered, should be paired with a "nuclear umbrella" as a deterrent, but a simple reliance on nuclear weapons could only lead to abhorrent and absurd results if the United States actually had to go to war—an eventuality that Nitze thought well within the scope of possibility (as did, unfortunately, air force brass like Curtis Lemay, who was all too willing to get in an atomic showdown with the Soviets).[21] Indeed, Nitze asserted that the Soviets presented a substantial military challenge, not just a political and economic one (as Kennan had held). Thus, while economy was central to Nitze's and NSC 68's strategic program, it was in every way subservient to calculations of necessary military force. It was, in the language of strategy, but a means to an end.

Still, Nitze's economics pushed him toward an ambitious, global agenda. As far back as the genesis of the Marshall Plan, he had held that the United States did not recognize just how global the postwar economic crisis really was. "Why not do it [an economic recovery program] on a broader scale?" he had asked the Truman administration during Marshall Plan deliberations. "The problem was a worldwide problem." To be sure, the United States had huge export surpluses. Other nations were buying US goods on credit, and they were not producing any substantial wealth of their own. This pattern, the so-called "dollar-gap" problem, risked a mammoth global economic crisis, another great depression, if nation after nation began to default.[22] Therefore, Nitze felt that budget hawks at home were missing the bigger economic picture. It would do no good for the United States to balance its budgets if overseas markets for US goods collapsed. Similarly, NSC 68 suggested that a sound domestic budget would do little if nations across the world were brought into the communist sphere, thus isolating the United States economically as well as politically.

But the more fundamental argument of NSC 68 was not a matter of theory as much as it was a matter of history, or interpretation of the latter. NSC 68 was penned on the heels of inauspicious global and domestic developments. The first year of the second Truman administration brought ample reason to accentuate rather than temper the ominous tones of the Cold War. On September 23, 1949, the president had solemnly announced that American aerial reconnaissance had detected a Soviet atomic explosion. Two weeks later, on October 7, the Soviets established the German Democratic Republic, thus quashing any hopes that had arisen after the May 1949 lifting of the Berlin blockade that Germany would be reunited. At virtually the same time, the Chinese Communist revolution culminated in Mao Tse-tung's announcement of the People's Republic of China. In the ensuing months, Communist China would become a point of ongoing diplomatic contention, with the Soviets walking out of the U.N. Security Council in the winter to protest Anglo-American objections to seating the new Chinese government in the U.N., followed by the February 1950 Soviet-China signing of a Treaty of Friendship.[23] Meanwhile, at home Joseph McCarthy was stirring up anticommunist sentiment with his infamous Wheeling, West Virginia, claim to have "in my hand a list of 205—a list of names that were made known to the Secretary of State as being members of the Communist Party and who nevertheless are still working and shaping policy in that State Department."[24] While McCarthy was drumming up charges, Alger Hiss, an old friend of Acheson, was being tried for perjury related to accusations of being a Soviet spy in the 1930s. All the while, the first major covert warfare incursions against the Soviets—by means of a CIA program that would drop foreign agents by parachute into Soviet territory—were proceeding disastrously. Fully aware of American designs, the Soviets were rounding up and executing the American-backed foreign agents as soon as they hit the ground.[25]

NSC 68 could thus argue with some plausibility that America was already at war—albeit for the time being nontraditional war—and ought to spend and strategize accordingly. It assumed not only Cold War communist successes, but also that the Soviets would start a hot war as soon as they were confident they could win one. In this respect, NSC 68 looked toward 1954, "a critical date," when the atomic arsenal of the USSR would, it was argued, reach sufficient capacity for a large-scale attack on the United States.[26] In its view the Cold War would therefore either be a prelude to hot war or a means of aggressively warding it off through political, economic, and military initiatives.

Crucial in this identification of a critical date was Nitze and his colleagues' belief in the possibility of *planning*. NSC 68 was the product of an epistemological realism, presuming as it did the possibility of sizing up data and reading history's signals so as to come up with a plausible plan for future action. What would worry Eisenhower in matters of national defense, and neoliberals in matters of economy—unforeseen consequences, insufficient data, and myriads of contingencies—were but problems to be overcome, if not mastered, for Nitze. Hence, in looking to 1954 as a critical date, NSC 68 applied a Keynesian epistemology to foreign policy problems, and planned accordingly.

Truman would eventually assent to its conclusions. Here the Korean crisis was not only crucial, but illustrative of a basic shift that took place within the Truman administration during the drafting of NSC 68. In a memo to Acheson, Kennan had been willing to shrug off communist incursions in Asia, insisting that such events "would not necessarily be fatal or irreparable . . . and no cause either for despair or lack of self-confidence on our part."[27] Acheson for a time seemed to concur. But a week after Kennan penned his memo to the secretary, Acheson told the National Press Club that America's "defensive perimeter" in the Pacific ran only "from the Ryukyus to the Phillipine Islands"—that is, it did not include South Korea—and that Washington would not embark on "foolish adventures" in the Pacific.[28] Indeed, the signals from the United States were so strong in this regard that in the run-up to the Korean War, Russia and North Korea assumed the United States would not intervene (though Mao warned them otherwise) and thus decided to proceed with their exploits.[29] NSC 68, however, would formalize a profound change in Washington's outlook, such that by the time the North Koreans began their bombardment, Truman felt it necessary to marshal US troops to the defense of South Korea. America was at war with communism, and now everyone would *see* it.

On December 16, 1950, the president declared a national emergency in words that echoed the creedal rhetoric and global logic of NSC 68. "*Whereas*," it warned, "if the goal of communist imperialism were to be achieved, the people of this country would no longer enjoy the full and rich life they have with God's help built for themselves and their children, . . . *Now, Therefore, I, Harry S. Truman,* president of the United States of America, do proclaim the existence of a national emergency, which requires that the military, naval, air, and civilian defenses of this country be strengthened as speedily as possible to the end that we may be able to repel any and all threats against our national security and to fulfill our responsibilities in the efforts being made through the United Nations and otherwise to bring about lasting peace."[30] Over the next three years, defense spending would jump from $13.7 billion to $52.8 billion, from 5% of gross domestic product (GDP) to 14.2%. Measured as a percentage of GDP, defense spending would not return to its 1950 level until 1977.[31]

Indeed, the overarching policy point of NSC 68 was that the crises of the Cold War called for a new wartime economy and society in the United States. What was needed was an effort like that seen in World War II. Central to it would be an aggressive military program, one that would go well beyond stockpiling atomic weapons to substantially strengthen conventional forces and extend their power globally. It was "essential," NSC 68 offered in a stunning plan for American global military hegemony, that the United States "provide an adequate defense against air attack on the United States and Canada and an adequate defense against air and surface attack on the United Kingdom and Western Europe, Alaska, the Western Pacific, Africa, and the Near and Middle East." This robust American military posture was essential to success, "as the ultimate guarantee of our national security" and "as an indispensable backdrop to the conduct of the policy of 'containment.'"[32]

To those devotees of The Road to Serfdom—however many or few there were in 1950—the course of the early Cold War could thus well have confirmed Hayek's prognosis that the warfare state would invent and reinvent reasons to survive and increasingly threaten to morph into an authoritarian state. Indeed, in the immediate alarm over the North Korean assault on South Korea, few would challenge what would amount to a disconcerting precedent in American politics: Truman would go to war without even caring to get congressional approval. It was a "police action," he and Acheson reasoned, and speed of its execution was more important than Constitutional procedures.[33] It would take but a few months, however, before political support for the increasingly ugly war would weaken, and the president would find himself the target of accusations of unlawful action, even tyranny. Truman's term would thus end where it began, amidst the political and ideological disorders of the American warfare state.

Eisenhower and the Deterrent State

The war in Korea was a disaster, and in 1952, Eisenhower campaigned for the presidency with a promise to end it. But Eisenhower's campaign as president would be set not just against large-scale martial misadventures abroad, but against the whole style of foreign policy that Truman, and before him Franklin Roosevelt, represented. As historian Kenneth Osgood, summarizing the tenor of Eisenhower's outlook, writes,

> The memory of the horrific costs of World War II and the unthinkable consequences of nuclear warfare meant that the Cold War, more than any other conflict in human history, was channeled into nonmilitary modes of combat, particularly ideological and symbolic ones. The importance of the ideological and symbolic factors in this conflict, then, in turn, made the Cold War even more all-embracing. Virtually every aspect of the American way of life— from political organizations and philosophical ideals, to cultural products and scientific achievements, to economic practices and social relationships—was exposed to scrutiny in this total contest for the hearts and minds of the world's peoples.[34]

Indeed, the New Look, as Eisenhower's foreign policy platform was branded, was less a dramatic revision of the budgetary economics of national security (as it is often supposed to be) and more a revaluation of the status of economy in national security and a corresponding aesthetic transformation of the national security state into the image of economy, a network of largely hidden systems and activities dispersed across the nation and the globe.[35] The New Look, that is, entailed the displacement of a culture of military iconography with a defensive and offensive logic premised on the rule of unrepresentable orders.

The New Look—the outlines of which were formalized in the fall of 1953 in NSC 162/2—called for a powerful nuclear weapons arsenal capable of inflicting "massive retaliatory damage" on the USSR, coupled with "a sound, strong, and growing economy" and the "maintenance of morale and free institutions" both at home and abroad.[36] The latter two objectives were anticipated in Eisenhower's public statements as far back as 1947, when he argued that the long-term security of the United States depended on the nation's economic vitality within the framework of a capitalist, competitive market system. Thus, while speaking at the American Legion Convention in New York in August 1947, Eisenhower—still chief of staff—went so far as to say, "Our nation is faced today with problems, present and future, which equal in scope and significance any it has hitherto met in 171 years of existence."[37] The crises, however, did not strictly come from abroad. They came, he explained, in part from those in the United States who accused the postwar administration of "'internationalism,' implying a lack of patriotism in those who struggle to maintain world conditions essential to the preservation of our own freedoms."[38] Eisenhower suggested that such domestic political strife was as dangerous to the future of the country as were aggressors abroad— protectionists, isolationists, pacifists, and the like threatened to undermine both the moral and physical strength of the nation. Americans instead needed to strive for "unity of action," through which the country could be "a veritable colossus in support of peace."[39]

But a "colossus" it would only virtually be, for the unity of action upon which Eisenhower would call would not have a visible form at all, not even a civic one. Rather Eisenhower would turn to economy, as he would over and over again in the years to come:

> Our competitive system is an essential feature of democracy, but the practice of competition gives no man, no group, the right to act for selfish and im- mediate gain, against the interest of the nation. Each of us must realize that whatever might weaken the whole will in the long term, defeat each part—no matter what the glitter of the immediate promise. Banker and borrower, in- dustrialist and worker, politician and farmer, civilian and soldier, must each keep his eyes upon the major good. All must acknowledge that in every prob- lem where is involved the welfare of America there can be one answer only. That answer must be given, not merely by emotional response to a patriotic hymn. It must be lived, every day, in the workaday actions and reactions of a hundred and forty million people. If we fail in this, there will be no real security for the United States, because eventually we could be so weakened by domestic strife that conquest from without would be little more than a formality.[40]

In one respect Eisenhower seemed to point here, as Truman and FDR had, to a republican fortress as a bulwark against insecurity. But this fortress was curiously devoid of any republican calls to distinctly *civic* duty and sacrifice, other than the rather nonrepublican refusal to participate in political strife. Instead, Eisenhower's sense of the civic here was thoroughly integrated with economic activity. Economy offered an ethos of individual effort and national cooperation free of political positioning and power play. Like his contempo- rary Hayek, Eisenhower presented the competitive system as the principal means of warding off the catastrophe of tyranny. Thus, Eisenhower concluded, "Within the workings of a free economy persons of similar interests organize for strength. . . . All must work together—or eventually we will work under the whip!"[41] Eisenhower's American fortress would be an economic one. Economy was not only the *means* of postwar American power; it was in a crucial sense its *end*.

The rub was in one's conception of the American way of life. Eisenhower consistently and uncritically understood the matter in fundamentally economic terms. Since "at the heart" of the American way life, he declared in testimony before the US Senate in 1950, was the "freedom of the individual, we must not so over-burden or tax the resources of the country that we practically enslave or regiment people in the effort to keep them from foreign aggression."[42] Americans were laborers, managers, owners, inventors and so on—to deprive them of a capitalist economy in which they were given a full range of economic possibilities would be to strip them of their basic freedom and thus defeat the purpose of national security. The claim was not only directed against the specter of the garrison state; it was aimed indirectly at New Deal Democrats and others eager to see the warfare state transformed back into the welfare state.[43] At the same time, economy was the basis of military power: drawing from his experience in World War II, the president held that the key to success in modern warfare—an age of "total war"—was a strong industrial base capable of producing in short-order tons upon tons of munitions and machines. Continuing a theme he pronounced in 1947, he argued, for example, in his 1950 Senate testimony, "To wreck our economy, would be as great a victory for the Soviets as they could remotely hope for in a war."[44] Eisenhower would displace the republican fortress with an economic one.

Hence, in NSC 162/2, the Eisenhower administration granted economy a distinct synthetic power, describing the means and ends of American security strategy in the language of economic productivity and free institutions. The problem before America, the document began, was twofold: "To meet the Soviet threat" and, "in doing so, to avoid seriously weakening the U.S. economy or undermining our fundamental values and institutions."[45] The way to do this, it reasoned, was (*a*) to organize a military posture around nuclear deterrence *together with* (*b*) maintenance of a sound, strong, and growing economy, capable of providing, through the operation of free institutions, the strength described in (*a*) above over the long pull and of rapidly and effectively changing to full mobilization if need be; and (*c*) maintenance of morale and free institutions and the willingness of the people to support the measures necessary for national security.[46]

The military imperative of a strong domestic economy, combined with Eisenhower's identification of capitalism with the American way of life, committed the president to a military-backed, global economic agenda. As he wrote to his future secretary of state, John Foster Dulles, months before his first inaugural, "The minimum requirement is that we are able to trade freely, in spite of anything Russia may do, with those areas from which we obtain raw materials that are vital to our economy."[47] But this commitment to a capitalist, competitive, market-based economy would leave the president in the quagmire of means and ends: the vitality of a "free" economy with global reach was a necessary ingredient of military strength, but military strength was needed to secure that strong economy. Could one be said to have priority over the other?

Asymmetrical nuclear retaliatory power offered at least in theory a way out of this quagmire, and it would be the linchpin of the Eisenhower administration's approach to national security. Nuclear weapons were seen by the administration as a more economical means of defending the United States than large standing armies (a case, as I have noted, that the air force had been making virtually since World War II ended), thus satisfying Eisenhower's own anti-Keynesian commitment to balanced budgets and low inflation, as well as pacifying to a degree the Taft Republicans, who vociferously resisted higher taxes or budget increases of any kind. In light of such philosophical commitments and political pressures, Eisenhower saw in nuclear weapons a more cost-effective means of maintaining a strong military posture.

But built into the Eisenhower administration's commitment to asymmetrical nuclear deterrence was a more immediate, catastrophic existential concern: making the Soviets think twice, indeed three times, about initiating a surprise nuclear attack. As far back 1949, when the Soviets began atomic bomb tests, the air force had been warning the White House of the possibility of a Soviet surprise nuclear attack.[48] For the Eisenhower administration, this was in some respects a convenient possibility, for it allowed the administration to press Taft Republicans for concessions on military-driven taxes and expenses: "The danger of an atomic Pearl Harbor is real," Eisenhower's budget-minded Secretary of Treasury George M. Humphrey told Congress in 1953, protesting Taft Republican efforts to cut taxes and thus cut defense spending even more severely than Eisenhower himself was already proposing.[49] But in less partisan respects, the fear of an atomic Pearl Harbor was the central national security anxiety of the 1950s, even before—but especially after—*Sputnik*. The possibility of sudden, spectacular catastrophe—more than the fall of foreign countries to communist rule—drove the Eisenhower administration's military planning.

And here the goal was to make policy that could, as much as possible, limit contingencies. In a manner that echoed the arguments of Eisenhower's neoliberal contemporaries regarding the economy, the president evinced a profound skepticism toward planning in war. "The very definition of an 'emergency' is that it is unexpected, therefore it is not going to happen the way you are planning," Eisenhower once remarked. "So, the first thing you do is to take all the plans off the top shelf and throw them out the window and start once more."[50] The best policy, the logic followed, was one that could as much as possible eliminate occasions for throwing the plans out the window. Asymmetrical nuclear deterrence was seen as such a policy. Its aim was to institute a law to the chaotic world of nations in the form of the demonstrable threat of an overwhelming force, and so prevent anarchy from erupting. It was, in this respect, consistent with Eisenhower's strategy at Little Rock—but here quite literally blown up in the iconic images of America's mushrooming nuclear tests.

In 1954, Eisenhower convened the Technical Capabilities Panel, or Killian committee, to address the worry of an atomic Pearl Harbor. Its goal was determine technological means of reducing American vulnerability.[51] The Killian committee wrote alarmingly of US susceptibility to a surprise attack, arguing that the nation would suffer "millions of causalities and crippling damage."[52] It concluded that America's commitment to nuclear deterrence needed to grow even stronger in light of these vulnerabilities. Later, a follow-up group convened by Eisenhower, the Gaither Committee, urged upon the administration a robust missile defense system, development of sophisticated early-warning radar systems, a widespread network of fallout shelters, and more advanced offensive nuclear weapons capabilities.[53] The Gaither Committee's recommendations arrived on the president's desk in the wake of the *Sputnik* crisis, helping bring a 10 percent increase in defense spending, accelerated ICBM and IRBM programs, the commissioning of the Polaris submarine system, installation of early warning radar systems, and the reorganization of Strategic Air Command forces into a more diffuse network of bases and air fields.[54]

Nevertheless, this would not free the president from his predicament. He had argued repeatedly that whatever might be done to defend the American way of life must not strip that way of life from the American people. Thus, as we have seen, he opposed the "regimentation" of the American economy, culminating in the feared garrison state, claiming that compromising economic freedom meant destroying the American way of life, so that America's leaders would have done the work of the Soviets for them. But in his commitment to nuclear weapons, Eisenhower risked far more: putting an end to the very *existence* of the United States in order to protect relative economic freedoms. Historian John Lewis Gaddis concludes that this wager, desperate as it seemingly was, was rooted in Eisenhower's overwhelming desire to avoid a nuclear war: "He believed that the best way to avoid an all-out nuclear war was *to make that the only military option available to the United States*."[55] Thus the quest to avoid "absolute war" meant making it the only viable choice, so that the Soviets would not only think thrice, but America's leaders would too. Asymmetrical nuclear deterrence therefore became for the president a technological means of eliminating, as much as possible, contingencies. Eisenhower's absolute commitment to nuclear weapons was a means of, as absolutely as possible, avoiding absolute war. Indeed, the New Look was rooted in a logic of *extremes*. Just as neoliberals like Hayek saw states as having a strong tendency to expand their coercive power to totalitarian proportions and so looked for a Law, so Eisenhower's New Look sought a Law by which to restrain nations from escalation into annihilation. But this Law was but a force.

In hindsight, however, nuclear deterrence afforded the Eisenhower administration perhaps even a more significant power, little commented upon: an *invisibility* of a kind, one gained not only through strategies of state secrecy, but also through the disassociation of the new Cold War from the soldierly iconicity of World War II. The New Look offered the means of developing robust military power apart from a national culture of militancy. Indeed, as Ira Chernus has remarked, in the nuclear age that Eisenhower established, "the traditional calls for courageous battlefield self-discipline were insufficient."[56] We might even say they were absurd, as battlefield courage would mean little in an apocalyptic war. Rather, the new Cold War, based on asymmetrical nuclear deterrence, would demand an altogether different sort of "soldierly confidence" from American citizens, one that "had to be maintained over a long haul that was neither war nor peace."[57] For the vast majority of Americans, this new soldierly confidence would be offered and indeed instituted by the administration in terms of the pursuit of an "American way of life" based on enterprising cooperation. Willingly or not, Americans were conscripted by Eisenhower into a program of what Chernus calls "apocalypse management," where war meant a kind of ultimate iconoclasm and, far more, nuclear annihilation, and thus had to be avoided if at all possible. "Peace" in this context meant pressing on with the American way of life in the dark shadow of that unrepresentable future.[58] The New Look indeed entailed a new *look* for the national security state.

To draw out the significance of this new look, we can return to Truman's ideal of the citizen-soldier. Amidst the turbulence of the postwar reorganization of America's defense structure, Truman pushed long and hard for universal military training (UMT), ultimately unsuccessfully. The reasons for its political failure were varied, but one major reason was an anxiety about normalizing World War II's militarization of American society. UMT, powerful voices argued, would "undercut the home, the family, and the school, replacing the democratic virtues they taught with a mindless military mentality and a habit of regimentation that were decidedly un-American."[59] Similarly, the long-term militarization of American society represented by UMT, some argued, would lead to the further undercutting of American society as "military research would monopolize the scientific manpower on which industry depended" and "corral corporate and university laboratories for military purposes."[60] Truman, in contrast, saw in UMT the possibility of a nation of citizen-soldiers living according to the republican virtues of discipline, duty, and sacrifice for the greater good. Indeed, he argued that the program would have the effect of breaking up the "political cliques that run the Army and Navy," returning America's military to its democratic roots.[61]

The significance of the controversy over UMT is not only in the arguments for or against, but in the liveliness of the debate itself. At stake in the UMT debates were *icons* of America, realized in the public and political imagination. Entrenched within the proposal was the symbolic significance of the citizen-soldier and all that it variously meant, both politically and historically. To some, it meant military concerns would overcrowd citizenly ones, but to others it meant that soldierly virtues would come to infuse, in a positive manner, democratic citizenship. The UMT issue offered Americans an occasion for political debate about the national security state as it came packaged, so to speak, in the iconography of the citizen-soldier.

The New Look avoided such culturally, historically, and politically rich iconographies. To be sure, the technologically infused networks of nuclear deterrence eventually turned out their own cultural iconographies.[62] But by constructing the deterrent system and placing it at the center of America's defense posture, the Eisenhower administration hid from view this profound form of American militarization, both literally—as silos were located in remote areas of the country, and weapons-related facilities built behind tall, ominous fences—and rhetorically, as Eisenhower urged upon the nation a sense of normalcy even amid the hot days of the Cold War. Thus, instead of fiery debates on the senate floor or in local newspapers over the virtues and vices of citizen military training, those who opposed nuclear militarization were largely left, in one way or another, in the halls of the absurd—either as they set up picket lines at remote facilities far from public view, or as they resorted to parody, camp, the grotesque, or other means of struggling to make visible what was willfully being kept invisible. Eisenhower thus destroyed not only a particular American iconography but the underlying logic of icons themselves, twice destroying the image. The New Look represented the aesthetic transformation of America's Cold War security posture. Whereas Truman's term in office ended with citizens again being made soldiers and sent to foreign lands, and with the return of a wartime economy, Eisenhower's ended with the president's cryptic warning against the "unwarranted influence" of the "military-industrial complex."[63] Americans, in an important sense, would have to learn to decode first, and debate later, this new nuclear and covert militarization of their society—they would have to learn to see the nature, meaning, and implications of Cold War national security quite apart from the aid of public light.

The Neoliberal Security State

With respect to its twentieth-century philosophical lineage, neoliberalism came out of the loosely organized effort of American and European intellectuals to restore, in theory at least, the rule of law to a Europe wrecked by fascist and police states. Neoliberalism's first intellectual war was against the (dis)order of arbitrary violence. Yet in the United States neoliberalism's intellectual battalion was quickly maneuvered rightward, where the economic critiques of Austrian economists like Hayek and Mises were summoned to attack the infrastructures and ideologies of the New Deal welfare state, and it would be in this battle, far more than that against the police state, that neoliberalism as we have come to know it would make its advances. In both cases, however, the *warfare* state presented a conundrum for neoliberals in the 1940s: on the one hand, it was a necessary means of defeating fascists, communists, and even socialists, but on the other it threatened to morph into the enemy, marshaling as it could all the economic and cultural energies of the nation into an implacable, planned order.

This, of course, was precisely the conundrum that Hayek was trying to work out in *The Road to Serfdom* and to warn Britain against. Hayek's solution was temporal, almost to the point of days on the calendar: in a season of national emergency, he argued, the warfare state was necessary, but upon the closure of the emergency—that is, upon victory—the nation needed to scrupulously dismantle the warfare state and restore a liberal order. Otherwise, the warfare state might very well become a more permanent, authoritarian condition, and the war against totalitarianism would be self-defeating. As Hayek warned, "It is Germany whose fate we are in some danger of repeating."[64] The warfare state must not become a more permanent state.

The risk of a more permanent warfare state was easy enough to envision in the 1940s, but the more general epistemological critique of Hayek and other neoliberals left them arguing not only against the warfare state, but also against socialism, the welfare state, communist influences, and other modes of "planning." But planning would not go away in the years after World War II. Indeed, in war-ravaged Europe the necessity of planning was, in the words of historian Tony Judt, the one thing on which "all were agreed," not the least Europe's occupier, the United States.[65] Hence "planners" were everywhere in the eyes of Hayek and other neoliberals, sometimes easy to see, but often not.

Influence, conditioning, ideas, and even *ideology* became watchwords in the neoliberal search for threats to liberal order. Thus, in his 1956 foreword to the American edition of *The Road to Serfdom,* Hayek presented his dilemma in psychological more than historical terms. Anticipating the charge of having been a false prophet in the first edition of *The Road to Serfdom* (he admitted that by 1956 England had had six years of socialist government and yet had not fallen into tyranny) he responded,

> But those who argue that this has disproved the thesis of *The Road to Serfdom* have really missed one of its main points: that the most important change which extensive government control produces is a psychological change, an alteration in the character of the people. This is necessarily a slow affair, a process which extends not over a few years but perhaps over one or two generations. The important point is that the political ideals of a people and its attitude toward authority are as much the effect as the cause of the political institutions under which it lives.[66]

If in 1945 the risk of planning was immediate, ten years later the road to serfdom had become for Hayek a matter of slow processes of cultural conditioning, calling in turn for forms of counterconditioning, "a revised conception of our social aims."[67] But this was a psychological project and not a strictly ideational one, precisely because it included an aesthetic dimension. While the ideational foundations of society had to be rebuilt, its aspirational horizons also needed to be redrawn, and its vision for society reimagined.

Eisenhower's conception of his Cold War mission, too, was psychological in the root sense of concerned with soul and spirit. As Jonathan P. Herzog has argued, Eisenhower oversaw an era when—in a curious reversal of the standard narrative of civil religion in America—the state strategically summoned the spiritual to do its Cold War political and ideological work. "Just as the Soviet elites during the Cold War considered traditional religious faith a hindrance to national interests and worked to destroy it, American elites considered religious faith a bulwark and worked to promote it."[68] To be sure, as Eisenhower's speech writer Emmet John Hughes once wrote, "Perhaps no adjective figured so prominently in his [Eisenhower's] political vocabulary as 'spiritual.'"[69] The crisis before America, the president suggested, was at root a spiritual crisis; its solution similarly spiritual. Eisenhower, like Hayek and many others, assumed that culture was constituted by values, and therefore the cultivation of values was paramount. They saw the warfare state and welfare state alike as threats to America's spiritual strength, displacing the virtues of the "spirit of enterprise" with the whip of command and control.[70]

Command and control, however, could not simply be dispensed with—not in a dangerous world possessed by hostile ideologies, atomic forces, and scarce resources. Thus, Eisenhower would reenvision the national security state, changing its appearance, doing this in part by turning from a hot war, Korea, back to cold war, which would be more and more covert war; and in part by revaluing economy as the site of America's Cold War struggles. Indeed, in his New Look three aspects of the ideology of neoliberalism were anticipated. First, *economy* was approached as an end, not just a means, of national policy. Economy thus assumed an ethical status consonant with ideologies of freedom, liberty, individualism, and willing cooperation (as opposed to the coercive power of the state). Second, the state's security powers were organized around a catastrophic emergency having the form of sudden, spectacular violence. The New Look did not, as Truman did in his second term, prepare a nation for war, supposing that a martial confrontation with the Soviets was imminent. Rather, its strategy of asymmetrical nuclear deterrence, covert action, and aggressive psychological warfare was premised on other great fears: a surprise nuclear attack from the Soviets; the idea that any conventional war of any size was highly likely to escalate into nuclear confrontation; and the more nebulous fear of a decline of Cold War morale in America. This, in turn, contributed to the New Look's third ideological aspect: it was premised on the power of privacy in the sense of being hidden away. Thus, rather than seeking to organize national culture around a republican ideal of the citizen-soldier, as Truman had done, and so make visible America's war with the Soviets, in the New Look Eisenhower sought to orient national culture toward economic productivity in a competitive system, leaving the (cold) war fighting to invisible orders that appeared in public only in emergencies or before the prospect of emergencies. It was not that Eisenhower sought to hide the Cold War. To the contrary, as with Hayek and other neoliberals, the Cold War provided the most powerful warrant for his insistence that America center its spiritual and material energies on furthering the free system. Rather, it was that Eisenhower sought to hide the coercive power of the state, except in occasions of emergency, instead turning the nation's gaze toward the wonders of the free-enterprise system.

Thus, in a *national security policy*, rather than economic policies per se, we have the rough outlines of a neoliberal state. Contemporary critics of neoliberalism have sought various ways of accounting for the relationship between neoliberalism and national security. Wendy Brown, for example, has suggested that the effects of neoliberal policies—from the depoliticization of political problems to a new emphasis on the efficiency of state action—prepare the ground for "the authoritarian features of neoconservative governance," including a staunch militarism.[71] Others have stressed that the logic of intervention advocated by neoliberals allows states to not only introduce market reforms but to enforce them, as needed, through military interventions. Manfred Steger and Ravi Roy thus stress that "the rise of neoliberalism would have been impossible without strong government action," including military action.[72] Others, like David Harvey, have suggested that the relationship between neoliberalism and national security forces comes down to the problem of anarchy inherent within neoliberalism, noting that the latter risks a "chaos of individual interests" to which the state can offer an antidote both by means of ideology—specifically, the ideology of patriotism—and through more direct means of coercion.[73]

In the New Look, however, we see another aspect of the neoliberal security state. There the relationship between the visible and invisible—a vital aspect of what Jacques Rancière calls "the distribution of the sensible," and a perennial variable of both politics and aesthetics—was dramatically reversed relative to America's experience of World War II and Korea.[74] In those hot wars, economic activity was subordinated to war efforts, and civic ethics allied with republican ideals of the citizen-soldier. Here, to be sure, *economy* represented an emergency order of a kind, summoned to address geopolitical crises, but it was primarily an instrumental one. In contrast, in Eisenhower's New Look, the war activities of the state were hidden within the patent productive power of capitalism, and national security became a secret emergency order to protect and preserve the capitalist state—where capitalism itself entailed an invisible order of market forces that stemmed from transcendental values and ideals.

Thus, to return to September 11 and its aftermath, Peter Alexander Meyers has observed that the War on Terror is in important respects "*a continuation of the Cold War.*"[75] Meyers refers to this general form of war as *civic war*, "a mongrel name suggesting a neoplastic attraction of opposites in which the political facts of the Citizen come to serve exactly that devastating form of human relationship they were meant to avoid."[76] Civic war entails the conscription of the ordinary activities of the citizen into a war effort, even as it assigns to the state extraordinary emergency powers. The tradeoff here, as Meyers argues, is not really between liberty and security, but between liberty and publicity.[77]

Indeed, in the New Look we had the vestiges of the neoliberal security state, a state that, in the United States at least, has lived alongside other manifestations of the national security state since the 1950s. The New Look offered in its aesthetic form a means of redressing the liberal tension between freedom and security, and that form was privatization. *Privatization* here refers not only to private contractors, private transactions, private conversations, and so on, but also and especially to the privation of publicity, of a public life (as Hannah Arendt so eloquently discussed in *The Human Condition* at the end of the Eisenhower years).[78] In the neoliberal security state, the classical tension between freedom and security is aesthetically mitigated as freedom is foregrounded in ideology and policy via the ethics of economy, even as the state's security apparatus is hidden from view, the latter left to appear only in epiphanic moments of sudden and spectacular catastrophe. Catastrophe itself therefore gains a normative aspect, alongside economy: catastrophe is the occasion for the revelation, the epiphanic publicity, of the state as an emergency order. We only *see* the state, that is, in the images of emergency.

Conclusion

In 1946, at the war's end, General Eisenhower addressed an audience at the Metropolitan Museum of Art in New York, beginning as follows:

> We have recently emerged from a bitter conflict that long engulfed the larger nations of the globe. The heroism and sacrifice of men on the fighting lines, and the moral and physical energies of those at home, were all devoted to the single purpose of military victory. Preoccupation in a desperate struggle for existence left time for little else.
>
> Now we enter upon an era of widened opportunity for physical and spiritual development, united in a determination to establish and maintain a peace in which the creative and expressive instincts of our people may flourish. The welcome release from the fears and anxieties of war will, as always, be reflected in a resurgence of attention to cultural values.[79]

That the victorious culmination of World War II marked for the victorious general the dawning of a new age is less remarkable than the contrast he drew here between the age passing and the age to come: that which was passing had "engulfed" the world of nations; the people of the United States had been focused on a "single purpose;" the "preoccupation" of the war squeezed in upon not only the nation's sense of space, but its sense of time. The war's end, then, represented a great "release," as well as a kind of psycho-spiritual relief, allowing Americans to redirect their "creative and expressive instincts" toward flourishing instead of the "desperate struggle for existence."

It is certainly not that Eisenhower was here placing these two eras on a scale of value, praising the latter over the former. Rather, he was engaged in a historicist aesthetic exercise, searching for the forms of national expression suitable to the times. Indeed, Eisenhower elsewhere presented America's efforts in World War II as entirely suited to that particular moment: "The wartime Army of the United States was a mass expression of America," he went so far as to say.[80] But postwar America needed new forms of expression, ones consonant with cultural values rather than the demands of survival.

But seven years later the New Look brought a powerful but largely invisible new order to the United States—and indeed to the world—that was organized around the prospect of a sudden, spectacular catastrophe in the form of surprise nuclear attack, an atomic Pearl Harbor. Cold War culture would hence be curiously tethered to the apocalyptic images of destruction, above all the mushroom cloud. At the same time, the New Look was a means of safeguarding an invisible, unrepresentable order of market-based capitalism. It offered the military power of a wartime economy without necessitating that the state reach into various corners of the economy, at least overtly. Indeed, Eisenhower's Cold War did reach far and wide into economy and society; but it did so disguised in the clothes of domestic housekeeping, so to speak: economics. Just as Eisenhower, upon assuming aspirations for civilian leadership, took off his general's stripes and pulled out his corporate blue suit, in assuming the presidency he put America's World War II military iconography in the closet of history and invented a new American style for national security, one that—like his vision of a harmonious but unrepresentable American economic colossus—disguised the security exigencies in the garb of domestic fulfillment and economic prosperity.

As with the rise of neoliberalism in later decades, it is easy, and indeed reasonable, to attribute this covert approach to a new American militarism to the unwarranted influence of corporate CEOs, air force brass, and think tanks like the RAND Corporation. To be sure, representatives of the new, nuclear-centric, military-industrial complex agilely maneuvered through the halls of Congress and the White House to sell America's leaders on the virtues of asymmetrical nuclear deterrence. But Eisenhower himself did not have to maneuver so carefully when addressing the American public. Rather—and far more successfully than Truman—he was able to offer his ambitious, world-historical (in light of the destruction it was built to bring) security strategy in the language of American values. Truman did his best to present his Cold War agenda in the language of republican citizenship, calling for the virtues of wartime duty and sacrifice. Eisenhower instead drew more successfully upon the language of individual responsibility and initiative, transforming liberty from an ideal to be embodied in the dutiful sacrifices of citizens into a spiritual principle in a larger national and fundamentally economic enterprise.

(Neo)Liberal Genealogies

In no country, it seems, has sudden and spectacular violence meant so much as in the United States in the last three-quarters of a century. Though in fact it has suffered far less from geopolitical insecurities than most countries on the globe, it has drawn disproportionate meaning from such insecurities, as the global, epochal significance of the Cold War and the War on Terror both attest. Shortly after bombs blasted at the 2013 Boston Marathon, Rafia Zakaria, a columnist for Pakistan's *Dawn*, wondered about this peculiar form of global inequality. "Boston is no different, no more or less tragic than the bombings that have razed the marketplaces of Karachi, the school in Khost, the mosque in Karbala," she wrote. "And yet it seems so. Attacks in America are far more indelible in the world's memory than attacks in any other country. There may be fewer victims and less blood, but American tragedies somehow seem to occur in a more poignant version of reality, in a way that evokes a more sympathetic response." Zakaria wondered if this was because the United States, relatively speaking, has suffered so little from such violence, if "the world's allocations of sympathy are determined not by the magnitude of a tragedy— the numbers of dead and injured—but by the contrast between a society's normal [*sic*] and the cruel aftermath of a terrorist event."[1] There is indeed something about the breaking in of spectacular violence that the relative security of the United States magnifies.

At the same time, it is clear that this reaction, both in the United States and abroad, has not been simply one of sympathy. Each violent spectacle has been followed by calls to remake American institutions (and sometimes even global ones, as in the case of September 11), accompanied by a range of revolutionary fervors and anxieties, so as to assure that such misfortunes will never happen again. While those abroad, who may have initially sympathized with America's plight, grow nervous with worry about America's response, citizens of the United States await another revolution in government structures and systems—sometimes with suspicion, sometimes with anticipation, sometimes with indifference. These governmental revolutions have been part and parcel of economic ones, as political legitimacy has become entangled with new post-trauma industries, markets, or—as after the Kennedy assassination—economic attitudes.

Yet, almost in the same breath, we are told that these catastrophes must not alter the American way of life, that America's freedoms and aspirations must remain constant through its revolutionary storms, that whatever is remade in the way of government structures and systems must not remake America. It seems to be taken for granted, not even argued, that America, in some fundamental sense, is not to be remade, and that the American way of life can survive, even thrive, independent of revolutions in government and economy. Government is but the shifting terrain of a transcendental quest; politics is but the mundane business of partisans and bureaucrats that exerts an unwelcome gravitational pull to be overcome; even new markets and economic attitudes are but the trivia of nationhood.

The quest has been nebulously social and explicitly apolitical. Catastrophes are occasions for Americans to experience their nationhood at two complementary emotional poles. First the shock. Joseph Masco argues that "the politics of shock are central to the conceptualization of the national security state as a distinct form of American power."[2] Shock connects Americans in a powerful, mass-mediated virtual experience *beyond* our many differences. But then there is the aftershock. Marita Sturken has described the aftershock in terms of the creation of a "comfort culture," one built on symbolic sites mass produced for consumers: sites like mini flags, yellow ribbons, and teddy bears. These sites affirm our innocence and re-present our trauma in miniature form, giving us "a sense of containment and control over an event" and even a "godlike position" over a small world.[3] Such comforts would seem to be a long way from the sublime. However, if the in the sublime we pass through the destruction of an image and, moreover, of the imagination, only to emerge at a top-limit with a sense of our superiority—in Kantian fashion—we can see how such practices of making all things small indeed conform to its logic.[4] Sudden, spectacular violence becomes a means by which to tokenize our world, not the least our *political* world; iconoclasm becomes a means of transcendence.

The inevitable politics that follow catastrophes, not to mention the politics of catastrophes, seem out of step with this sublime spirit. Amid the comforts of the sublime, the artifice of politics seems to represent a loss of innocence, a fall, as necessary as it may be. There is indeed something inauthentic about such political processes vis-à-vis national purpose and the American way of life. They cannot be but artificial. But that this artifice is felt *as a loss*, even a fall, is indicative of a larger national condition—what I have been arguing is a neoliberal condition.

That no country in the last four decades of the twentieth century was more receptive to the rhythms and rhetorics of neoliberalism than the United States is consistent with the transcendental quests of the period. For neoliberalism too entailed a discourse of transcendence and an attack on representation. However, in this final chapter, I argue for more than complicities between the discourse of violent spectacles and that of neoliberalism. I explore the liberal genealogy of neoliberalism, so as to suggest that the national pieties, rhythms, and rhetorics peculiar to the American response to violent spectacles from the Kennedy assassination through September 11 represented, in a certain sense, a completion or fulfillment of the liberal project—not its only possible fulfillment, and certainly not its ultimate one, but a completion nevertheless. This chapter is philosophical in orientation, and my goals in it seemingly conflicted: on the one hand, I want to normalize neoliberalism by placing it within a liberal tradition, suggesting its genetic place within liberal culture, particularly in the United States. On the other hand, I want to consider the severity and indeed strangeness of its logic by stressing the way its leaps into the transcendent lead to a form of political inauthenticity as a means of redressing political crises. In what is no more than a sketch, I proceed in this chapter in three steps, reaching across several centuries: first, I look at the shifting status of political artifice in the seventeenth and eighteenth centuries; then I look at the distinctive contribution of neoliberal theory to the critique of political artifice, and finally I consider the way in which neoliberal theory puts a distance between politics and economy, which together would no longer represent a hybrid order (political-economy) but two distinct and competing orders. I conclude by returning to the power of the violent spectacle in America vis-à-vis the neoliberal condition.

From Another Nature, to Art over Nature, to Nature over Art

Seventeenth-century England may seem like an unlikely place to begin a discussion of neoliberalism, but as the first great revolutionary period of the modern era, it was also a period of profound upheavals in political thought and practice, upheavals that neoliberals themselves would cite as the beginning of their own story. In this regard, Thomas Hobbes, as has been widely recognized, was a pivotal and representative figure. In my brief discussion here, I want to consider Hobbes's revaluation of the artificial nature of politics and rhetoric, and consequently of the nature of representation. My goal is to provide a backdrop for what would become the liberal revolution in the eighteenth century and ultimately to consider what was "new" in neoliberalism as liberalism confronted internal and external crises in the twentieth century.

Whether we are referring to the representation of an idea, an interest, or a people, politics is always presented with the problem of representation. For a long time, this problem was worked out in two interrelated fields, politics and rhetoric—both of which enjoyed a pivotal if not always central place within philosophy (broadly conceived). Thus Aristotle considered under the former the various types of government, the nature and duties of citizenship, sorts of constitutions, and other structural elements through which political representation was realized, and under the latter the ethical and strategic aspects of speech in which representation was realized. Politics structured regularities, whereas rhetoric arbitrated contingencies. What was true of Aristotle remained true in political thought all the way up until the time of Hobbes: social order, invariably considered a product of political order, was achieved through systems of representation realized at the intersection of governing structures and norms of speech.

The humanistic tradition in the seventeenth century took the general position that both politics and rhetoric were arts. In claiming this, however, they did not suggest a strong opposition between art and nature. Rather, following Cicero and drawing on Christian conceptions of creation, they conceived of art—be it the art of politics or the art of poetry—as a qualitative transformation of nature rather than its antidote. Thus, Sidney could offer "poesy" as "in effect *another nature*."[5] Hobbes challenged this idea. For him, the natural condition was a war-filled one. The central *political* problem, therefore, was how to overcome the state of nature. Politics was an art, or artifice, by which to counteract the hostile condition of nature. Rhetoric, meanwhile, had for him a dual status: on the one hand, it represented a natural human ability by which to sway others through the power of words; on the other hand, it could be approached—as Hobbes did in his *Breife* on the art of rhetoric—as an artificial mechanism by which to counteract nature.[6] Thus, just as Hobbes would overcome the war-filled state of nature through the artifice of politics, so he would overcome the natural propensity of humans to manipulate and bend the wills of other humans through speech via the art of rhetoric—an art which really amounted to an art of *representation*, for representation was for him both the internal psychological end and the external means of the artifice of rhetoric.

So Hobbes broke quite noticeably with the humanist tradition.[7] The domain of the artificial was for him the means by which to overcome the domain of the natural. Politics became an artificial order by which to overcome an anarchic natural order. Representation, though rooted in natural psychological capacities, became within the *civitas* also the product of artifice. Through it, society came to order, as the famous frontispiece of *Leviathan* suggested. Hobbes, moreover, did not miss the theological implications of his new political science. Just as the political order entailed for him the artificial displacement of a natural social condition, so it also entailed an artificial religion opposed to scholastic natural theology, with the *civitas* both an artificial creation that imitates the original creation of God and a kind of church, regulating piety and morality.[8]

After Hobbes, however, there was yet another significant revaluation of nature and artifice vis-à-vis society and politics, one that was neither humanistic nor Hobbesian in its conclusions. Here we find something of the beginning of a distinctly liberal perspective on these matters. Locke's *Essay Concerning Human Understanding*, which begins famously by asserting the *tabula rasa*, sharply divided the power of God-given natural reason from the misleading artifice of human language in the formation of true knowledge. Locke retained the Hobbesian opposition between nature and art, in contrast with the humanists, but reversed their respective valuations: nature registered positively, but artifice—especially as it stemmed from language—negatively. Locke did not therefore have a simplistically benign view of nature. He too saw it as fallen. However, the state of nature was not for him equivalent to a state of war, as it had been with Hobbes. Rather, in nature humans find themselves in an imperfect state of society, one that, as the humanists held, could be improved not through art but through reliance on natural reason.[9]

So too Adam Smith, in his *Theory of Moral Sentiments*, offered an argument for the natural capacities of humans to feel sympathy for others, even if such natural sympathy is fundamentally motivated by a form of self-interest:

> How selfish soever [*sic*] man may be supposed, there are evidently some principles in his nature, which interest him in the fortune of others, and render their happiness necessary to him, though he derives nothing from it except the pleasure of seeing it. Of this kind is pity or compassion, the emotion which we feel for the misery of others, when we either see it, or are made to conceive of it in a very lively manner; ... for this sentiment, like all the other original passions of human nature, is by no means confined to the virtuous and humane, though they perhaps may feel it with the most exquisite sensibility. The greatest ruffian, the most hardened violator of the laws of society, is not altogether without it.[10]

By contrast, Smith typically presented artifice in the *Theory of Moral Sentiments* in a negative light, as the means by which we exasperate, manipulate, or otherwise distort the natural passions, even associating artifice with violence over and against sincerity and justice.[11] The artificial (though certainly not the artificer, or maker of products for trade) had a similarly negative valence in *The Wealth of Nations*, where, for example, Smith sharply criticized the settlement laws of England for instituting "artificial boundaries" that distort the distribution of wages in the labor market.[12] It is the "policy of Europe," Smith argues more generally, that occasions all sorts of inequalities "by not leaving things at perfect liberty."[13] Here the artificial political order Hobbes celebrated is conceived as bringing about social and economic harm.

Thus, whereas Hobbes, in constructing an argument for the legitimacy of the artificial state, sought to elevate the distinctly political within broader society, liberalism began a process of substitution, displacing the political at each conceivable turn with the social and, above all, the economic.[14] Politics proper, Hobbes argued, was concerned with sovereign authority, citizenship, and law; rhetoric with strategies of suasion that could bring the people to conform to law.[15] Locke and his liberal successors, however, sought solutions for the calamities of Europe in the extra-governmental powers of society itself.[16] As Sheldon Wolin writes, "Gradually society came to be conceived simultaneously as an entity distinct from political arrangements and as the shorthand symbol of all worthwhile human endeavor; and . . . these developments left little scope and less prestige for the political. The political became identified with a narrow set of institutions labeled 'government,' the harsh symbol of the coercion necessary to sustain orderly social transactions."[17]

For the classical economists of the eighteenth century, such as Adam Smith, *economy* became shorthand for the social order realizable apart from politics and for human flourishing more generally. Above all, the division of labor suggested to Smith the possibility of a providentially granted, *undirected* social order, one achieved quite apart from governmental authority.[18] At the same time, rhetoric became increasingly marginalized, a means of manipulation. Locke himself famously dismissed rhetoric in the *Essay on Human Understanding*, declaring "all the artificial and figurative application of Words Eloquence hath invented perfect cheats" (much as Protestant iconoclasts would characterize catholic icons).[19] Later eighteenth-century approaches to rhetoric—whether in Adam Smith, Hugh Blair, or George Campbell—were not so contemptuous; they did, however, tend to leave rhetoric to gentlemanly refinement rather than the rough business of political representation.

Fascinated with a new science that was at once mechanical and theologically tethered—eventually reaching an apogee in Paleyian science—liberal philosophy thus attributed an order to society that was nonpolitical, non-rhetorical, and nonrepresentable. This Paleyian world, of course, did not last. Darwinian science exposed the dark underbelly of nature, and so the social too began to take on more ominous hues. The social evolutionism, the ruthless industrialism, and the laissez-faire capitalism of the nineteenth century were no less rooted in the idea of a nonpolitical, nonrhetorical, nonrepresentable social order than was the free-market advocacy of Adam Smith; it is just that that order became far more unforgiving. And it is here that one story of neoliberalism can be said to begin. For neoliberalism entailed an attempt, even with Darwin's unsettling disclosures of nature in view, to recover for society an optimistic Paleyian outlook.

The End of Laissez-Faire

In a 1926 lecture at Oxford, John Maynard Keynes foretold the "end of *laissez-faire*." Offering an account of the development of economic thought since Adam Smith much like the one I just summarized, Keynes polemically concluded,

> Let us clear from the ground the metaphysical or general principles upon which, from time to time, *laissez-faire* has been founded. It is *not* true that individuals possess a prescriptive "natural liberty" in their economic activities. There is *no* "compact" conferring perpetual rights on those who Have or on those who Acquire. The world is *not* so governed from above that private and social interest always coincide. It is *not* so managed here below that in practice they coincide. It is *not* a correct deduction from the principles of economics that enlightened self-interest always operates in the public interest. Nor is it true that self-interest generally *is* enlightened; more often individuals acting separately to promote their own ends are too ignorant or too weak to attain even these. Experience does *not* show that individuals, when they make up a social unit, are always less clear-sighted than when they act separately.[20]

Quoting Edmund Burke, Keynes went on to argue that the problem of social order brought us back to "one of the finest problems in legislation, namely, to determine what the State ought to take upon itself to direct by the public wisdom, and what it ought to leave, with as little interference as possible, to individual exertion."[21] Thus, Keynes argued for bringing back the political to the social. So, too, he hinted at the need for the return of the rhetorical. Feelings, thought, and speech were out of order in the laissez-faire society, he argued. We may feel one thing, think another, and say a third thing. Hence, in a manner consistent with I. A. Richards's "new rhetoric," Keynes noted,

"Confusion of thought and feeling leads to confusion of speech," and argued that reform needs to begin with a "candid examination of our own inner feelings in relation to the outside facts," and a search for forms of speech consistent with both. Keynes was hardly optimistic or triumphal here; his was a call to become more serious and sober about the problems of society. But he did look toward a general realignment of politics, rhetoric, and epistemology, or legislation, speech, and practical knowledge.

A decade later Walter Lippmann, in his *An Inquiry into the Principles of the Good Society*—the text provided the occasion for the fateful first meeting of neoliberals in Paris in 1938—refuted this realignment. Lippmann argued that limitations on human knowledge demanded severe restraints on the scope and power of politics. He presented government planners, who sought to understand social processes, as the single greatest threat to human freedom, if not social order. As an alternative, he argued for a market economy, realized most pristinely in the division of labor, as a means of a relatively stable and harmonious social order independent of demands on human knowledge. Lippmann did not, however, argue for a return to laissez-faire, which he thought was based on a "fallacy" that presumed freedom could only be realized apart from law.[22] He instead sought a legislated order that would create conditions for the market to operate efficiently and thus vouchsafe human freedom. Against the backdrop of laissez-faire liberalism, Lippmann's argument represented something new, something Keynes had not even considered: a fusion of social optimism with epistemological skepticism. But in another way the argument here was quite old, as Lippmann's epistemological critique and social optimism here recalled that of sixteenth-century iconoclast theologies and later theories of the sublime, as it focused on the way a realization of the limits of the powers of the imagination, and by extension representation, could be the epiphanic key to new forms of social order. In a pointed moment, Lippmann noted that the social planner could not even represent to himself the social and economic processes that went into making his own breakfast; such processes "would be beyond the understanding of any mind," he scoffed. Thus, what of the planner's attempt to "draw up plans for the direction of society"?[23] The limits of politics therefore must conform to the limits of the human imagination: "The essential limitation, therefore, of all policy, of all government, is that the human mind must take a partial and simplified view of existence. The ocean of experience cannot be poured into the little bottles of our intelligence."[24]

With this Lippmann began his quest for a new liberalism, or neoliberalism. A year after the publication of his book the Colloque Lippmann was held in Paris and attended by the likes of Hayek, Mises, Michael Polanyi, and

Raymond Aron. Lippmann and his colleagues considered how to revolutionize liberalism in light of the catastrophes of world war, economic depression,
fascism, and communism. The Colloque Lippmann was the source of the
term *neoliberalism*, and it began the long organizing process that would lead,
eventually, to the first meeting of the Mont Pèlerin Society in April 1947.[25]
As that momentous meeting drew near, Hayek published *The Road to Serfdom*, elaborating as follows on the themes of Lippmann. "The point which
is so important is the basic fact that it is impossible for any man to survey
more than a limited field, to be aware of the urgency of more than a limited
number of needs. Whether his interests center round his own physical needs,
or whether he takes a warm interest in the welfare of every human being
he knows, the ends about which he can be concerned will always be only
an infinitesimal fraction of the needs of all men." "This," Hayek continued,
"is the fundamental fact on which the whole philosophy of individualism is
based." As if to stress what was new to this neoliberalism, he further clarified,
"It does not assume, as is often asserted, that man is egoistic or selfish or
ought to be. It merely starts from the indisputable fact that the limits of our
powers of imagination make it impossible to include in our scale of values
more than a sector of the needs of the whole society."[26]

  The limits of our powers of imagination: Hayek offered this claim as a polemical point in *The Road to Serfdom*, but he presented it as a theoretical
conclusion in his little-known *The Sensory Order* (1952). The book, a work
of psychology, stemmed from Hayek's extensive interest in the problems of
knowledge and perception.[27] In it, he presented what can well be read as a broken view of human psychology, one where the internal psycho-physiological
sensory order and the external, worldly physical order have no representable
relation to each other. The problem for Hayek was twofold. First, the sensory and physical orders were two distinct orders (though both ultimately
operated within the larger physical field), with different sorts of operations,
creating something like the distinction between reality (the physical order)
and appearance (the sensory order). Second, whatever models or pictures
we might develop of the relation between the sensory and physical orders
would itself be a proximate product of the sensory order; thus, to understand
how the mind or imagination brings about a representation would itself require that the mind produce a representation, and so on *ad infinitum*. Thus,
we could never validate a representation as such; we could, however, test its
predictive capacity, and thus build an empirical science built on laws or principles rather than valid representations or models.[28]

  The assertion of the limits of the powers of the imagination vis-à-vis
social order was the distinctive claim of neoliberals (rather than Smithian

claims for natural human sympathy or providential social mechanisms). Social processes, it was argued, could not be legitimately represented. The social
is beyond imagination, and within the larger context of economy was indeed
sublime. However, as we see, neither Lippmann nor Hayek therefore gave up
the task of social theory before their epistemological skepticism. To the contrary, both argued that it was well within human capacities to understand
the laws or general principles behind social processes, even if they could not
be represented. Thus, Lippmann sought the common principles that stood
behind "the division of labor, democracy, and the method of common law"
in order to build a new liberalism.[29] Hayek likewise sought what he referred
to as principles of liberty.[30] Here, we might say, they unwittingly followed the
iconoclastic logic of the Kantian sublime: we can think what we cannot see.

Lippmann's *Inquiry* is particularly instructive for thinking about what
would come of neoliberalism in this regard. The book suggested three possible futures. The first, and most pressing, would be a future of violent tyranny. Here, Lippmann's "road to serfdom" was even more severe than Hayek's
would be: "Thus, by a kind of tragic irony, the search for security and a rational society, if it seeks salvation through political authority, ends in the most
irrational form of government imaginable—in the dictatorship of casual
oligarchs, who have no hereditary title, no constitutional origin or responsibility, who cannot be replaced except by violence."[31] The second future the
Inquiry imagined was a progressive, technocratic one:

> The time may come when the higher logic will have been sufficiently devel-
> oped to enable thinkers to analyze the whole relevant social order, and from
> the analysis to predict successfully the real, not merely the apparent and im-
> mediate, effect of a political intervention. Not until then will it be possible
> to contemplate a planned society consciously directed. It is not merely that
> we do not have to-day enough factual knowledge of the social order, enough
> statistics, censuses, reports. The difficulty is deeper than that. We do not pos-
> sess the indispensible logical equipment—the knowledge of the grammar and
> the syntax of society as a whole—to understand the data available or to know
> what other data to look for.[32]

Lippmann suggested here a future where technology comes to compensate
for the apparent innate limits of the human mind. "The successful analysis of
a great society," he admitted, "can perhaps be imagined by the mathematical
logicians."[33] But it is not the future that Lippmann himself would imagine in
the *Inquiry*, nor would it be the future his neoliberal successors would offer.
They were deeply skeptical of what Lippmann would call "the gods of the
machine," instead seeking a more organic liberal future.[34] That future would

be one where the impossibility of any image, set of images, imagination, or image-machine adequate to the representation of society would give way to the law of economy.

And this would require a faith. Lippmann, writing in the face of totalitarian violence in Europe and what he saw as an overbearing federal administrative apparatus in the United States, wrote that his was a lost generation in need of a new faith:

> The cause of civilization does not now rest upon . . . strong convictions but rather upon helpless forebodings of disaster, and an impotent longing for peace and dignity. For the masses of men consent reluctantly to the great re-action toward arbitrariness, but nonetheless they consent, having no positive faith which springs from the roots of their being with which they can whole-heartedly challenge it. Though they feel that they are sinking into barbarism, their judgment is confounded, their minds disoriented in the tangle of ab-stractions, technicalities, claims and counter-claims through which they are supposed to find their way.[35]

Thus, a "polestar" was needed, rather than "many perplexing lights."[36] That polestar would be the "inviolability of the human person," and inviolability that had in the history of liberalism led from "the general dominion of men over men" to the dominion of an impersonal order, and could do so again.[37]

Politics and Economics

Thus neoliberal theory was not, as is too often assumed, merely a cover for a return to laissez-faire capitalism. Neoliberalism, moreover, should not be approached only as a "vehicle for the extension of class power," let alone as a straightforward extension of capitalism.[38] Rather, in light of this discussion, we can now see that it entailed a distinct social philosophy, one that can be placed within the larger liberal tradition. In the face of the political disasters of Europe and its colonial extensions, neoliberalism sought to tame the political by working from economic postulates to social principles, all apart from the artificial representations typical of the social and human sciences as well as the preponderance of political processes. Neoliberalism, we might say, emerged in a war between *Wissenschaften*.

But here neoliberalism has less to do with political economy than with the space between politics and economics. From a neoliberal perspective, the long history of liberalism has too often muddled the distinction. Politics must be regulated by the economic, rather than confused with it. Economic principles lead to political solutions, both with respect to specific social conflicts and crises, and in the broader sense of the solution to the problem of the nature and limits of the political generically. In order to regulate the political, economics must hold within itself the basic capacities of the political. It must be able to fulfill the basic social functions of the political and rhetorical— that is, to structure regularities and arbitrate contingencies. Within a liberal culture, these regularities must at least seem to be based upon the principle of *equality*, whereas the arbitration of contingencies must offer the possibility of differentiation amid the general rule of equality.

Contractual, rights-based politics has generally presumed in one form or another rule among equals. Even Hobbes began here to develop his absolutist theory. For him politics entailed the art (or science as the case may be) of actualizing rule among equals by, somewhat paradoxically, assigning them differing roles.[39] The basic tasks Hobbes brought to political philosophy proper—determining the nature and function of sovereign authority, the duties of citizenship, and the scope and power of law—had to do with transforming a society of equals into a determinate order through a structure of rule.[40] This was a distinctive *political* task. Importantly, the interplay between equality and differentiation within the contractual tradition depended not, as is sometimes claimed, on absolute principles, but on contingent and pragmatic (or functional) considerations. When approaching the question of politics, Hobbes and his contractual successors have asked, given a set of political purposes and a social context, what differing roles are required in order to fulfill those purposes? Here claims of *necessity*, that vital watchword of modern politics, were rooted in prudential judgment, and thus could by their very nature be challenged. (Hobbes, for one, held that when a person's life was at stake he, and one would hope *she*, could challenge the judgment of the sovereign. Much later, Carl Schmitt simply turned this Hobbesian logic on its head, asserting that he who is able to prudentially judge a state of emergency *is* the sovereign.) When, *within* the political domain, the factors that determine the differentiation of roles among equals cease to be contingent and pragmatic, or when necessity is given an absolute status, we witness the ideological transformation of the political. Political ideologies *misrepresent* political purposes and the rule of equals in the service of particular interests. Indeed, political ideologies are possible (and we might add rampant) because politics is functionally dependent upon representation.

Neoliberal economics too addresses the interplay between equality and differentiation, but begins not by postulating the equality of persons, but a common measure, the basic monetary unit. Moreover, it looks not to contingent and pragmatic considerations in differentiating roles within the social order but to an inviolable and seemingly providential mechanism, the division of labor, ultimately determined by impersonal market forces. Here, necessity is rooted in a quantifiable, objective logic of scarcity, or supply and demand. Finally and crucially, there is no real economic equivalent to political ideology, for whereas the latter depends on misrepresentation (or, more accurately, *mal*representation) the former rests on a flat and uniform representation, *money*, as a means of measure. In the perfectly efficient, ideal economy of neoliberal economists, money lacks the potential for misrepresentation simply because it lacks any aesthetic quality at all; it is simply a standard measure.

Hence, while both liberal politics and neoliberal economy depend on the interplay between equality and differentiation, the space between politics and economy is *the space of representation*. Neoliberalism—in theory, as a broader discourse, and as a condition—has rejected representation in accounting for social processes and, by extension, historical events. As Hayek suggested in *The Sensory Order* and Milton Friedman argued in "The Methodology of Positive Economics," descriptive theories of social processes are valid only as long as they *function* predictively: "A theory or its 'assumptions' cannot possibly be thoroughly 'realistic' in the immediate descriptive sense so often assigned to this term. A completely 'realistic' theory of the wheat market would have to include not only the conditions directly underlying the supply and demand for wheat but also the kind of coins or credit instruments used to make exchanges; the personal characteristics of wheat-traders such as the colour of each trader's hair and eyes, his antecedents and education, the number of members of his family, their characteristics, antecedents, and education, etc."[41] Friedman thus called not for thicker theories of social processes; to the contrary, he dismissed any concern at all with representational realism in economic theory, arguing in a seemingly pragmatic vein that the only value a theory had was its predictive capacity. But pragmatism this was not, as Friedman assumed the presence of a foundational reality that ultimately determined the validity of a theory. Friedman's target was the domain of representation rather than, as pragmatists have targeted, the domain of reality, as he argued that the relative descriptive (we might even say *aesthetic*) quality of a given representation of a social or historical process was irrelevant to its scientific status. Thus, if legitimation crises entail crises *in* representation, neoliberalism centers on a more fundamental crisis *of* representation. It is not a particular representation or even a broader structure of representation that is in question, but representation itself.

Here one wishes that this crisis *of* representation was theoretically anomalous, peculiar to the radical agenda of particular class interests. But it is not. It has been a latent if not always realized aspect of the larger liberal tradition, which began in part by questioning the social role of artifice and the artificial. Rousseau's critique has long been paradigmatic. He argued that the sovereignty, consisting essentially in the general will, "cannot be represented for the same reason it cannot be alienated," for the general will "is itself or something else; there is no middle ground."[42] For Rousseau, politics begins, and indeed ends, with the unbroken expressions of the collective will. Representation, because it is always divided, would divide the will, making politics indirect and thus undemocratic and quite possibly authoritarian. More recent theorists of democratic culture, from Benjamin Barber to Robert Bellah, have followed Rousseau in skeptical accounts of political representation. Barber writes, "Representation is incompatible with freedom because it delegates and thus alienates political will at the cost of genuine self-government and autonomy."[43] Similarly, Bellah's "civil religion" can be understood as an account of the American attempt to transcend the inevitable brokenness or dividedness of politics through an unbroken transcendental discourse.

The neoliberal critique of representation is therefore consistent with a wider liberal critique of representation. However, as its critique is specifically rooted in epistemology, it is also different. Its concern is not with the will of the people; indeed, its concern is not with the people at all. Rather, it is with two poles of a theoretical reality: the individual, on the one hand, and the social processes that give him or her sustenance, on the other. Thus, there is within neoliberalism a *twofold* critique of representation, one that indeed comes very near to the critiques of the representation of the deity put forward by iconoclasts in the Protestant Reformation. First, there is the claim that no representation is adequate to the complexity of social and political processes, but second there is the consequent claim that representation is in constant danger of creating the illusion of knowledge where in fact there is none. Thus, the world of representations—for there *are* invariably representations—is a world of tokens, unreal representations that make no further claim upon us, or idols, unreal representations that claim veracity.

Conclusion

Economy is in neoliberalism a cosmos, a cyclical order of creative destruction that transcends the contingencies of politics, biology, history, and locality. It requires, in stoic fashion, an indifference to the particulars, reserving respect only for the universals. It leaves all that appears on the surface—above all, politics and government—mere tokens of a background *tertia*.[44] It thus moves from an ontology to an ideology of iconoclasm. Within the iconoclastic moment, neoliberalism and where-were-you-when? events come together in a "conspiracy to protect the ineffable."[45]

If these violent spectacles have meant so much in American political culture since the advent of the Cold War, it is in part because they assert, in a kind of optimistic but negative civil theology, the impossibility of any representation adequate to American nationhood, a nationhood now indivisible from economy. Americans have managed these traumas by subordinating political means of their redress to discourses of transcendence and explicitly consumer-oriented practices. These violent eruptions thus expose the artificial as mere artifice, the equivalent to mere rhetoric. And as such they make room for revolutions in government—revolutions motivated by specific interests—without those revolutions appearing fateful for national destiny.

At the same time, those revolutions in government appear under the auspices of an emergency order. The artificial thus returns with Hobbesian force, but not as a means of overcoming an unregulated, spontaneous order, but as a means of reinforcing it at the point of its distinctive *political* crisis. It is not so much the return of a Law—a Reason, a God—from a realm beyond representation as it is the return of the Law within the realm of representation to protect the province of the unrepresentable. The state, however, appears here as but a token, both in the sense of an accidental and arbitrary representation (though a necessary appearance) and in the sense of authenticating the higher, unrepresentable order by means of its symbolic work.

We might even call it *rhetorical* work, for neoliberalism has from the outset been a faith in need of propagation. Friedman wrote in 1951 as World War II was becoming a memory and the Cold War was heating up, "Ideas have little chance of making much headway against a strong tide; their opportunity comes when the tide has ceased running strong but has not yet turned. This is, if I am right, such a time, and it affords rare opportunities to those of us who believe in liberalism to affect the new direction the tide takes. We have a new faith to offer; it behooves us to make it clear to one and all what that faith is."[46] Rhetoric is here, however, not a substantive component of social order. Rather, like the state, it appears in a moment of crisis to turn the tide, so to speak. It is, to use Friedman's description of the state under old-style liberalism, "purely instrumental and has no significance in and of itself."[47]

Lippmann wrote of a generation where "helpless forebodings of disaster, and an impotent longing for peace and dignity" had displaced "strong convictions" in directing social energies and action. Neoliberalism, he supposed,

would reverse this. Friedman, however, saw in social crises occasions to rhetorically redirect social aspirations. That is, forebodings of disaster and long-
ings for peace could be occasions for directing convictions rather than their
substitutes. Thus, to return to the question of the particular power of spectacular violence in America, these where-were-you-when? events have not
only shocked as they break into a relatively tranquil American normalcy, they
have also been powerful rhetorical occasions to offer images of an order that
is, by virtue of its apolitical character, beyond such violent acts. This higher
order both relativizes the magnitude of the violence in question by keeping it
within the domain of the artificial and offers a faith in a transcendent order
that neither guns, nor mechanical failures, nor missiles can destroy.

Conclusion

Image and representation; catastrophe and iconoclasm; economy and sublimity—my argument in these pages has relied on a critical vocabulary gleaned from the outer edges and inner concerns of liberal theory since the Enlightenment. I cannot well condense the arguments of this book into a few discrete conclusions. I will, however, engage in several meta-reflections on its key terms and arguments, offering them with frequent reference to Hayek, himself a kind of meta-thinker of the neoliberal social project. As a social imaginary, neoliberalism has relied on "normative notions and images that underlie [social] expectations."[1] My aim here is to reflect on these normative notions and images so as to sketch the pivotal features of the neoliberal imaginary.

The Idolatry of the State

Liberalism has relied, as much as any political worldview, on representation (paradigmatically seen in the image). This is evident not the least in the varied connotations and denotations of *representation* in liberal societies—a key word in aesthetic, political, and, civil religious discourses. If *representation* is a slippery term, it is because it circulates so smoothly and widely within liberal societies. Yet liberalism is hardly settled on the matter of representation. To begin with, there are different forms and structures of representation, such as the difference between what Ankersmit refers to as "mimetic" and "aesthetic" representation, the latter "broken" but still more true to actual political representation than the dream of one-to-one mimetic correspondence. In this book, I have worked with a terminology drawn from a related but in some respects different domain of representation—theology, including political theology—to suggest that representation is not just a matter of structures and logics between the represented and the representation, but also a matter of power and status, specifically with respect to our disposition before the image.

Liberalism's anxieties about the power and status of the image are most evidently seen in the various attempts to overcome the logic of representation altogether. Liberal cultures have spawned a variety of anti-representational theories and discourses in a variety of forms: romantic subjectivities of intuition and immediacy; deontological ethical, political, and economic philosophies that would in an *a priori* manner begin from law rather than, in deliberative fashion, lead to it; direct democracy; postmodern theories; and the subject of this book, neoliberalism. Liberalism has thus left this basic question of social order unresolved: Are the means and mechanisms—the *powers*—of social order to be represented? If so, are they then subject to design (or planning)? And if so, does design render them artificial and thus in turn challenge their legitimacy? These are the questions that have proved generative for neoliberalism. It has answered the first and foremost question in the negative: Are the powers of social order to be represented? But it has done so because it has answered the latter two questions affirmatively: representation calls for artifice, and artifice is the source of legitimation crises.

But there is a crucial exception here—the mechanisms of social order are to be unrepresentable *except* when the state appears to support, serve, and above all protect the invisible market order. Indeed, Hayek and Friedman not only agreed on this; it is this inclusion of the appearance of the state in social order that they used to distinguish their neoliberal project from laissez-faire economics. Friedman wrote, "A new faith must avoid errors. It must give high place to a severe limitation on the power of the state to interfere in the detailed activities of individuals; at the same time, it must explicitly recognize that there are important positive functions that must be performed by the state. The doctrine sometimes called neo-liberalism . . . is such a faith."[2] Neoliberalism reserved a role for the state within a calculus of "social costs" wherein "the preservation of competition" is the measure.[3] The state's role had a negative and a positive aspect. Negatively, whatever it might do must not interfere with competition; positively, it acts legitimately when it acts to preserve and further competition. Such is the appearance of the state in the neoliberal imaginary.

Catastrophes of various kinds—ecological, natural, economic, or political—would seem to represent a major challenge to the supremacy of invisible orders, for as social and political experiences, catastrophes call for accountability, an explanation typically having the form of a discourse of responsibility. But impersonal social forces cannot be responsible, if only because they are incapable of responding to calls for accountability. Impersonal social forces are *agents*, in a sense approximating that of chemical agents, but they are not *actors* in the sense of responsible, and indeed visible, beings. Neoliberalism's innovation relative to laissez-faire economics is at this point: the state is the political actor summoned to protect, and when necessary *appear* to protect, an impersonal and invisible social agency. As such, the state serves two basic social functions: it appears in moments of crisis as an emergency order to preserve or otherwise actively further a market-based social order, *and* it serves as an actor to be held accountable, responsible, answerable, and thus satisfy a basic social and political need.

But what does the state represent? At best the interest of the market; at worst, nothing but its own coercive power. In this way neoliberalism, though wrought out of a wish to put an end to the overextension of the state's coercive power, in fact brings the state back to that power as its only effective and legitimate aspect. "The state would police the system," Friedman declared, and that would sum its legitimate function.[4] The state appears as an instrument of necessity, rather than freedom. As such, we have a remarkable reversal of the ancient Greek distinction that Arendt discusses between the *polis* and the *oikos* ("household," from which we get the word *economics*).[5] In the neoliberal vision, politics is the space of necessity, and economics is the space of freedom. And this reversal also entails a transformation of the status and significance of the world of appearances, which the Greeks associated with the distinctly political life—and thus freedom—as opposed to the hidden necessities of the household. Within the Greek conception, the possibility of a rupture between the *agathos* and the *kalos*, the "good" and the "beautiful," is part of what made citizens free: things should be as they appear, but they are sometimes not. The *oikos*, on the other hand, was a space deprived of such brokenness, if only because it was a space without *kalos*, without beauty. Neoliberalism would divorce freedom from the world of appearances altogether and offer instead an unrepresentable, inviolable realm as the domain of freedom.

Privatization

Thus, one way to reflect on the history of liberalism and democracy is to consider the shifting nature and status of representation.[6] Indeed, it was "symbols of sovereignty," Habermas argues, that were originally *public* in medieval Europe. The feudal lord—the holder of what we would today understand as both political and economic power—represented his power publicly: "He showed himself, presented himself as the embodiment of an ever present 'higher' power."[7] Feudal power participated in a system of iconicity, as did theocentric power. But so did later liberal societies, though in an appreciably transformed manner. "In the first modern constitutions the catalogues of fundamental rights," Habermas continues, "were a perfect image of the liberal model of the public sphere," asserting as they did significant private rights and clear limits on public authority. Liberal societies found a certain iconicity not only in founding documents, but in a more general mode of political participation: supervision. It was the role, Habermas argues, of private individuals to *see* the state, and so regulate its activities by leaving open the question of its legitimacy. The state's role was to represent faithfully citizens and their rights, and its legitimacy rested on its perceived fidelity. Liberalism thus rested on a more fundamental right, one so taken for granted as to be left unasserted in its political constitutions: the right, as Nicholas Mirzoeff has recently formulated it, *to look*.[8] In turn, it presumed representation—that is, things to be looked *at*, and indeed through. Liberalism, with republicanism, put representation to use—not only in the form of elected officials, but the press, public opinion, and representative literatures, arts, and so on.

Yet it is hard to imagine a liberalism that does not in some way cede itself to the economic. It was, as Sheldon Wolin has written, liberalism that in the eighteenth century reduced politics to "a narrow set of institutions labeled 'government,' the harsh symbol of the coercion necessary to sustain orderly social transactions," while elevating economics to the supreme social science.[9] Economy became sublime (and the sublime became economic) as it seemed to be able to carry out what the magisterial rulers of prior centuries could not: namely, a providentially granted ordering order (*ordo ordinans*) for society. *Pace* Wolin, however, that economy offered an impersonal order did not necessarily therefore mean the end of politics or even political philosophy. As Yaron Ezrahi has written, "Technicalizing actions [as in economics], in the sense of rendering them impersonal, disciplined means to designated ends, has generated ways not only to purify public action from personalized uses of political power but also to enhance it as 'representative.' As a method for alienating actions from their agents, for making actions detachable from persons, instrumentalism has given support to the claim that individuals can be trusted as agents 'acting for' other persons, that individual actors can generate public actions."[10] Indeed, the rise of economics meant new possibilities for political legitimation. As long as social processes could be in some sense measured and mastered—or, in Ezrahi's word, "technicalized"—political agents and agencies could claim for themselves a legitimate instrumental agency.

In fact, as Wolin published the first edition of his *Politics and Vision* in 1960, this seemed to be the destiny of liberalism: he wrote of the rise of the organization in his own time—close kin to Max Weber's notion of rationalization—not as the displacement of politics with economics, but rather as the "the diffusion of the political," or "the absorption of the political into non-political institutions and activities" (e.g., corporations, trade unions, and universities).[11] It seemed to Wolin at the time, as to Arendt and Habermas, that this was the course of the near future: liberal society would be increasingly organized into managerial structures that would sublimate the political within large-scale administrative apparatuses that claimed for themselves an impersonal, scientific legitimacy.[12]

Yet, at the same time Wolin was writing, Hayek was arguing against precisely such a course in *The Constitution of Liberty*. Claiming the tradition of liberalism to vindicate his position, Hayek reminded readers of the dark side of a technicalized society.[13] It had only been but a decade and a half since Hitler had turned a portion of the so-called population under his power into the equivalent of laboratory rats, and as Hayek wrote, reports emanated from the east of similar atrocities in the Soviet empire. *Organization* carried the connotations not merely of technicalization and instrumentalization, but of the worst social and political disasters of modernity.

Hence, in Hayek's work and those of his successors, economy took on a cosmic hue. Associated with both liberty and liberalism, it allied itself in Cold War America to what may have been the ultimate charismatic term of the age, *freedom*. Indeed, in 1953 Richard Weaver wrote of freedom,

> The greatest sacrifices that contemporary man is called upon to make are demanded in the name of "freedom"; yet the referent which the average man attaches to this word is most obscure. Burke's dictum that "freedom inheres in something sensible" has not prevented its breaking loose from all anchorages. And the evident truth that the average man, given the choice between exemption from responsibility and responsibility, will choose the latter, makes no impression against its power. The fact, moreover, that the most extensive use of the term is made by modern politicians and statesmen in an effort to get men to assume more responsibility (in the form of military service, increased taxes, the abridgment of rights, etc.) seems to carry no weight either. The fact that what the American pioneer considered freedom has become wholly impossible to the modern apartment-dwelling metropolitan seems not to have damaged its potency. Unless we accept some philosophical interpretation, such as the proposition that freedom consists only the discharge of responsibility, there seems no possibility of a correlation between the use of the word

and circumstantial reality. Yet "freedom" remains an ultimate term, for which people are asked to yield up their first-born.[14]

In *freedom* America possessed a transcendent term, itself free from the sensible and circumstantial, that had the power to summon and justify collective sacrifice. Weaver was thinking, of course, of sacrifice to the nation, but it would not be long before sacrifice in the name of freedom could be summoned in the name of impersonal market forces. Indeed, neoliberalism differentiated itself from nationalism in part along these lines—it was a postnationalist, global market ideology. Thus, when several decades later Ronald Reagan addressed the nation in the immediate aftermath of the *Challenger* explosion, claiming, "That's the way freedom is, and we wouldn't change it for a minute," the claim could be taken as a traditional statement of Cold War patriotic pride.[15] Yet, given the place of the *Challenger* adventure within a project aimed at privatizing space exploration, Reagan's statement meant from a programmatic view that the sacrifice of the *Challenger* crew was made on behalf of free enterprise.

That this latter sort of freedom is hard to see on the surface of Reagan's speech (it requires some uncovering and contextualization) is consistent with the broader sense of privatization in which Reagan was invested—privatization as freedom from publicity. Neoliberalism would mean not only freedom from representation but even from the logic of non-representation. Indeed, in a 1946 essay, "Individualism: True and False," Hayek offered a Weaver-like lament over the ambiguities of key cultural terms, but one that departed significantly from Weaver in its underlying claim.

> The difficulty which we encounter is not merely the familiar fact that the current political terms are notoriously ambiguous or even that the same term often means nearly the opposite to different groups. There is the much more serious fact that the same word frequently appears to unite people who in fact believe in contradictory and irreconcilable ideals. Terms like "liberalism" or "democracy," "capitalism" or "socialism," today no longer stand for coherent systems of ideas. They have come to describe aggregations of quite heterogeneous principles and facts which historical accident has associated with these words but which have little in common beyond having been advocated at different times by the same people or even merely under the same name.[16]

Whereas Weaver would complain of words that had broken free of any reference, Hayek here protested of words that had "contradictory and irreconcilable" references. The difference is seemingly slight, but in fact it was quite significant: for Weaver, the problem was the *loss* of representation, whereas for Hayek, it was the *incoherence* of representation. The former thinker would seek to resuscitate representation; the latter, to either straighten it out or—as the case would be for neoliberals—to abandon it altogether.

The Disposition of the Sublime

If liberalism, more than any other sort of political culture, puts representation to use, it is thus more than a bit odd that liberal culture should turn against representation, finding it inadequate to its purposes. However, it may be the centrality of representation in liberal cultures that makes them so hungry for the sublime, for that which is beyond representation. For representation is precarious: easily contestable, readily falsifiable, its truths are as soft as flesh and as fleeting as time. At the same time, representation has extraordinary power: the capacity to persuade, to woo, even to all but compel. Thus, the worry about the aestheticization of politics, hardly unique to critiques of European fascism, contains two opposing anxieties: one preoccupied with the weakness of the image, the other with its strength.[17] Indeed, it has been typical of liberal political culture, from Rousseau onward, to undermine the conditions of its own possibility by attacking the image in the name of the sublime. The sublime has been like a rearguard formation, able to protect liberal cultures from behind, so to speak. Just when representation's dual quality of precariousness and power would seem to make liberalism vulnerable to a fatal assault, the sublime appears, offering a transcendental reality beyond representation as the essence of the liberal project—a being, or more often a *becoming*, that is indefatigable because it is unrepresentable.

Just so, amid the symbolic upheavals of the Cold War and the doomed postwar apogee of Wolin's "age of organization," the political sublime reappeared, initially in that neo-Rousseauean American civic piety that Bellah described as "at its best is a genuine apprehension of universal and transcendent religious reality," then in the discourse of Reagan's America, and then again in a post–Cold War moment, amid the trauma of September 11. The 1960s to the 1990s were indeed decades when political representation was hotly debated in American political culture—in civil rights movements, in the fights between the religious right and secular left, and in debates over multiculturalism—but these debates, as Daniel Rodgers has argued of the era more generally, were components of "a great age of fracture," the "disaggregation" of representations of America.[18] If there was to be an active, effective, and unifying political discourse in this era, it would have to be a discourse of the sublime.

And so arose the apparent need for an "antirationalistic" individualism, as Hayek called it. The term *individualism*, he argued, had been distorted by advocates and opponents alike. Opponents (namely, socialists) had equated it

with an antisocial selfishness and greed; advocates (namely, "false" individu-
alists; he names them as the Encyclopedists, Rousseau, and the physiocrats)
had used a Cartesian rationalistic individualism to justify social-planning
projects leading to "socialism or collectivism."[19] Hayek argued against both,
offering an "antirationalistic" individualism—or a "true individualism" (one
he claimed was in keeping with the thought of such figures as John Locke,
Edmund Burke, Bernard Mandeville, David Hume, Josiah Tucker, Adam Ferguson, Adam Smith, and Alexis de Tocqueville).[20] "True individualism" was
deeply skeptical of any and all attempts to realize human social processes in
institutions or representations. Rather, it rested on the disposition of "humil-
ity" toward macro-social phenomenon, seeing them not as human creations
but as the products of "impersonal and anonymous social processes."[21] Humans, in turn, should limit their concerns to the local (in keeping with their
epistemic and political limitations), and governments should limit their activities to "the enforcement of abstract principles," or "rules," that delimit a
"sphere of responsibility" wherein free action can thrive.[22]

Thus, for Hayek, it was not so much that there is no such thing as society,
as Margaret Thatcher would claim, but rather that the social was beyond representation, and any representation (or theory) that did not begin with this
admission was false, indeed idolatrous. The insight of the true individualist
is that "the spontaneous collaboration of free men often creates things which
are greater than their individual minds can ever fully comprehend."[23] Therefore, "if left free, men will often achieve more than individual human reason
could design or foresee."[24] Thus, Hayek articulates the disposition:

> The fundamental attitude of true individualism is one of humility toward the
> processes by which mankind has achieved things which have not been de-
> signed or understood by any individual and are indeed greater than individual
> minds. The great question at this moment is whether man's mind will be al-
> lowed to continue to grow as part of this process or whether human reason
> is to place itself in the chains of its own making. What individualism teaches
> us is that society is greater than the individual only in so far as it is free. In so
> far as it is controlled or directed, it is limited to the powers of the individual
> minds which control or direct it.[25]

Only an attitude appropriate to the sublime can be consonant with a culture
of freedom, as freedom is itself for Hayek the experience of, and participation
within, spaces and processes beyond human epistemic capacities. To be free is
to participate in the ineffable. For to know is to determine, to determine is to
design, and to design is to enslave. Freedom thus entails a form of submission,

submission to the unknown. Free civilization, he argued, requires a "readiness ordinarily to submit to the products of the social process which nobody has designed and the reasons for which nobody may understand." Otherwise submission is serfdom.[26]

It was a stark choice, and an equally stark view, one that may appear more justified in light of the stark realities of twentieth-century Europe. Still, its starkness should not be minimized. Hayek was not just challenging police states and totalitarianisms, he was challenging the political more generally as a robust sphere for collective human life, putting in its place the economic. The economic was not just a way of delimiting certain natural human processes of acquisition and exchange; it was, for Hayek, a way of delimiting a legitimate epistemic field, a field we can indeed claim to *know*. An "indisputable intellectual fact," he wrote, concerns "the constitutional limitation of man's knowledge and interests, the fact that he *cannot* know more than a tiny part of the whole of society and therefore all that can enter into his motives are the immediate effects which his actions will have in the sphere he knows."[27] Knowledge, to be legitimate, must somehow be *immediate*. "All man's mind can effectively comprehend are the facts of the narrow circle of which he is the center."[28] Thus, for all of Hayek's protesting against Cartesianism, he began with the Cartesian epistemic postulate, only to extend it, ever so uncritically, into a romantic idealization of local, spontaneous social knowledge. The economic for Hayek found its roots in an Arcadian scene, only to be transformed into a sublime system through the mysterious market processes of aggregation. *That's* the way freedom is.

The Icon of Iconoclasm

How have the bloody and fiery spectacles meant so much in the neoliberal imaginary? Hayek might say all images are *made*, and as such are not only inadequate to meaning, but inauthentic, even dangerous. Thus, they become authentically meaningful only in their destruction. The resources for the argument are within liberalism. We see hints of it, to be sure, in Habermas's notion that legitimacy can only come from the ground up in the form of "consensus," and the corollary suppositions that "there is no administrative production of meaning" and that all state "ideology planning" will be self-defeating. The images produced by the state, Habermas suggests, are not only inadequate, they are inauthentic.[29] Meanwhile, Habermas's postmodern nemesis, Lyotard, assumed a similar stance toward the image in positing representation as an inherently totalizing, and thus dangerous, power.

Lyotard's celebration of the sublime of the avant-garde of high modernism was as sure a testament as we can find that the only authentic image is the image destroyed.[30]

Still, my argument has been that neoliberalism, as it developed in America as a social philosophy and social imaginary, made particularly powerful use of the assumption of the inadequacy of the image to meaning. Indeed, the Cold War and post–Cold War catastrophic images of "state ideology planning" I have considered—not only JFK's assassination, the *Challenger* explosion, and *9/11*, but Little Rock and *Sputnik*—have appeared as images that prove the inadequacy and inauthenticity of the image. All images, indeed representations, are fabrications ("creations" and "constructions," to use Hayek's words) that can never claim for themselves a reliable relationship to reality, but must be content merely to serve as tokens within an ineffable process. The only legitimate political images are those that prove this point. The only legitimate political rhetoric is a rhetoric of transcendence.

That this particular neoliberal tokenization of the image was realized amid an era characterized by an explosion in image-technologies suggests that the "great persuasion" of neoliberalism may have drawn strength from the inflationary pressures, to use economic language, put on the image. Did its overproduction threaten its value? Like investors dumping dollars and running to gold, the retreat to the invisible and private has undeniably been a valuable ideological resource for the United States as a neoimperial power. A culture consumed with the image may also be a culture tired of the image, or at least dismissive of it. In suggesting that social and economic processes, let alone principles and values, cannot be penetrated by the image, neoliberalism offered the freedom of the ineffable as an alternative to the Burkean idea that freedom inheres in something sensible.

Similarly, the ascendency of neoliberalism (is it now in its descent?) cannot be divorced from the geopolitical culture of the past sixty-plus years. The proliferation of images and image-technologies in the 1950s was not simply a phenomenon of new, innovative means of media production: it was inseparable from the cultural and political efforts of the United States to create for the world an image of America. The project was doomed to crash in on itself: the dual weakness and power of the image meant that images could never do enough, even though—as at Little Rock—they could for some like Eisenhower do far too much. America, if it were to win the Cold War, would have to move beyond the image, a rhetorical strategy that Eisenhower and Reagan, more than any other Cold War presidents, perfected. Indeed, that Reagan, the Hollywood actor turned president, was more conditioned to image-logics than any other Cold War president enabled him to communicate what was beyond the image. Here was a president who believed in the capacity of images to evoke a realm of experience, feeling, and indeed life beyond representation—but not through the heroic iconicity of the big-screen star, but rather, in B-movie style, through a cumulative affect that interchangeable images can produce.[31]

Thus the paradox of the icon of an iconoclasm is in important respects resolved in the neoliberal imaginary. For if images are inadequate to meaning, and can be inauthentic and dangerous, neoliberalism has succeeded not only in displacing the political field of representation with the ineffable economic field of the market, but has conditioned us to tolerate *catastrophes that cannot be seen* as somehow more real, true, and authentic. September 11 was an important transition point here, for in it we were met with a catastrophe about which we had, or presumed to have, full information—even as it was happening "live." Here the images of the destruction of images, as spectacular as they were, were indeed tokens used to organize information about the new globalized world that much of the rest of the world had known for decades, but Americans had a hard time seeing. The information pointed to unseen lands in South Asia, the Middle East, and North Africa, and to an unseen force—terror. From such mysterious realms came America's great threat, and to such invisible places we would take the unrepresentable War on Terror.

But there was as yet an even more invisible catastrophe on the horizon— one that cost as much, if not more, in lives and livelihoods worldwide than has America's War on Terror: the Great Recession. The economic collapse of 2008 was seemingly saturated in data but immune to representation of the political or aesthetic sort. It was the product not only of invisible market forces but of that conspiracy to protect the ineffable that we know as neoliberalism. Indeed, there were no cameras present. I cannot tell you where I was in 2008 when the economy crashed. I did not see and could not hear the bubbles bursting. Lehman Brothers, Bear Stearns, and Goldman-Sachs offered no iconic public representatives—persons or objects—through which to be seen. They, like the ineffable market in which they participated and which they manipulated, worked in a realm beyond such representational recognition. And hence their fall was in important respects a sight unseen, though its reverberations were felt everywhere on the globe. Here we had found a point of authentic submission, submission to the unknown. Here we had become ready to, in Hayek's words, "submit to the products of the social process which nobody has designed and the reasons for which nobody may understand."[32]

Postscript and Acknowledgments

In discussing or circulating this work, I have been asked several times now what constructive alternative I might offer against the critique of the prior pages. This is a challenging request, largely because the critique I have offered is in a significant respect a critique of liberalism, and to offer an alternative to liberalism at the present time seems implausible and, even more, reckless. I am well aware of the fact—indisputable, I think—that the clearest alternatives to liberalism offered in the last century were not only no better, they were far worse. I do not want to appear like an ungrateful child before a good, if imperfect, parent. So, for the moment at least, I would say that I have no constructive alternative to offer beyond this: a liberalism tempered by the social-democratic norms of equity and equality, and even more by the civic-republican values of representation, citizenly virtue, and the responsibility of leaders to the people. Neoliberalism, as a social imaginary, projects a world where such norms, values, and virtues are, ideally, irrelevant to the successful functioning of society. When this social imaginary functions ideologically, it can and has become an insidious means of protecting the interests of wealth and power from public interests. To this I object most firmly. But the best alternative is, for now at least, but a tempered and justice-oriented liberalism.

This said, I do think that we would benefit a good deal from some educational alternatives, beginning with a revival of interest in the "art" of the liberal arts, and indeed of the sciences and engineering. The legitimation crises I have been addressing are, in their essence, crises in the status and significance of the image as a product of *art* or the *artificial*. We live in a curious moment where the artificial has at once become our taken-for-granted, perhaps even natural, future (whether we are talking about artificial life, artificial intelligence, or artificial implants) and one of the least studied and least valued subjects of the day. I work on a campus that values the arts, including the liberal arts, but does not seem to believe that ultimately they are really all that valuable to society—at least not if we measure the university's commitments by its faculty and capital expenditures. This trend does not seem likely to change, not in our neoliberal regnum, precisely because in that regnum art (*artes, technê*) is valued so slightly, and indeed—apart from a curious fascination with design—is held in quiet but powerful suspicion. The most radical thing I might say, then, is that we need a multidisciplinary school for the artificial in all of its aspects. This would include a substantive revival of the liberal arts.

Again, I risk looking ungrateful. In fact, I am very grateful to my university for the years it has generously supported my non-grant-generating work. This book would not exist apart from the support of the University of Illinois and my great colleagues in the Department of Communication. I want to especially thank Cara Finnegan, an outstanding thinker who took special time with the manuscript to offer, as always, insightful, sharp, but encouraging feedback. Numerous graduate students in the Department provided significant help on this project along the way (often funded by the Department of Communication): special thanks to Jillian Klean Zwilling, Marissa Bambrey Wolfe, Sabrina Marsh, Ian Hill, Rohini Singh, Courtney Caudle, and Mary Grace Hebert. My undergraduate student Joanna Chromik did crucial editorial work on the manuscript at a critical time. And Dave Tewksbury and John Caughlin have been very supportive departmental leaders, making my time at Illinois fruitful. A number colleagues at Illinois outside the department have been wind behind my sails, as the saying goes: Cliff Christians, Jon Ebel, Scott Althaus, and above all my co-conspirator at Illinois, Kevin Hamilton, who has been an intellectual partner and a dear friend. His conversations and collaboration pervade this work, especially its latter portions. Elsewhere at the University of Illinois, I received institutional support that contributed to this project from the Illinois Program in Research in Humanities, the Center for Advanced Study, and the Vice-Chancellor's Office for Research (thanks especially to the fantastic moral support of Nancy Ableman!). As I wrote this, I was working on a different project sponsored by the National Endowment for the Humanities, and that project very much informed this work.

My thinking about catastrophes in modern America, in fact, began some moons ago in graduate school, where Rosa Eberly, Tom Benson, Jorge Reina Schement, and Stephen Browne were remarkable mentors. My main disciplinary community, rhetorical studies, is full of amazing minds: thanks especially to Brandon Inabinet and Nathan Crick for long conversations about this project, and especially to Dave Tell—an amazing friend, conversation

partner, and fellow traveler. Katya Haskins has been a great disciplinary col-
league over these years—thanks Katya! Marty Medhurst has always been
there in the background, and sometimes the foreground, pushing me along
in my Cold War interests. Thanks Marty. Chad Wellmon at the University of
Virginia offered very helpful critical feedback on the manuscript at a crucial
time. Thanks Chad, and I will be coming back for more. Thanks also to Josh
Yates and Jay Tolson at Virginia for support and encouragement. Gary Mack
at the JFK Assassination Museum in Dallas aided me in finding some needed
research materials. Thanks also to the archivists at the Dwight D. Eisenhower
Library, the Truman Library, and the National Archives in College Park. I
suspect you are underpaid for your public service. I hope books like this serve
as a form of reward, if not compensation.

I owe and wish to give all kinds of thanks to Doug Mitchell and his com-
patriots Tim McGovern and Kyle Adam Wagner at the University of Chicago
Press. Doug's enthusiasm for this project came as somewhat of a surprise to
me, but it has kept me drumming when my arms were growing tired. Doug
secured a couple of amazing outside readers for the project. One has remained anonymous. To that reader I want to offer a hearty thank you and say
that you made this book substantially better. The other reader, I learned after
the fact, was Robert Hariman. Bob has been crucial to the progress of this
project in many ways, beginning when I first read his work some time back
and thought, "Gosh I want to be able to that!" Thanks, Bob, for being both a
critic and a champion.

Thanks also to the crew the Press brought together to produce this book.
Ashley Pierce has guided me through the art of publicity; Mary Corrado and
Nicholas Murray have artfully guided me through edits upon edits, proofs
upon proofs; and Brian Chartier has truly made visible the art of the book.

I live amid a number of downright good friends—some near, some far
off. They keep me writing as they keep me thinking and believing. They know
who they are. Here I just want tap out, as my message across the wire, "Thank
you! Friendship is shelter."

My kids have watched me grey a bit over the last several years, perhaps
attributing it to the stress their very active lives put on me. In fact, they keep
me young and restless. Thanks Graham, Will, and Mariclare. I love you each
very much and can't wait to see what God has in store for you, trusting that
whether it is pleasant, difficult, or just plain perplexing, you'll do well in it.
Finally, this book is dedicated to Linda for the very best reason there is: love.

Notes

Preface

1. Taylor, *Modern Social Imaginaries*, 23.

2. For cultural history on catastrophe in America and Europe, see Rozario, *Culture of Calamity*; Biel, *American Disasters*; Hoffman and Oliver-Smith, *Catastrophe & Culture*; Huet, *Culture of Disaster*.

3. For historiographical material on neoliberalism, see Harvey, *Brief History of Neoliberalism*; Steger, *Neoliberalism*; Burgin, *Great Persuasion*; Mirowski and Plehwe, *Road from Mont Pèlerin*.

4. See Friedman, "Neo-Liberalism."

5. Mirzoeff, *Right to Look*.

Introduction

1. Baudrillard, "Spirit of Terrorism."

2. White, *Content of the Form*.

3. Baudrillard, "Spirit of Terrorism."

4. Thus these disasters may, with some qualification, be called artificial disasters as opposed to natural ones. Of course, the latter are never wholly natural, shaped as they are by human artifice—whether it be building construction or the culture of political communities. Nevertheless, the disasters I am concerned with in this book—these where-were-you-when? events—are characterized by a conspicuous artificiality (in the sense of *artifice*): both the object of destruction and the means of its destruction are manifestly artificial. And as we will see, neoliberal theory, too, was concerned with the artificial.

5. Rozario, *Culture of Calamity*, 136–38.

6. Weaver, *Language Is Sermonic*, 88.

7. Ibid., 100.

8. Ibid., 211.

9. Ibid., 105–9.

10. Rodgers, *Age of Fracture*, 24.

11. Ibid., 25.

12. Jameson, "Postmodernism"; Jameson, *Postmodernism*.

13. Jameson, *Postmodernism*, 6.

14. Longinus, *On the Sublime*, sec. 36.

15. Borgerhoff, *Freedom of French Classicism*, ix.

16. Thus Rozario argues that the idea of "creative destruction" is central to the cultural significance of disasters in America. See Rozario, *Culture of Calamity*, 3, 17–18, 26.

17. Rozario, *Culture of Calamity*, 10, 20.

18. Lippmann, *Inquiry*, 174.

19. Burgin, *Great Persuasion*, 186–214. Friedman used "radical liberal" to describe his own economic philosophy; see Burgin, 176–77.

20. In addition to Burgin, Daniel Stedman Jones has offered a very helpful account of the persuasive efforts of leading neoliberals, including Hayek and Friedman. See his *Masters of the Universe*.

21. Steger, *Neoliberalism*, 11.

22. Hayek and Mises, of course, have long been treated by their champions more as representatives of a social philosophy than of a strict economic theory. But not until relatively recently have scholars begun to unpack the intellectual lineages of the movement. Intellectual histories include Burgin, *Great Persuasion*; Caldwell, *Hayek's Challenge*; Jones, *Masters of the Universe*.

23. Lippmann, *Inquiry*, 19.

24. Ibid., 22.

25. Ibid., 24.

26. Ibid., ix.

27. Ibid., 20.

28. Harvey, *Brief History of Neoliberalism*, 12–13.

29. Boorstin, *The Image*, xiii.

30. McLuhan, *Understanding Media*, 294–95.

31. Ibid., 294.

32. Simpson, *Under the Hammer*, chap. 1.

33. "Modern Art Was CIA 'Weapon.'"

34. Ibid.

35. Simpson, *Under the Hammer*, 28. In chapter 1, Simpson offers a fine meditation on the relationship between abstract expressionism, iconoclasm, and America's Cold War.

36. Taylor, *Modern Social Imaginaries*, 23.

37. Brown, "American Nightmare."

38. The rhetoric of economics is now a well-trod field. For some foundational work, see Klamer, McCloskey, and Snow, eds., *Consequences of Economic Rhetoric*; McCloskey, *Rhetoric of Economics*; Aune, *Selling the Free Market*.

39. Harvey, *Brief History of Neoliberalism*, 3.

40. Rozario, *Culture of Calamity*, 85.

41. Ibid., 24.

42. For the connection between providential processes and social processes, see Milbank, *Theology and Social Theory*.

43. Schumpeter, *Capitalism, Socialism, and Democracy*.

44. Ankersmit, *Aesthetic Politics*, 23.

45. Ibid., 92–93, 94, 99.

46. Ibid., 32–34, 45–48.

47. On the historical connection of the Austrian school of economics to game theory, see Kelly, "Mises, Morgenstern, Hoselitz, and Nash."

48. Burke, *Rhetoric of Motives*, 22–23.

49. Ibid., 22.

50. Mitchell, *Cloning Terror*, 60.

51. Lyotard, *Postmodern Condition*, 81.

52. On neoliberalism and game theory see Kelly, "Mises, Morgenstern, Hoselitz, and Nash."

53. Venturi, *Learning from Las Vegas*, 50.

54. Friedman, "Methodology of Positive Economics," 43.

Chapter One

1. Fraser, "Crossing the Color Line," 234; Goldzwig and Dionisopolous, "Crisis at Little Rock," 190.

2. Eisenhower, "President's News Conference."

3. Eisenhower, "Executive Order 10730."

4. Eisenhower, "Radio and Television Address."

5. DeLuca and Peeples, "From Public Sphere to Public Screen"; Taylor, "Politics of Recognition."

6. Allen, *Talking to Strangers*, 21.

7. Arendt, "Reflections on Little Rock," 198.

8. Eisenhower, "Radio and Television Address."

9. Osgood, *Total Cold War*.

10. James Simpson discusses Eisenhower's advocacy of abstract American art during the Cold War, arguing that such art "offered the perfect aesthetic response, by way of diametrical opposition, to Soviet Realism" (see Simpson, *Under the Hammer*, 28). There's no question that such Cold War oppositions played a role in a more general suspicion of the image in Eisenhower's Cold War. What interests me here, however, is not the suspicion itself but its ideological resources within the liberal tradition.

11. Chomsky, *Profit over People*; Harvey, *Brief History of Neoliberalism*; Harvey, *Condition of Postmodernity*; Jameson, "Postmodernism"; McChesney, Meiksins Wood, and Foster, eds., *Capitalism and the Information Age*; Steger, *Neoliberalism*.

12. Habermas, *Legitimation Crisis*.

13. Ibid., 70.

14. Ibid.

15. Ibid.

16. Ibid., 73, 75.

17. Ibid., 73.

18. Friedland and Alford, "Bringing Society Back In," 234.

19. Pollitt, "Bureaucracies Remember," 199–200.

20. Margaret Thatcher, "Interview for *Woman's Own*." So too in *The Fatal Conceit: The Errors of Socialism*, Hayek claimed that the word *social*, used in its adjectival sense to qualify nouns ranging from *justice* to *order* and *good* was, quoting Charles Curran, a "semantic fraud" (Hayek, *Fatal Conceit*, 118). For Friedrich Hayek's direct influence upon Thatcher, see Ranelagh, *Thatcher's People* (e.g., ix, 174–76).

21. My account here relies on that in Burgin, *Great Persuasion*, 87–90. Bruce Caldwell also provides a helpful overview of its publication history in his introduction to the 2007 edition of *The Road to Serfdom* published by the University of Chicago Press.

22. Burgin, *Great Persuasion*, 89.

23. From the condensed version of Hayek's *Road to Serfdom* as it appeared in the April 1945 edition of *Reader's Digest*, 45.

24. Ibid., 36.

25. Hayek, *Road to Serfdom*, 104.

26. The *Look* version of *The Road to Serfdom* was published in February 1945. It can be accessed at http://www.mises.org/books/TRTS/.

27. Caldwell, "Introduction," 32.

28. Ibid.

29. Hayek, *Constitution of Liberty*, 107.

30. Ibid., 108.

31. This phrase appears often in *The Road to Serfdom* (e.g., 73).

32. Hayek, *Confusion of Language*, 10–11.

33. Ibid.

34. Wolin, *Politics and Vision*, 305. Of course, the great eighteenth-century French champion of natural society was Jean-Jacques Rousseau. Hayek, however, departed from Rousseau in that the former had a decidedly positive view of progress, property, law, and so on, in contrast with Rousseau's skeptical view of such features of developed civilization.

35. Hayek, *Constitution of Liberty*, 57.

36. Ibid.; Friedman, "Neo-Liberalism," 7.

37. See Hayek, *Economic Freedom*.

38. Hayek, *Confusion of Language*, 16; emphasis added.

39. Hayek, *Road to Serfdom*, 139.

40. Ibid., 73.

41. Ibid., 72.

42. Habermas, *Communication*, 178; Hayek, *Road to Serfdom*, 134.

43. Hayek, *Road to Serfdom*, 95.

44. Friedman, "Methodology of Positive Economics," 15.

45. Ibid., 23.

46. Ibid., 35.

47. Hayek, *Road to Serfdom*, 102.

48. Schumpeter, *Capitalism, Socialism, and Democracy*, 83.

49. Habermas, *Communication*, 179; Hayek, *Individualism and Economic Order*, 8.

50. Habermas, *Communication*, 179.

51. See Rawls, *Theory of Justice*, esp. 4–11, 48–54, 73–78.

52. For a helpful comparison/contrast of Rawls and Hayek (one that takes a slightly different approach than I do), see Lister, "'Mirage' of Social Justice."

53. Habermas, *Communication*, 179.

54. Salazar, "Rhetoric Achieves Nature," 81.

55. Ankersmit, *Aesthetic Politics*, 28.

56. Ankersmit, *Political Representation*, 2; Ankersmit, *Aesthetic Politics*, 28, 45.

57. Ankersmit, *Aesthetic Politics*, 53.

58. Ibid., 28.

59. Ibid., 46.

60. Ibid., 45–51.

61. Mitchell, *What Do Pictures Want?* xiii.

62. For a fascinating psychological account of the problem, see Hayek, *Sensory Order*.

63. See Friedman, "Methodology of Positive Economics."

64. Ibid., 24–25.

65. Mirzoeff, *Watching Babylon*, 68.

66. Tully, *Strange Multiplicity*, 135.

67. Urbinati and Warren, "Concept of Representation," 388, 392.

68. Stout, *Democracy and Tradition*.

69. It is for this same reason that secrecy is so harmful to a democracy and that history (including journalism) is so crucial to democratic health. As Frank Ankersmit writes in his profound defense of historical narration, "Secrecy is a great evil in forms of knowledge having a public function. . . . Public debate is, to a large extent, a discussion of what is good and evil for a democratic society. Thanks to its incompatibility with secrecy, history offers a better platform for such a discussion than any other discipline. However, it will never give us certainty; history will always give us mere opinions, *doxai* that are only 'probable' in the Aristotelian sense. Certainty in this domain can be achieved only at the price of abandoning publicity for secrecy" (Ankersmit, *Political Representation*, 34). Here we should remember that *doxa* in Aristotle's day referred not only to "opinion" but to "appearance," even "glory." This conjunction of opinion and appearance is at the heart of democratic health. Without *both* there simply is no platform for public debate.

70. Hobbes, *Man and Citizen*, 227.

71. See Hobbes, *Leviathan*, 13–31.

72. See O'Gorman, "Hobbes."

73. Hariman and Lucaites, *No Caption Needed*, 3.

74. Fraser, "Identity, Exclusion, and Critique," 313–14.

75. Hariman and Lucaites, *No Caption Needed*, 39–48.

76. Nietzsche, "On Truth and Lies," 116.

77. Ibid., 116–18.

Chapter Two

1. Colomina, *Domesticity at War*, 239.

2. Newman, "Sublime Is Now," 553.

3. Rozario, *Culture of Calamity*, 136.

4. Fousek, *To Lead the Free World*, 26–27.

5. Eisenhower, "Annual Message."

6. Whitfield, *Culture of the Cold War*, 91.

7. Almost every historical discussion of iconoclasm, including Karlstadt's, cites as foundational the Mosaic prohibition in Exodus 20. The prohibition troubled the Christian church as early as the third century CE, when theologians like Tertullian and Origen warned against the use of images in piety, fully cognizant, as they were, of the role of images in the emperor cult (see Mangrum and Scavizzi, "Introduction: The Debate on Images," 5). Their ideas reverberated through the iconoclastic controversies of eighth- and ninth-century Byzantium (contributing to the split between Rome and Constantinople), controversies that were in many respects inaugurated from outside the Christian Church—which had, despite the efforts of Tertullian and Origen, reorganized the emperor cult into a rich material piety. In 721, Caliph Yazid II issued an edict prohibiting the use of images in worship for Christians and Muslims alike (Jews already stood as witnesses against such practices). Some sixty years after the Caliph's edict, John of Jerusalem, in defense of images, argued at the Second Council of Nicaea (787) that Yazid II's prohibitions were

those of a "sinful tyrant" who "stripped the Churches of God unsparingly," and, more broadly, that the subsequent iconoclastic politics of Christian emperors were the result of the theological and political impurities brought by Jews and Muslims (Barnard, *Background of the Iconoclastic Controversy*, 17). John of Jerusalem thus argued that the iconoclastic Christian bishops of the eighth-century had been led astray by exposure to the iconoclastic thinking of the Muslims and Jews—a view that went on to reverberate in modern historiography of the period, which sometimes placed blame for the iconoclastic controversies of eighth- and ninth-century Byzantium on "the influence of Oriental ideas alien to the Byzantine tradition" (1). The Byzantine church ended up reinstating the use of images in piety and reasserting imperial authority, positing—as I discuss above—a subtle distinction between the legitimate use of icons and the illegitimate use of idols (Freedburg, "European and Byzantine Iconoclasm," 167).

8. Karlstadt, "Removal of Images," 22–23; emphasis added.

9. *Oxford English Dictionary*, 2nd ed. (1989), s.v. "icon"; online version: http://www.oed.com .proxy2.library.uiuc.edu/Entry /90879>. (First published in *New English Dictionary*, 1899.)

10. Eire, *War Against the Idols*, 2.

11. Mitchell, *Iconology*, 1–2; Mondzain, *Image, Icon, Economy*, 12–13, 66; Simpson, *Under the Hammer*, 22–23.

12. Or, as Mitchell writes, pictures "want." See Mitchell, *What Do Pictures Want?* xv.

13. Besançon, *Forbidden Image*, 149. Besançon writes of Gregory: "The image is rhetorical in the strong sense. It persuades, it instructs, it moves, it pleases. It counsels (deliberative mode), it accuses or defends (legal mode), it praises or blames (epideictic mode): the categories of Ciceronian rhetoric perfectly apply to Gregory's program" (150). The arguments of the Byzantine iconodules, and of Pseudo-Dionysius and Bonaventure in Latin Christianity, who "wanted the image to be a rung in the ladder allowing the soul to move from the material to the spiritual sphere," too can be found well within the rhetorical tradition, from Plato's *Phaedrus* to Longinus's *Peri Hypsous* (Besançon 150; see also 154–57). For a discussion of participation versus instrumentalism in theories of the icon, see Besançon, *Forbidden Image*, 96–123.

14. Besançon, *Forbidden Image*, 123 (see also 66).

15. Plato ascribed something like inauthenticity to sensible images, and to be sure, after Plato, "all the enemies of the image will employ Platonic arguments" (ibid., 36). But, as Besançon suggests, the Platonic charge of inauthenticity may be directed toward a form of iconophilia, as it "completely justifies man's desire to contemplate divine beauty" in its claim that sensible images are inauthentic representations of the divine (36).

16. Renaissance humanists like Erasmus also worried that the arts, because they were divine in origin, might be taken *as* divine. Thus humanists drew careful distinctions between the inner and outer, the representation and the represented, and spirit and matter. On the important role of Erasmus in these distinctions, see Eire, *War Against the Idols*, 28–53. However, for radical reformers, their more moderate counterparts, and humanists alike, the question of images and their destruction returned relentlessly to anxieties about subservience and lordship, and freedom and authority, and thus was inseparable from questions about the broader character of sociopolitical order. On Erasmus's opposition to images, see Eire, *War Against the Idols*. That the removal of images from churches in the Reformation was a delicate *political* matter is seen in Melanchthon's reticence to pursue such a policy, worried as he was that such actions would alienate political powers from the reformers (see Mangrum and Scavizzi, "Introduction," 10–11). Of the interconnectedness of religious and political motivations for European iconoclasm of the sixteenth and seventeenth centuries, David Freedberg has written that though iconoclasm

was framed theologically, it "almost always had a significant political dimension" (Freedburg, "European and Byzantine Iconoclasm," 167).

17. Wandel, *Voracious Idols*, 26. For an argument for the inevitable connection between Calvinistic theology and a politically motivated iconoclasm, see Eire, *War Against the Idols*, 279–304.

18. Ankersmit, *Aesthetic Politics*, 28.

19. Anderson, *Imagined Communities*, 6.

20. On Virginia's Natural Bridge and the new American nationalism, see Nye, *American Technological Sublime*, 17–33. For a fascinating and insightful reading of the iconicity of the "Times Square Kiss," see Hariman and Lucaites, *No Caption Needed*, 67–87.

21. Hariman and Lucaites, *No Caption Needed*, 39–40.

22. Simpson, *Under the Hammer*, 11, 120.

23. Eire, *War Against the Idols*, 2.

24. Here I refer the reader to the expansive sense of political representation in Ankersmit, *Political Representation*, which does not shy away even from the aesthetic.

25. Besançon, *Forbidden Image*, 209.

26. Shelley, *Literary and Scientific Men of France*, 288.

27. Brody, *Boileau and Longinus*, 85.

28. Burke, *Philosophical Enquiry*, 44.

29. Ibid., 53, 59–65.

30. Ibid., 62.

31. Ibid., 112.

32. Ankersmit, *Aesthetic Politics*, 46, 53, 119–20.

33. Burke, *Reflections*, 77.

34. A reading of Burke's *Enquiry* that pursues themes similar to those that I do here appears in Mitchell, *Iconology*, 116–49, 165–66. Mitchell stresses that Burke seems to want to reserve the artificial, or artistic, sublime for verbal arts, despairing, for example, of the potential for painting to achieve the sublime (126). Nevertheless, Burke's nonartificial sublime remains intensely oriented toward the visual field, and very much sets the standard for sublimity more generally. Verbal arts are more suited to its artificial achievement only because they have the unique artistic capacity for creating intensities of associations that defy any *clear* (visual) representation without appearing forced or as the products of mere artifice (as Burke believes that painting tends to do).

35. Kant, *Observations*.

36. This suggestion is not a mere trick based on a clever rhyme. The nominalization of *divine*, Besançon reminds us (following Werner Jaeger), seems to have originated with Anaximander, who used it to describe a central abstraction, the *archê*, the limitless first principle of the cosmos (see *Forbidden Image*, 19). Thus, when Kant replaces the divine with the sublime, he participates in this tradition of interchanging philosophical abstractions and theological concepts.

37. Kant, *Critique of Judgment*, 83.

38. Ibid., 84.

39. Ibid., 83.

40. Ibid., §26, §27, and §39.

41. Ibid., 108; emphasis in original.

42. Ibid., 101; emphasis added.

43. Ibid., 46.

44. Ibid., 102.

45. Ibid., 103.

46. Ibid., 49.

47. Burke, *Philosophical Enquiry*, 62.

48. Anderson, *Imagined Communities*.

49. Kant, *Critique of Judgment*, 115. This passage can be read alongside Kant's "An Answer to the Question: What Is Enlightenment?" which gives a fuller picture of Kant's notion of political maturation. The essay appears in Kant, *Perpetual Peace*.

50. Here Kant, as I discuss further below, is following Rousseau, who in *On the Social Contract* argues that "the general will" is the only possible resolution to the political problem of representation: "Find a form of association that defends and protects the person and goods of each associate with all the common force, and by means of which each one, uniting with all, nevertheless obeys only himself and remains as free as before" (Rousseau, *On the Social Contract*, translated by Judith Masters, 53). Any *symbolic* solution to the problem, Rousseau argues, needs to be strictly subordinated to the idea of the general will, consistent with Rousseau's generally ambivalent attitude toward material culture.

51. Kant, *Critique of Judgment*, 115; emphasis added.

52. For the broader iconoclastic tendencies of the Enlightenment, see Simpson, *Under the Hammer*, 11 and 116.

53. Burke, *Philosophical Enquiry*, 62; emphasis added.

54. Kant, *Critique of Judgment*, 121; emphases added. The phrase "*species finalis accepta, non data*" is glossed as "The appearance of finality is assigned, not given" by Guyer in Kant, *Critique of the Power of Judgment*, 161.

55. Rousseau, *Social Contract*, 135.

56. Thus Rousseau writes of the Sovereign, "While it can compel no one to believe them [the articles of the civil profession of faith], it can banish from the State whoever does not believe them—it can banish him, not for impiety, but as an anti-social being, incapable of truly loving the laws and justice, and of sacrificing, at need, his life to his duty. If any one, after publicly recognising these dogmas, behaves as if he does not believe them, let him be punished by death: he has committed the worst of all crimes, that of lying before the law" (ibid.).

57. Ibid., 23–26, 55.

58. Ibid.

59. Wills, *Lincoln at Gettysburg*, 90.

60. Wilson, *American Sublime*.

61. Nye, *American Technological Sublime*, 24.

62. Bellah, "Civil Religion in America," 3.

63. Ibid., 12.

64. See Bellah, "Civil Religion in America by Robert N. Bellah." Online at http://www.robertbellah.com/articles_5.htm.

65. See O'Gorman, *Spirits of the Cold War*, chap. 4.

66. Bellah, "Civil Religion in America," 17.

67. Eisenhower, "Farewell Radio and Television Address."

68. Ibid.

69. Ibid.

70. As Joe Kennedy said in an interview just before Jack's 1960 presidential campaign began, "Jack is the greatest attraction in the country today. I'll tell you how to sell more copies of a book. Put his picture on the cover. Why is it that when his picture is on the cover of *Life* or *Redbook* they sell a record number of copies? You advertise the fact that he will be at a dinner and you

will break all records for attendance. He can draw more people to a fundraising dinner than Cary Grant or Jimmy Stewart. Why is that? He has more universal appeal" (quoted in Lubin, *Shooting Kennedy*, 6.).

71. Boorstin, *The Image.*

Chapter Three

1. Lubin, *Shooting Kennedy*, 1–2.

2. Ibid., 1, 4, 15.

3. Kennedy, *Inaugural Address.*

4. Zelizer, *Covering the Body*, 129.

5. Sontag, "Image-World," 351.

6. Charney, "In a Moment," 281.

7. Ibid., 287, 290, 292.

8. Ibid., 292.

9. Ibid., 290.

10. Thompson, *Six Seconds in Dallas*, 6.

11. Thompson, "Oral History Interview," 15.

12. Charney, "In a Moment," 292.

13. Black, "Secrecy and Disclosure," 135.

14. Ibid.

15. Fetzer, *Great Zapruder Film Hoax.*

16. Others have been unable to learn this as well. For example, Gary Mack, curator at the Sixth Floor Museum in Dallas, told me that not even Richard Stolley, the *Life* editor who acquired the film from Zapruder, knows who made the editorial decisions for the issue. I had the opportunity to speak with Stolley on November 14, 2013, on a radio program where he was a guest, and I a caller. He confirmed that he did not know who made the editorial decisions, but said that the decision-making group certainly would have included high-level *Life* executives, including not only Jackson but also Henry Luce himself. The radio program is available at https://will.illinois.edu /focus/program/the-day-kennedy-died-a-conversation-with-former-life-editor-richard-stolley.

17. Zapruder, *Image of an Assassination.*

18. For an account of Jackson's propagandistic style, see chapter 3 of my *Spirits of the Cold War.*

19. Like many other Americans, my mother preserved the issue in a sturdy box.

20. After *Life* extracted the thirty-one frames from the Zapruder film, it was put in a safe. The action may have expressed more than journalistic paternalism. *Life* clearly was interested in protecting its market from the intrusion of television. Print media in general at this time saw television as an awkward, unprofessional, and obnoxious intruder in their business. A few months before Kennedy's assassination, the International Press Institute formally refused to admit radio and television reporters into their society, arguing that they were not "bona fide journalists" (Zelizer, *Covering the Body*, 27). The professional tension was exasperated by television's growing importance in American life. By the summer of 1960, 88 percent of American homes had television sets (27). Kennedy himself had helped turn the nation toward television, converting his press conference room to a television set (28).

21. Lubin, *Shooting Kennedy.*

22. Horkheimer and Adorno, *Dialectic of Enlightenment*, 248.

23. Kant, *Critique of Judgment*, sec. 28, 102.

24. Battersby, "Stages on Kant's Way"; Freeman, *Feminine Sublime*; Yeager, "The 'Language of Blood'"; Zylinska, *On Spiders*.

25. Battersby, "Stages on Kant's Way," 229.

26. Horkheimer and Adorno, *Dialectic of Enlightenment*, 248.

27. "Assassination of President Kennedy," 24. Zelizer also notes how the text does not refer to the amateur source for the photos. She argues that this silence was motivated by a desire on the part of *Life* to prop the authority and credibility of journalists, who, by failing to shoot any images of their own, had missed "the scoop" (Zelizer, *Covering the Body*, 68–69).

28. Zapruder, *Image of an Assassination* (interview with Phil Chamberlain).

29. "Assassination of President Kennedy," 23.

30. Ibid.

31. Ibid.

32. Ibid.

33. Ibid.

34. Ibid.

35. Ibid.

36. Holton, ed., "Mass Culture and Mass Media"; Kornhauser, *Politics of Mass Society*; Mills, *Power Elite*; Shils, "Theory of Mass Society"; Stillman and Pfaff, *Politics of Hysteria*.

37. Canetti, *Crowds and Power*, 15.

38. Ibid., 15–16.

39. Ibid., 237.

40. Ibid., 248.

41. Ibid., 255.

42. Ibid., 248.

43. Ibid., 254.

44. Holland, "After Thirty Years," 191.

45. U.S. President's Commission, *Report of the Warren Commission*, 4.

46. Ibid., 19.

47. Ibid., 100.

48. Ibid.

49. Ibid.

50. Ibid., 110.

51. Holland, "After Thirty Years," 192.

52. Farrell, "Sizing Things Up," 6. See also Farrell, "Love and Theft After 9/11."

53. Rivera, *Good Night America*.

54. Wrone, *Zapruder Film*, 69.

55. Ibid., 65.

56. Scott, *Deep Politics*, 6–7.

57. Kant, *Critique of Judgment*, sec. 29, 116.

58. Rivera, *Good Night America*.

59. I would hardly claim that *Good Night America*'s appeal to an affective ground through which to experience American nationhood was novel. To the contrary, it is arguably as old as the rise of American nationhood itself. Robert A. Ferguson, in *Law and Letters in American Culture*, locates one of its origins in the oratory of Daniel Webster, which he claims influentially articulated "an emotional basis for national identification" and thus challenged a republican identity premised on "intellectual right" (231). What is distinctive about *Good Night America*, and the 1970s in the United States more generally, is the darkness of the emotional basis—*Good Night*

America suggests that conspiracy rhetoric in this period was less about accounting for the parts and whole of a disordered Cold War state and more about creating ominous affective national ties, dark sentiments, across desperate groups of people feeling disenfranchised by the Cold War state. See Ferguson, *Law and Letters in American Culture*, chap. 8.

60. Elshtain, *Limits of Politics*, 5.

61. Taylor, *Sources of the Self*, 374; Taylor, *Hegel*, chap. 1.

62. See Taylor, *Ethics of Authenticity*.

63. Rivera, *Good Night America*.

64. Ibid.

65. Sontag, "Image-World," 355.

66. I realize that in addressing the function of conspiracy theory, I am touching upon a robust scholarly literature, and that I hardly do justice to it here. The most influential study, of course, has been Richard Hofstadter's *The Paranoid Style in American Politics*. Two important recent corrections of (as well as complements to) Hofstadter's argument are Goldberg, *Enemies Within*, and Pfau, *Political Style of Conspiracy*.

67. Burke, *Philosophy of Literary Form*, 52.

68. Medhurst, "Oliver Stone's *JFK*," 140–41.

69. Stone and Sklar, *JFK*.

70. Ibid.

71. Medhurst, "Oliver Stone's *JFK*," 135.

72. Ibid., 134.

73. Stone and Sklar, *JFK*.

74. Ibid.

75. Cavell, *Pursuits of Happiness*.

76. Plato, *Symposium*, 210e, 211b.

77. Habermas, *Legitimation Crisis*, 70.

78. Jameson, *Postmodernism*, 355.

79. MacIntyre, *After Virtue*, 31.

Chapter Four

1. Upon entering office, Eisenhower's National Security Council initially accepted Robert Oppenheimer's recommendation that the administration adopt "a policy of candor toward the American people by revealing fully the dangers engendered by the atomic arms race" (quoted in Tudda, *Truth Is Our Weapon*, 57). But it did not take long for the administration to transform this would-be policy of candor into a means of sending the Soviets a message regarding the destructive power of America's nuclear arsenal. For more on Operation Candor, see Chernus, *Eisenhower's Atoms for Peace*; and Hewlett and Holl, *Atoms for Peace*.

2. Nye, *American Technological Sublime*, 226.

3. "Missile and Satellite Hearings."

4. Snead, *Gaither Committee*, 80.

5. Mieczkowski, *Eisenhower's Sputnik Moment*, 140.

6. McDougall, *Heavens and the Earth*, 7.

7. Turner, *Frontier in American History*, 2.

8. Ibid., 2.

9. Ibid., 3.

10. Ibid., 1.

11. Jameson, *Postmodernism*, xx.

12. Nixon, "Address to the Nation."

13. Locke, *Two Treatises of Government*, para. 184.

14. Bush, *Science, the Endless Frontier*.

15. Osgood, *Total Cold War*, 323.

16. Ibid., 328; see pp. 323–53 for an excellent account of the propaganda dimensions of the early US-USSR space race.

17. Ibid., 332.

18. Ibid.

19. Trento, *Prescription for Disaster*, 4–6.

20. Young, Silcock, and Dunn, *Journey to Tranquility*, 90–91.

21. Kennedy, "Special Message," 9.

22. Mindell, *Digital Apollo*, 258–59.

23. Ibid., 12.

24. Ibid.

25. Young, Silcock, and Dunn, *Journey to Tranquility*, 158.

26. Bush, *Science, the Endless Frontier*.

27. See Prelinger, *Another Science Fiction*.

28. Kennedy, "Special Message," 9.

29. Patterson, *Grand Expectations*, 453.

30. Jasanoff, *The Fifth Branch*, 3.

31. Ibid.

32. Reagan, "Inaugural Address."

33. Jameson, *Postmodernism*, 84.

34. Reagan, "Inaugural Address."

35. Jameson, *Postmodernism*, 78.

36. Williams, *Television*.

37. Rogin, *Ronald Reagan, the Movie*, 3, 7. Rogin notes that even Reagan's near death by assassination was thoroughly embedded in this conflation between movies and reality. "As confirming evidence of [Reagan's own conviction of] the power of film, John W. Hinckley Jr., imitating the plot of the movie *Taxi Driver*, deliberately shot the president on the day of the Academy Awards [at which Reagan was going to make a taped appearance]. Obsessed with *Taxi Driver*, Hinckley had seen it repeatedly and had cast himself in the role of its isolated, deranged, and violent protagonist. Like the character played by Robert De Niro, Hinckley became a gun freak. Like him, he determined to win the woman he loved—Jodie Foster—by assassinating a political leader" (3).

38. Rodgers, *Age of Fracture*, 32.

39. Ibid., 33.

40. Ibid., 32.

41. Rogin, *Ronald Reagan, the Movie*, 8.

42. Jameson, *Postmodernism*, 18.

43. Williams, *Television*, 86–96.

44. Rodgers, *Age of Fracture*, 34.

45. Reagan, "Inaugural Address."

46. Reagan, "Farewell Address."

47. Jasinski, "Antithesis and Oxymoron," 122.

48. Ibid., 128.

49. Kant, *Critique of Judgment*, sec. 25, 88; his emphasis.

50. Reagan, "Remarks During a Visit."

51. Kant, *Critique of Judgment*.

52. Reagan, "Remarks at the Johnson Space Center."

53. Ritter and Henry, *Ronald Reagan*, 4.

54. Mister, "Reagan's Challenger Tribute"; Ritter and Henry, *Ronald Reagan*.

55. Auer, "Acting Like a President," 119.

56. Noonan, *What I Saw*, 255–56.

57. Keyworth, "The Future of Space," 26.

58. Ibid.

59. Ibid., 28.

60. Noonan, *What I Saw*, 255.

61. Reagan, "Space Shuttle *Challenger*."

62. Ibid.

63. Noonan, *What I Saw*, 255–56.

64. Rousseau, *Social Contract*, 177.

65. Ankersmit, *Aesthetic Politics*, 92–93; O'Gorman, "Aristotle's Phantasia."

66. Reagan, "Space Shuttle *Challenger*."

67. Ibid.

68. Ibid.

69. Reagan, "Space Shuttle *Challenger*."

70. Noonan, *What I Saw*, 262.

71. Reagan, "Space Shuttle Challenger."

72. Ibid.

73. Hariman and Lucaites, *No Caption Needed*, 255.

74. Ibid., 244.

75. Rogin, *Ronald Reagan, the Movie*, 7.

76. Arendt, *Human Condition*, 2.

Chapter Five

1. "New monumentality" refers to the thesis (or mere suggestion?) of Robert Venturi, De-nise Scott Brown, and Steven Izenour that the future of architecture lay in the displacement of the "old monumentality" of big, high, open spaces with "low, glittering-in-the-dark, enclosed mazes and alcoves," as in Las Vegas. See Venturi, Brown, and Izenour, *Learning from Las Vegas*, 55. Frederic Jameson proclaimed Venturi's book a "manifesto" for the postmodern (Jameson, *Postmodernism*, 2).

2. Giuliani, "9/11 Speech."

3. Ibid.

4. Ibid.

5. Office of Public Affairs, "Fact Sheet."

6. Bush, "Strikes Against Al Qaida."

7. Bush, "Terrorist Attacks of September 11."

8. Anderson, *Imagined Communities*, 7.

9. Friedman, *World Is Flat*.

10. See Bolter and Grusin, *Remediation*.

11. See Jameson, *Postmodernism*, 355; Zelizer, *Covering the Body*.

12. The phrase "prodigious . . . display of synchronicity" is from Jameson, *Postmodernism*, 355.

13. All quotations were transcribed by the author from video recordings of the CNN television broadcast anchored by Aaron Brown and Judy Woodruff, US edition, September 11, 2001. Hereafter cited as CNN broadcast, September 11. They were verified at http://edition.cnn.com /TRANSCRIPTS/0109/11.html.

14. CNN broadcast, September 11.

15. Tsang, *The Sublime*, 41.

16. Jameson, *Postmodernism*, 6, 34–37.

17. Reynolds and Barnett, "'America Under Attack,'" 92.

18. A different historical frame that might have been invoked is Hiroshima. In the days after September 11 a few comparisons to Hiroshima were drawn in the media, as it clearly had distinct visual parallels with the World Trade Center attacks; and the term *ground zero* was consistent with the vocabulary of atomic warfare. However, the collective memory of Hiroshima in the United States is one of last-resort means and bears a sense of shame. Moreover, it lacks the phoenix-like form of Pearl Harbor. Thus, despite its vivid visual resemblance, Hiroshima was not invoked as a frame for historical perspective in CNN's coverage.

19. Clausewitz et al., *On War*.

20. This typological distinction between iconic and iconoclastic cultures is pursued as well, and with great insight, by James Simpson in *Under the Hammer*.

21. Bodnar, *Remaking America*.

22. CNN broadcast, September 11.

23. See Hediger and Vonderau, *Films That Work*; for a look into this postwar world, see Congrès international de photographie et cinématographie, "Photographie et cinématographie"; International Congress on High-Speed Photography, *Proceedings*.

24. Of course, film is a receptive medium (of light and chemicals), but film, as Sontag argued, receives in order to possess—it is, we might say, informed, and thus ends in a discrete image or piece of information that in turn needs to be made "part of a system of information, fitted into schemes of classification and storage" (Sontag, *On Photography*, 156.). The information network transforms all inputs into data, most typically in the forms of ones and zeros. Here again we come to a flatness, a reduction (and indeed a kind of destruction) of things to their most generic informational bits and pieces. Thus Steven Harnad can write of computation what cannot quite be written of film:

> Computation is interpretable symbol manipulation. Symbols are objects that are manipulated on the basis of rules operating only on the symbols' shapes, which are arbitrary in relation to what they can be interpreted as meaning. Even if one accepts the Church/Turing Thesis that computation is unique, universal and very near omnipotent, not everything is a computer, because not everything can be given a systematic interpretation; and certainly everything can't be given every systematic interpretation. But even after computers and computation have been successfully distinguished from other kinds of things, mental states will not just be the implementations of the right symbol systems, because of the symbol grounding problem: The interpretation of a symbol system is not intrinsic to the system; it is projected onto it by the interpreter. This is not true of our thoughts." (Harnad, "Computation," [http://cogprints.org/1592/1/harnad94 .computation.cognition.html; accessed April 11, 2012].)

25. Manovich, *Language of New Media*, 56.

26. CNN broadcast, September 11.

27. Ibid.

28. Ibid.

29. Siegel, "In Hollywood Style."

30. Deggans, "Mayhem Unfolded in Waves," 18.

31. Laurence, "Television," 12.

32. Saunders, "TV Captured Unfolding Terror," 50.

33. Ostrow, "TV Coverage Seeks Balance," A4.

34. Pease, *New American Exceptionalism*, chap. 5.

35. Niebuhr, *Irony of American History*, 2.

36. My reference to "blank spots on the map" is drawn from Paglen, *Blank Spots on the Map*. My reference to the proliferation of invisible camps is drawn from Mirzoeff, *Watching Babylon*, sec. 3.

Chapter Six

1. McDaniel, "Fantasm," 55.

2. Hogan, *A Cross of Iron*, 70.

3. See Luce, "The American Century"; Haslam, *Russia's Cold War*, 37–41; O'Gorman, *Spirits of the Cold War*, 148–56.

4. George Kennan, "Long Telegram."

5. Haslam, *Russia's Cold War*, 80–82.

6. Truman, "Special Message."

7. Ikenberry, *Liberal Leviathan*.

8. Hogan, *Cross of Iron*, 50.

9. Ibid., 124; see also 122–25, 197–208, 267–75.

10. For more on the stoic character of these virtues, see O'Gorman, *Spirits of the Cold War*, 21–74.

11. See Hammond, "NSC 68." For further reflections on the history, rhetoric, and logic of NSC 68, see May, ed., *American Cold War Strategy*; and Robert P. Newman, "NSC."

12. See MacIsaac, *Strategic Bombing*.

13. Gaddis, *George F. Kennan*, 361.

14. Nitze, *From Hiroshima to Glasnost*, xv.

15. Ibid., xviii.

16. Ibid., xv.

17. NSC 68, in Drew, *NSC-68*, 39. All my references to NSC 68 and its later revisions refer to this volume.

18. Ibid., 47.

19. Gaddis, *Strategies of Containment*, 91–93. Nitze would disavow the connection between his recommendations in NSC 68 and deficit spending, arguing instead for higher taxes as a way to offset bigger defense budgets (see his "Grand Strategy of NSC-68," in Drew, *NSC-68*, 14).

20. Wells, "Sounding the Tocsin," 123.

21. In one of the first Policy Planning Staff papers issued under Nitze's PPS, Nitze told the secretary of state, "Stalin's election speech of 1946 was an open declaration of hostility and since that time the USSR has given every sign that it neither intends to abandon the struggle, other than on its own terms, nor pause in its prosecution. In the choice of tactics, the USSR has shown a willingness to employ at any given moment any maneuver or weapon which holds promise

of success." Nitze went on to say that while there was no indication from Moscow of plans "to launch in the near future an all-out military attack on the West," there could be no assurances that they would not turn to a "use of force in local areas, which might lead to an accidental outbreak of general military conflict" (see Nitze, "Recent Soviet Moves," 145–46). For Nitze's later comments on the "nuclear umbrella," see "BBC Interview with Paul H. Nitze."

22. Rearden and Smith, Interview with Paul H. Nitze (13 April 1983).

23. In fact, despite the signing of their Treaty of Friendship, relations were quite chilly between the Soviets and China. "To the outer world China and the USSR were now one. Yet those privy to the actual state of relations understood that this was inherently an unstable relationship" (Haslam, *Russia's Cold War*, 126).

24. My summary of events in the fall of 1949 and winter of 1950 here is based on Wells, "Sounding the Tocsin," 117. See also Joseph McCarthy, "Speech of Joseph McCarthy."

25. Weiner, *Legacy of Ashes*, 43–47.

26. Drew, *NSC-68*, 53.

27. George F. Kennan, "Memorandum by Kennan to Acheson" (January 6, 1950), 132.

28. Haslam, *Russia's Cold War*, 125.

29. Ibid., 127–28.

30. Truman, "Proclamation 2914."

31. Gaddis, *Strategies of Containment*, 393.

32. Drew, *NSC-68*, 88, 54.

33. Hogan, *Cross of Iron*, 50.

34. Osgood, *Total Cold War*, 2.

35. Eisenhower took office in January, 1953. In 1952 defense spending had reached 13.2% of gross domestic product (GDP), up from 7.4% in 1951. Eisenhower would never get defense spending down to anything approaching 1951 numbers. In 1953 defense spending went up to 14.2%, dipping back down in 1954 to 13.1%. The following year, it dipped further down to 10.8% of GDP; from 1956 to 1959 it hovered at or just above 10%; and in 1960 and 1961 it would go down further to 9.3% and 9.4% of GDP respectively, but it would not be until 1965 in the Johnson administration that defense spending would sink below 8.5% of GDP. Thus, despite the legacy of Eisenhower's Republican budget-mindedness, the Democratic administrations immediately before and after him in fact proved to have much better track records on defense spending. See Gaddis, *Strategies of Containment*, 393–94, for the numbers.

36. National Security Council, NSC 162/2, October 30, 1953 (pp. 4–5), NSC Series, box 6, Dwight D. Eisenhower Library. Available online at https://www.fas.org/irp/offdocs/nsc-hst/nsc-162-2.pdf.

37. Treuenfels, *Eisenhower Speaks*, 248.

38. Ibid., 249.

39. Ibid., 254.

40. Ibid., 254–55.

41. Ibid., 255.

42. Snead, *Gaither Committee*, 18.

43. Treuenfels, *Eisenhower Speaks*, 255.

44. Snead, *Gaither Committee*, 18.

45. National Security Council, NSC 162/2, October 30, 1953, 1.

46. Ibid., 5–6.

47. Gaddis, *Strategies of Containment*, 130.

48. Snead, *Gaither Committee*, 33. This would have been a suicide mission, as Soviet bombers well into the mid-1950s were not capable of two-way missions to North America. An attack on Europe, on the other hand, could have been pulled off without such a suicidal sacrifice.

49. Hogan, *Cross of Iron*, 396.

50. Gaddis, *Strategies of Containment*, 171.

51. Snead, *Gaither Committee*, 35–36.

52. Ibid., 38.

53. Ibid., 2.

54. Ibid., 3.

55. Gaddis, *Strategies of Containment*, 173.

56. Chernus, *Eisenhower's Atoms for Peace*, 82.

57. Gaddis, *Strategies of Containment*, 173.

58. Chernus discusses Eisenhower's "apocalypse management" in both *Eisenhower's Atoms for Peace* and *Apocalypse Management*.

59. Hogan, *Cross of Iron*, 9.

60. Ibid.

61. Ibid., 124.

62. See O'Gorman and Hamilton, "At the Interface."

63. Eisenhower, "Farewell Radio and Television Address."

64. Hayek, *Road to Serfdom*, 58.

65. Judt, *Postwar*, 67.

66. Hayek, *Road to Serfdom*, 48.

67. Ibid., 52.

68. Herzog, *Spiritual-Industrial Complex*, 5.

69. Hughes, *Ordeal of Power*, 152.

70. Eisenhower, "Special Message."

71. Brown, "American Nightmare," 705.

72. Steger, *Neoliberalism*, 49.

73. Harvey, *Brief History of Neoliberalism*, 82–83.

74. Rancière, *Politics of Aesthetics*, 12–13.

75. Meyers, *Civic War*, 7; emphasis in original.

76. Ibid., 7.

77. Ibid., 10.

78. Arendt, *Human Condition*, 58.

79. Treuenfels, *Eisenhower Speaks*, 81.

80. Ibid., 105.

Chapter Seven

1. Zakaria, "Tragedies of Other Places."

2. Masco, *Theater of Operations*, 6.

3. Sturken, *Tourists of History*, 2.

4. The language of bottom- and top-limits here is borrowed from Tsang, *The Sublime*.

5. Sidney, "Defence of Poesy," 216, line 177; I discuss Hobbes's approach to art (contra nature), focusing on the question of rhetoric, in O'Gorman, "Hobbes."

6. O'Gorman, "Hobbes."

7. Skinner, *Reason and Rhetoric.*

8. Hobbes, *Leviathan*, chap. 42.

9. Locke, *Human Understanding*; Wolin, *Politics and Vision*, 307–9.

10. Smith, *Adam Smith*, 11.

11. Ibid., 3.5, p. 150; see also 1.3, p. 42; 3.4, p. 139; 4.1, p. 162.

12. Smith, *Wealth of Nations*, 193–94.

13. Ibid., 163.

14. Wolin, *Politics and Vision*, 288–89.

15. Ibid., 288; O'Gorman, "Hobbes."

16. Wolin, *Politics and Vision*, 290.

17. Ibid., 291.

18. Ibid.; Smith, *Wealth of Nations*, 9–10. On Scottish classical economics and theologies of providence, see Milbank, *Theology and Social Theory.*

19. Locke, *Human Understanding*, 508.

20. Keynes, *End of Laissez-faire*, 36.

21. Ibid.

22. Lippmann, *Inquiry*, 186.

23. Ibid., 30.

24. Ibid., 30–31.

25. Burgin, *Great Persuasion*, 67.

26. Hayek, *Road to Serfdom*, 102. Alfred Korzybski and the movement known as General Semantics expressed a very similar concern about the limits of the human powers of imagination in the 1930s. Korzybski worried about "our inability to separate the pictures in our heads and the communicative processes that put them there from material reality itself" (Turner, *Democratic Surround*, 22–23). In fact, as Fred Turner discusses at length in *The Democratic Surround*, the whole matter of mass *perception* was one that drove a range of theories and initiatives in the 1940s, 1950s, and 1960s among the US cultural elite, from Margaret Mead to Marshall McLuhan. This was, of course, related to the crises of the status and significance of the image that I have been discussing in these pages, but it was not precisely the same movement. Whereas the elite whom Turner discusses wanted to shape, form, and even manage human psychology, thus tackling the subjective conditions for a thriving free society, the neoliberals I have been discussing wanted to shape, form, and regulate the objective conditions of human society vis-à-vis law and the economy. Their concerns were, to a degree, identical; but their solutions very different.

27. As Hayek wrote of the book in the preface, "It is the outcome of an idea which suggested itself to me as a very young man when I was still uncertain whether to become and economist or a psychologist" (*Sensory Order*, v).

28. Ibid.; see especially 4–6, 13–19, 191–94.

29. Lippmann, *Inquiry*, 374.

30. Hayek, *Constitution of Liberty.*

31. Lippmann, *Inquiry*, 105.

32. Ibid., 33.

33. Ibid.

34. Ibid., 7.

35. Ibid., 371.

36. Ibid.

37. Lippmann, *Phantom Public*, 374, 378.

38. Harvey, *Brief History of Neoliberalism*, 31.

39. I offer here a brief and general account of the political in order to stress the space between politics and economics. I am fully aware of its incompleteness, particularly as it offers no specific discussion of the most important notion of sovereignty, especially as it relates to law.

40. Wolin, *Politics and Vision*, 288.

41. Friedman, "Methodology of Positive Economics," 32.

42. Rousseau, *Social Contract*, translated by Judith R. Masters, 198.

43. Barber, *Strong Democracy*, 145.

44. See Ankersmit, *Aesthetic Politics*.

45. I borrow the phrase "conspiracy to protect the ineffable" from Sedley, *Sublimity and Skepticism*.

46. Friedman, *Indispensable Milton Friedman*, 6.

47. Ibid., 11.

Conclusion

1. Taylor, *Modern Social Imaginaries*, 23.

2. Friedman, "Neo-Liberalism," 7.

3. Hayek, *Road to Serfdom*, 87.

4. Friedman, "Neo-Liberalism," 7.

5. Arendt, *Human Condition*, 28–37.

6. See, for example, Ankersmit, *Political Representation*; Urbinati, *Representative Democracy*; and the enormously influential book by Pitkin, *Concept of Representation*.

7. Habermas, "Public Sphere," 50.

8. Mirzoeff, *Right to Look*.

9. Wolin, *Politics and Vision*, 291.

10. Ezrahi, *Descent of Icarus*, 41.

11. Wolin, *Politics and Vision*, 353.

12. Arendt, *Human Condition*, 38–49; Habermas, "Public Sphere."

13. In the aftermath of the French Revolution, Burke warned in his "Letter to a Noble Lord" of those in England, like the physiocrats in France, who would turn science into a means of politics: "These philosophers are fanatics; independent of any interest, which if it operated alone would make them much more tractable, they are carried with such a headlong rage towards every desperate trial, that they would sacrifice the whole human race to the slightest of their experiments," adding, "Ambition is come upon them suddenly; they are intoxicated with it, and it has rendered them fearless of the danger, which may from thence arise to others or to themselves. These philosophers consider men in their experiments, no more than they do mice in an air pump, or in a recipient of mephitick gas" (270). See his "Letter to a Noble Lord" in Burke, *Works*, 258–74.

14. Weaver, *Language Is Sermonic*, 107.

15. Reagan, "Space Shuttle Challenger."

16. Hayek, *Individualism and Economic Order*, chap. 1.

17. The "aestheticization of politics," of course, is most closely associated with Walter Benjamin's critique of fascism.

18. Rodgers, *Age of Fracture*, 3.

19. Hayek, *Individualism and Economic Order*, 4, 8–11.

20. Ibid., 4, 8.

21. Ibid., 8.

22. Ibid., 14, 16–18.

23. Ibid., 7.

24. Ibid., 11.

25. Ibid., 32.

26. Ibid., 23.

27. Ibid., 14.

28. Ibid.

29. Habermas, *Legitimation Crisis*, 70.

30. See the appendix to Lyotard, *Postmodern Condition*.

31. Rogin, *Ronald Reagan, the Movie*, 4–7.

32. Hayek, *Individualism and Economic Order*, 23.

Bibliography

Allen, Danielle S. *Talking to Strangers: Anxieties of Citizenship Since Brown v. Board of Education.* Chicago: University of Chicago Press, 2004.

Anderson, Benedict. *Imagined Communities: Reflections on the Origin and Spread of Nationalism.* Rev. ed. London: Verso, 2006.

Ankersmit, F. R. *Aesthetic Politics: Political Philosophy Beyond Fact and Value.* Stanford, CA: Stanford University Press, 1996.

————. *Political Representation.* Stanford, CA: Stanford University Press, 2002.

Arendt, Hannah. *The Human Condition.* Chicago: University of Chicago Press, 1998.

————. "Reflections on Little Rock." In *Responsibility and Judgment,* edited by Jerome Kohn, 193–213. New York: Schocken Books, 2003.

"The Assassination of President Kennedy." *Life,* November 29, 1963.

Auer, J. Jeffery. "Acting Like a President; or, What Has Ronald Reagan Done to Political Speaking?" In *Reagan and Public Discourse in America,* 93–120. Tuscaloosa: University of Alabama Press, 1992.

Aune, James Arnt. *Selling the Free Market: The Rhetoric of Economic Correctness.* New York: Guilford Press, 2001.

Barber, Benjamin R. *Strong Democracy: Participatory Politics for a New Age.* Berkeley: University of California Press, 2003.

Barnard, Leslie W. *The Graeco-Roman and Oriental Background of the Iconoclastic Controversy.* Leiden: Brill, 1974.

Battersby, Christine. "Stages on Kant's Way: Aesthetics, Morality, and the Gendered Sublime." In *Race, Class, Gender, and Sexuality: The Big Questions,* edited by Naomi Zack, Laurie Shrage, and Crispin Sartwell, 227–47. Oxford: Blackwell, 1998.

Baudrillard, Jean. "The Spirit of Terrorism." Online at *The European Graduate School;* http://www.egs.edu/faculty/jean-baudrillard/articles/the-spirit-of-terrorism/. Last modified November 2, 2001.

"BBC Interview with Paul H. Nitze" (July 19, 1983). Paul H. Nitze Papers, 1922–1998, box 118, folder 6. Library of Congress, Washington, DC.

Bellah, Robert N. "Civil Religion in America." *Daedalus: Journal of the American Academy of Arts and Sciences* 96, no. 1 (1967): 1–21.

———. "Civil Religion in America by Robert N. Bellah." Online at http://www.robertbellah .com/articles_5.htm (accessed May 26, 2012).

Besançon, Alain. *The Forbidden Image: An Intellectual History of Iconoclasm*. Chicago: University of Chicago Press, 2001.

Biel, Steven, ed. *American Disasters*. New York: New York University Press, 2001.

Black, Edwin. "Secrecy and Disclosure as Rhetorical Forms." *Quarterly Journal of Speech* 74, no. 2 (1988): 133–50. doi: 10.1080/00335638809383833.

Bodnar, John. *Remaking America: Public Memory, Commemoration, and Patriotism in the Twentieth Century*. Princeton, NJ: Princeton University Press, 1992.

Bolter, Jay David, and Richard Grusin. *Remediation: Understanding New Media*. Cambridge, MA: MIT Press, 1999.

Boorstin, Daniel Joseph. *The Image; or, What Happened to the American Dream*. New York: Atheneum, 1962. Later published as *The Image: A Guide to Pseudo-Events in America*. New York: Vintage Books, 1992.

Borgerhoff, E. B. O. *The Freedom of French Classicism*. Princeton, NJ: Princeton University Press, 1950.

Brody, Jules. *Boileau and Longinus*. Geneva: E. Droz, 1958.

Brown, Aaron, and Judy Woodruff, "Ramifications of Planned Attack on the U.S.," CNN, aired September 11, 2001. Online at http://edition.cnn.com/TRANSCRIPTS/0109/11/bn.37.html.

Brown, Wendy. "American Nightmare: Neoliberalism, Neoconservatism, and De-Democratization." *Political Theory* 34, no. 6 (2006): 690–714. doi:10.1177/0090591706293016.

Burgin, Angus. *The Great Persuasion: Reinventing Free Markets Since the Depression*. Cambridge, MA: Harvard University Press, 2012.

Burke, Edmund. *A Philosophical Enquiry into the Origin of Our Ideas of the Sublime and Beautiful*. New York: Oxford University Press, 1990.

———. *Reflections on the Revolution in France*. New York: Oxford University Press, 2009.

———. *The Works of the Right Hon. Edmund Burke: With a Biographical and Critical Introduction*. London: Samuel Holdsworth, 1837.

Burke, Kenneth. *The Philosophy of Literary Form*. New York: Vintage, 1957.

———. *A Rhetoric of Motives*. Berkeley: University of California Press, 1969.

Bush, George. "George W. Bush: Address before a Joint Session of the Congress on the United States Response to the Terrorist Attacks of September 11." *The American Presidency Project*. Online at http://www.presidency.ucsb.edu/ws/index.php?pid=64731&st=&st1=#axzz1wqs EXLe9 (last modified September 20, 2001).

———. "George W. Bush: Address to the Nation Announcing Strikes Against Al Qaida Training Camps and Taliban Military Installations in Afghanistan." *The American Presidency Project*. Online at http://www.presidency.ucsb.edu/ws/index.php?pid=65088&st=&st1=#axzz1wqs EXLe9 (last modified October 7, 2001).

Bush, Vannevar. *Science, the Endless Frontier: A Report to the President*. Washington, DC: Government Printing Office, 1945.

Caldwell, Bruce. *Hayek's Challenge: An Intellectual Biography of F. A. Hayek*. Chicago: University of Chicago Press, 2004. http://public.eblib.com/EBLPublic/PublicView.do?ptiID=515738.

———. "Introduction." In *The Road to Serfdom: Text and Documents*. Definitive ed. Vol. 2 of *The Collected Works of F. A. Hayek*. Chicago: University of Chicago Press, 2007.

Canetti, Elias. *Crowds and Power*. New York: Penguin, 1973.

Cavell, Stanley. *Pursuits of Happiness: The Hollywood Comedy of Remarriage*. Cambridge, MA: Harvard University Press, 1981.

Charney, Leo. "In a Moment: Film and the Philosophy of Modernity." In *Cinema and the Invention of Modern Life*, 279–94. Berkeley: University of California Press, 1995.

Chernus, Ira. *Apocalypse Management: Eisenhower and the Discourse of National Insecurity*. Stanford, CA: Stanford University Press, 2008.

———. *Eisenhower's Atoms for Peace*. College Station: Texas A&M University Press, 2002.

Chomsky, Noam. *Profit over People: Neoliberalism and Global Order*. New York: Seven Stories Press, 1999.

Clausewitz, Carl Von. *On War*. Oxford: Oxford University Press, 2007.

Colomina, Beatriz. *Domesticity at War*. Cambridge, MA: MIT Press, 2007.

Congrès international de photographie et cinématographie ultra-rapides, Pierre Naslin, and Jean Vivié. "Photographie et Cinématographie Ultra-rapides Actes Du 2ème Congrès International de Photographie et Cinématographie Ultra-rapides, Paris, Septembre 1954." Paris: Dunod, 1956.

Deggans, Eric. "On TV, Mayhem Unfolded in Waves." *St. Petersburg Times*, September 12, 2001.

DeLuca, Kevin Michael, and Jennifer Peeples. "From Public Sphere to Public Screen: Democracy, Activism, and the 'Violence' of Seattle." *Critical Studies in Media Communication* 19, no. 2 (2002): 125–51. doi: 10.1080/07393180216559.

Drew, Nelson, ed. *NSC-68: Forging the Strategy of Containment*. Washington, DC: National Defense University, 1994.

Eire, Carlos M. N. *War Against the Idols: The Reformation of Worship from Erasmus to Calvin*. Cambridge: Cambridge University Press, 1989.

Eisenhower, Dwight D. "Annual Message to the Congress on the State of the Union, February 2, 1953." *The American Presidency Project*. Online at http://www.presidency.ucsb.edu /ws/?pid=9829.

———. "Executive Order 10730—Providing Assistance for the Removal of an Obstruction of Justice within the State of Arkansas, September 24, 1957." *The American Presidency Project*. Online at http://www.presidency.ucsb.edu/ws/?pid=75572.

———. "Farewell Radio and Television Address to the American People," January 17, 1961, *The American Presidency Project*. Online at http://www.presidency.ucsb.edu/ws/?pid=12086 #axzz1w0soEIeo.

———. "The President's News Conference, July 17, 1957." *The American Presidency Project*. Online at http://www.presidency.ucsb.edu/ws/?pid=10839.

———. "Radio and Television Address to the American People on the Situation in Little Rock, September 24, 1957." *The American Presidency Project*. Online at http://www.presidency .ucsb.edu/ws/?pid=10909.

———. "Special Message to the Congress Recommending Amendments to the Atomic Energy Act, February 17, 1954." *The American Presidency Project*. Online at http://www.presidency .ucsb.edu/ws/?pid=10163.

Elshtain, Jean Bethke. *Augustine and the Limits of Politics*. Notre Dame, IN: University of Notre Dame Press, 1998.

Ezrahi, Yaron. *The Descent of Icarus: Science and the Transformation of Contemporary Democracy*. Cambridge, MA: Harvard University Press, 1990.

Farrell, Thomas B. "Love and Theft After 9/11: Magnification in the Rhetorical Aftermath." In *Rhetorical Democracy*, edited by Gerard A. Hauser and Amy Grim. Mahwah, NJ: Lawrence Erlbaum Associates, 2004.

———. "Sizing Things Up: Colloquial Reflection as Practical Wisdom." *Argumentation* 12, no. 1 (1998): 1–14. doi:10.1023/A:1007747321075.

Ferguson, Robert A. *Law and Letters in American Culture.* Cambridge, MA: Harvard University Press, 1984.

Fetzer, James H., ed. *The Great Zapruder Film Hoax: Deceit and Deception in the Death of JFK.* Chicago: Catfeet Press, 2003.

Fousek, John. *To Lead the Free World: American Nationalism and the Cultural Roots of the Cold War.* Chapel Hill, NC: University of North Carolina Press, 2000.

Fraser, Cary. "Crossing the Color Line in Little Rock: The Eisenhower Administration and the Dilemma of Race for U.S. Foreign Policy." *Diplomatic History* 24, no. 2 (2000): 233–64. doi:10.1111/0145–2096.00211.

Fraser, Nancy. "Identity, Exclusion, and Critique: A Response to Four Critics." *European Journal of Political Theory* 6, no. 3 (July 1, 2007): 305–38. doi:10.1177/1474885107077319.

Freedburg, David. "The Structure of European and Byzantine Iconoclasm." In *Iconoclasm: Papers Given at the Ninth Spring Symposium of Byzantine Studies, University of Birmingham, March 1975,* edited by Anthony Bryer and Judith Herrin, 165–77. Birmingham, UK, Centre for Byzantine Studies: University of Birmingham, 1977.

Freeman, Barbara Claire. *The Feminine Sublime: Gender and Excess in Women's Fiction.* Berkeley: University of California Press, 1995.

Friedland, Roger, and Robert Alford. "Bringing Society Back in: Symbols, Practices, and Institutional Contradictions." In *The New Institutionalism in Organizational Analysis,* edited by Walter W. Powell and Paul DiMaggio, 232–66. Chicago: University of Chicago Press, 1991.

Friedman, Milton. *The Indispensable Milton Friedman: Essays on Politics and Economics.* Edited by Lanny Ebenstein. New York: Regnery Publishing, 2012.

———. "The Methodology of Positive Economics." In *Essays in Positive Economics,* 3–43. Chicago: University of Chicago Press, 1953.

———. "Neo-Liberalism and Its Prospects." In Friedman, *Indispensible Milton Friedman,* 3–9.

Friedman, Thomas. *The World Is Flat: The Globalized World in the Twenty-First Century.* New York: Penguin, 2006.

Gaddis, John Lewis. *George F. Kennan: An American Life.* New York: Penguin, 2011.

———. *Strategies of Containment.* New York: Oxford University Press, 2004.

Giuliani, Rudy. "9/11 Speech to the United Nations General Assembly Special Session on Terrorism." *American Rhetoric.* Online at http://www.americanrhetoric.com/speeches/rudygiuliani 911unitednations.htm (accessed June 4, 2012).

Goldberg, Robert Alan. *Enemies Within: The Culture of Conspiracy in Modern America.* New Haven, CT: Yale University Press, 2001.

Goldzwig, Steven R., and George N. Dionisopolous. "Crisis at Little Rock: Eisenhower, History, and Mediated Political Realities." In *Eisenhower's War of Words,* 189–221. East Lansing: Michigan State University Press, 1994.

Habermas, Jürgen. *Communication and the Evolution of Society.* Boston, MA: Beacon Press, 1979.

———. *Legitimation Crisis.* Boston, MA: Beacon Press, 1975.

———. "The Public Sphere: An Encyclopedia Article (1964)." Translated by Sara Lennox and Frank Lennox. *New German Critique* 1, no. 3 (1974): 49–55.

Hammond, Paul Y. "NSC 68: Prologue to Rearmament." In *Strategy, Politics, and Defense Budgets,* edited by Warner R. Schilling, Paul Y. Hammond, and Glenn Snyder, 267–378. New York: Columbia University Press, 1962.

Hariman, Robert, and John Louis Lucaites. *No Caption Needed: Iconic Photographs, Public Culture, and Liberal Democracy.* Chicago: University of Chicago Press, 2007.

Harnad, Stevan. "Computation Is Just Interpretable Symbol Manipulation; Cognition Isn't." *Minds and Machines* 4, no. 4 (1994): 379–90. doi:10.1007/BF00974165.

Harvey, David. *A Brief History of Neoliberalism.* New York: Oxford University Press, 2005.

———. *The Condition of Postmodernity: An Enquiry into the Origins of Cultural Change.* Malden, MA: Wiley-Blackwell, 1991.

Haslam, Jonathan. *Russia's Cold War: From the October Revolution to the Fall of the Wall.* New Haven, CT: Yale University Press, 2011.

Hayek, F. A. *The Confusion of Language in Political Thought.* Institute of Economic Affairs Occasional Papers, no. 20. London: Institute of Economic Affairs, 1968.

———. *The Constitution of Liberty.* Chicago: University of Chicago Press, 1960.

———. *Economic Freedom and Representative Government.* London: Institute of Economic Affairs, 1973.

———. *The Fatal Conceit: The Errors of Socialism.* Chicago: University of Chicago Press, 2011.

———. *Individualism and Economic Order.* Chicago: University of Chicago Press, 1948.

———. *The Road to Serfdom: Text and Documents.* Definitive ed. Vol. 2 of *The Collected Works of F. A. Hayek.* Chicago: University of Chicago Press, 2007.

———. *The Sensory Order: An Inquiry into the Foundations of Theoretical Psychology.* Chicago: University of Chicago Press, 1952.

———, and *Reader's Digest*, eds. *The Road to Serfdom: The Condensed Version of The Road to Serfdom by F. A. Hayek as It Appeared in the April 1945 Edition of Reader's Digest.* London: Institute of Economic Affairs, 1945.

Hediger, Vinzenz, and Patrick Vonderau, eds. *Films That Work: Industrial Film and the Productivity of Media.* Amsterdam: Amsterdam University Press, 2009.

Herzog, Jonathan P. *The Spiritual-Industrial Complex: America's Religious Battle Against Communism in the Early Cold War.* New York: Oxford University Press, 2011.

Hewlett, Richard G., and Jack M. Holl. *Atoms for Peace and War, 1953–1961: Eisenhower and the Atomic Energy Commission.* Berkeley: University of California Press, 1989.

Hobbes, Thomas. *Leviathan.* Cambridge: Cambridge University Press, 1996.

———. *Man and Citizen: De Homine and De Cive.* Indianapolis, IN: Hackett, 1991.

Hoffman, Susannah M., and Anthony Oliver-Smith, eds. *Catastrophe & Culture: The Anthropology of Disaster.* Santa Fe, NM: School of American Research Press, 2002.

Hofstadter, Richard. *The Paranoid Style in American Politics.* New York: Vintage, 1952.

Hogan, Michael J. *A Cross of Iron: Harry S. Truman and the Origins of the National Security State, 1945–1954.* New York: Cambridge University Press, 1998.

Holland, Max. "After Thirty Years: Making Sense of Assassination." *Reviews in American History* 22, no. 2 (1994): 191–209.

Holton, Gerald, ed. "Mass Culture and Mass Media." *Daedalus: Journal of the American Academy of Arts and Sciences* 89, no. 2 (1960).

Horkheimer, Max, and Theodor W. Adorno. *Dialectic of Enlightenment.* New York: Continuum, 1972.

Huet, Marie-Hélène. *The Culture of Disaster.* Chicago: University of Chicago Press, 2012.

Hughes, Emmet John. *The Ordeal Of Power: A Political Memoir Of The Eisenhower Years.* New York: Atheneum, 1963.

Ikenberry, G. John. *Liberal Leviathan: The Origins, Crisis, and Transformation of the American World Order.* Princeton, NJ: Princeton University Press, 2012.

International Congress on High-Speed Photography, and Society of Photo-optical Instrumentation Engineers. *Proceedings of the International Congress on High-Speed Photography*. New York: Academic Press, 1957.

Isaacson, Walter, and Evan Thomas. *The Wise Men: Six Friends and the World They Made*. London: Simon & Schuster, 2012.

Jameson, Frederic. "Postmodernism; or, the Cultural Logic of Late Capitalism." *New Left Review*, no. 146 (August 1984): 53–92.

———. *Postmodernism; or, the Cultural Logic of Late Capitalism*. Durham, NC: Duke University Press, 1991.

Jasanoff, Sheila. *The Fifth Branch: Science Advisers as Policymakers*. Cambridge, MA: Harvard University Press, 1998.

Jasinski, James. "Antithesis and Oxymoron: Ronald Reagan's Figurative Rhetorical Structure." In *Reagan and Public Discourse in America*, edited by Michael Weiler and W. Barnett Pearce, 121–34. Tuscaloosa, AL: University of Alabama Press, 1992.

Jones, Daniel Stedman. *Masters of the Universe: Hayek, Friedman, and the Birth of Neoliberal Politics*. Princeton, NJ: Princeton University Press, 2012.

Judt, Tony. *Postwar: A History of Europe Since 1945*. New York: Penguin, 2006.

Kant, Immanuel. *Critique of Judgment*. 2d ed., rev. London: Macmillan, 1931.

———. *Critique of the Power of Judgment*, edited by Paul Guyer. Translated by Paul Guyer and Eric Matthews. New York: Cambridge University Press, 2001.

———. *Observations on the Feeling of the Beautiful and the Sublime*. Berkeley: University of California Press, 1960.

———. *Perpetual Peace and Other Essays*. Indianapolis, IN: Hackett, 1983.

Karlstadt, Andreas Rudolff-Bodenstein von. "On the Removal of Images." In *A Reformation Debate: Karlstadt, Emser, and Eck on Sacred Images: Three Treatises in Translation*, edited by Bryan D. Mangrum and Giuseppe Scavizzi, 19–25. Renaissance and Reformation Texts in Translation, 5. 2nd ed., rev. Toronto: Centre for Reformation and Renaissance Studies, 1998.

Kelly, Yvan J. "Mises, Morgenstern, Hoselitz, and Nash: The Austrian Connection to Early Game Theory." *Quarterly Journal of Austrian Economics* 12, no. 3 (2009): 37–42.

Kennan, George F. "Long Telegram, February 22, 1946." Harry S. Truman Administration File, Elsey Papers, p. 15. *Harry S. Truman Library and Museum*. Online at http://www.truman library.org/whistlestop/study_collections/coldwar/documents/index.php?pagenumber=1& documentdate=1946–02–22&documentid=6–6&studycollectionid=coldwar (accessed October 9, 2012).

———. "Memorandum by Kennan to Acheson" (January 6, 1950). In *Foreign Relations of the United States*. Vol. 1. *National Security Affairs; Foreign Economic Policy*, edited by Neal H. Petersen, John P. Glennon, David W. Mabon, Ralph R. Goodwin, and William Z. Slany. Washington, DC: US Government Printing Office, 1950.

Kennedy, John F. *The Inaugural Address*. Washington: Colortone Press, 1965.

———. "Special Message to the Congress on Urgent National Needs, May 25, 1961." *John F. Kennedy Presidential Library & Museum*. Online at http://www.jfklibrary.org/Asset-Viewer /Archives/JFKPOF-034–030.aspx (accessed May 26, 2012).

Keynes, John Maynard. *The End of Laissez-faire: The Economic Consequences of the Peace*. Amherst, NY: Prometheus Books, 2004.

Keyworth, George A. "The Future of Space: Looking Ahead in Space." *IEEE Spectrum* 20, no. 9 (1983): 80–84.

Klamer, Arjo, Donald N. McCloskey, and Robert M. Snow, eds. *The Consequences of Economic Rhetoric.* Cambridge: Cambridge University Press, 1988.

Kornhauser, William. *The Politics of Mass Society.* Glencoe, IL: Free Press, 1959.

Laurence, Robert P. "Television Brought the Full Horror Home." *San Diego Union-Tribune,* September 12, 2001.

Lippmann, Walter. *An Inquiry into the Principles of the Good Society.* Boston: Little, Brown, 1937.

———. *The Phantom Public.* New York: Harcourt Brace, 1925.

Lister, Andrew. "The 'Mirage' of Social Justice: Hayek Against (and for) Rawls." CCSJ Working Papers Series, SJ017. Online at http://social-justice.politics.ox.ac.uk/materials/SJ017_Lister _MirageofSocialJustice.pdf (last modified June 2011).

Locke, John. *An Essay Concerning Human Understanding.* Oxford: Clarendon Press, 1975.

———. *Two Treatises of Government.* Edited by Peter Laslett. 3rd ed. Cambridge, UK: Cambridge University Press, 1988.

Longinus, Cassius. *On the Sublime.* Translated by John M. Crossett and James A. Arieti. New York: E. Mellen Press, 1985.

Lubin, David M. *Shooting Kennedy: JFK and the Culture of Images.* Berkeley: University of California Press, 2003.

Luce, Henry R. "The American Century." *Life,* February 17, 1941.

Lyotard, Jean-Francois. *The Postmodern Condition: A Report on Knowledge.* Minneapolis: University of Minnesota Press, 1984.

MacIntyre, Alasdair. *After Virtue.* Notre Dame, IN: University of Notre Dame Press, 1984.

MacIsaac, David. *Strategic Bombing in World War Two: The Story of the United States Strategic Bombing Survey.* New York: Garland, 1976.

Mangrum, Bryan D., and Giuseppe Scavizzi. "Introduction: The Debate on Images at the Beginning of the Reformation." In *A Reformation Debate: Karlstadt, Emser, and Eck on Sacred Images: Three Treatises in Translation,* edited by Bryan D. Mangrum and Giuseppe Scavizzi, 1–18. 2nd ed., rev. Renaissance and Reformation Texts in Translation, no. 5. Toronto: Centre for Reformation and Renaissance Studies, 1998.

Manovich, Lev. *The Language of New Media.* Cambridge, MA: MIT Press, 2002.

Masco, Joseph. *The Theater of Operations: National Security Affect from the Cold War to the War on Terror.* Durham, NC: Duke University Press, 2014.

May, Ernest R., ed. *American Cold War Strategy: Interpreting NSC 68.* Boston: Bedford Books, 1993.

McCarthy, Joseph. "Speech of Joseph McCarthy, Wheeling, West Virginia, February 9, 1950." Online at http://historymatters.gmu.edu/d/6456 (accessed February 27, 2015).

McChesney, Robert W., Ellen Meiksins Wood, and John Bellamy Foster, eds. *Capitalism and the Information Age: The Political Economy of the Global Communication Revolution.* New York: Monthly Review Press, 1998.

McCloskey, Deirdre N. *The Rhetoric of Economics.* 2nd ed. Rhetoric of the Human Sciences. Madison, WI: University of Wisconsin Press, 1998.

McDaniel, James P. "Fantasm: The Triumph of Form (an Essay on the Democratic Sublime)." *Quarterly Journal of Speech* 86, no. 1 (February 2000): 48–66.

McDougall, Walter A. *The Heavens and the Earth: A Political History of the Space Age.* New York: Basic Books, 1985.

McLuhan, Marshall. *Understanding Media: Extensions of Man.* New York: McGraw-Hill, 1964.

Medhurst, Martin J. "The Rhetorical Structure of Oliver Stone's *JFK.*" *Critical Studies in Mass Communication* 10, no. 2 (1993): 128–43.

Meyers, Peter Alexander. *Civic War & the Corruption of the Citizen.* Chicago: University of Chicago Press, 2008.

Mieczkowski, Yanek. *Eisenhower's Sputnik Moment: The Race for Space and World Prestige.* Ithaca, NY: Cornell University Press, 2013.

Milbank, John. *Theology and Social Theory: Beyond Secular Reason.* Oxford, UK: Blackwell, 2006.

Mills, C. Wright. *The Power Elite.* New York: Simon and Schuster, 1956.

Mindell, David A. *Digital Apollo: Human and Machine in Spaceflight.* Cambridge, MA: MIT Press, 2008.

Mirowski, Philip, and Dieter Plehwe. *The Road from Mont Pèlerin: The Making of the Neoliberal Thought Collective.* Cambridge, MA: Harvard University Press, 2009.

Mirzoeff, Nicholas. *The Right to Look: A Counterhistory of Visuality.* Durham, NC: Duke University Press, 2011.

———. *Watching Babylon: The War in Iraq and Global Visual Culture.* London: Routledge, 2012.

"Missile and Satellite Hearings." In *CQ Almanac 1958.* 14th ed., 11-669–11-671. Washington, DC: Congressional Quarterly Press, 1959. Online at http://library.cqpress.com/cqalmanac /cqal58-1340132 (accessed February 27, 2015).

Mister, Steven M. "Reagan's Challenger Tribute: Combining Generic Constraints and Situational Demands." *Central States Speech Journal* 37, no. 3 (1986): 158–65.

Mitchell, W. J. T. *Cloning Terror: The War of Images, 9/11 to the Present.* Chicago: University of Chicago Press, 2010.

———. *Iconology: Image, Text, Ideology.* Chicago: University of Chicago Press, 1986.

———. *What Do Pictures Want?: The Lives and Loves of Images.* Chicago: University of Chicago Press, 2005.

"Modern Art Was CIA 'Weapon.'" *The Independent.* Online at http://www.independent.co.uk /news/world/modern-art-was-cia-weapon-1578808.html (last modified October 22, 1995; accessed August 30, 2013).

Mondzain, Marie-José. *Image, Icon, Economy: The Byzantine Origins of the Contemporary Imaginary.* Cultural Memory in the Present. Stanford, CA: Stanford University Press, 2005.

Newman, Barnett. "The Sublime Is Now." In *Theories of Modern Art: A Source Book by Artists and Critics,* 552–53. Berkeley: University of California Press, 1968.

Newman, Robert P. "NSC (National Insecurity 60): Nitze's Second Hallucination." In *Critical Reflections on the Cold War: Linking Rhetoric and History,* edited by Martin J. Medhurst and H. W. Brands, 55–94. College Station: Texas A&M University Press, 2000.

Niebuhr, Reinhold. *The Irony of American History.* Chicago: University of Chicago Press, 2008.

Nietzsche, Friedrich. "On Truth and Lies in a Nonmoral Sense." In *The Nietzsche Reader,* edited by Keith Ansell Pearson and Duncan Large, 114–23. Malden, MA: Wiley-Blackwell, 2006.

Nitze, Paul H. *From Hiroshima to Glasnost: At the Centre of Decision : A Memoir.* New York: Weidenfeld and Nicolson, 1990.

———. "Recent Soviet Moves" (February 8, 1950). In *Foreign Relations of the United States.* Vol. 1. *National Security Affairs; Foreign Economic Policy,* edited by Neal H. Petersen, John P. Glennon, David W. Mabon, Ralph R. Goodwin, and William Z. Slany. Washington, DC: US Government Printing Office, 1950.

Nixon, Richard. "Richard Nixon: Address to the Nation on the War in Vietnam," *The American Presidency Project,* November 3, 1969. Online at http://www.presidency.ucsb.edu/ws/index .php?pid=2303&st=&st1=#axzz1w1Dg1Nfw.

Noonan, Peggy. *What I Saw at the Revolution.* New York: Random House, 1990.

National Security Council. *NSC 162/2* (October 30, 1953). NSC Series, box 6. Dwight D. Eisenhower Library, Abilene, Kansas.

Nye, David. *American Technological Sublime.* Cambridge, MA: MIT Press, 1994.

O'Gorman, Ned. "Aristotle's *Phantasia* in the *Rhetoric*: Lexis, Appearance, and the Epideictic Function of Discourse." *Philosophy and Rhetoric* 38, no. 1 (2005): 16–40.

———. "Hobbes, Desire, and the Democratization of Rhetoric." *Advances in the History of Rhetoric* 16, no. 1 (January 2013): 1–28. doi:10.1080/15362426.2013.763737.

———. *Spirits of the Cold War: Contesting Worldviews in the Classical Age of American Security Strategy.* Rhetoric and Public Affairs Series. East Lansing: Michigan State University Press, 2012.

———, and Kevin Hamilton. "At the Interface: The Loaded Rhetorical Gestures of Nuclear Legitimacy and Illegitimacy." *Communication and Critical/Cultural Studies* 8, no. 1 (2011): 41–66. doi:10.1080/14791420.2010.543986.

Office of Public Affairs. "Fact Sheet: International Contributions to the War Against Terrorism." *Department of Defense.* Online at http://www.defense.gov/news/jun2002/d20020607 contributions.pdf (last modified June 14, 2002).

Osgood, Kenneth. *Total Cold War: Eisenhower's Secret Propaganda Battle at Home and Abroad.* Lawrence: University Press of Kansas, 2008.

Ostrow, Joanne. "TV Coverage Seeks Balance of Sensitivity, Censorship." *Denver Post,* September 16, 2001, A4.

Paglen, Trevor. *Blank Spots on the Map: The Dark Geography of the Pentagon's Secret World.* New York: Penguin, 2009.

Patterson, James T. *Grand Expectations: The United States 1945–1974.* New York: Oxford University Press, 1996.

Pease, Donald E. *The New American Exceptionalism.* 1st ed. Minneapolis: University of Minnesota Press, 2009.

Pfau, Michael William. *The Political Style of Conspiracy: Chase, Sumner, and Lincoln.* East Lansing: Michigan State University Press, 2005.

Pitkin, Hanna Fenichel. *The Concept of Representation.* Berkeley: University of California Press, 1967.

Plato. *The Symposium.* New York: Penguin, 1988.

Pollitt, Christopher. "Bureaucracies Remember, Post-Bureaucratic Organizations Forget?" *Public Administration* 87, no. 2 (2009): 198–218. doi:10.1111/j.1467–9299.2008.01738.x.

Prelinger, Megan. *Another Science Fiction: Advertising the Space Race 1957–1962.* New York City: Blast Books, 2010.

Rancière, Jacques. *The Politics of Aesthetics.* Translated by Gabriel Rockhill. London: Continuum, 2006.

Ranelagh, John. *Thatcher's People: An Insider's Account of the Politics, the Power and the Personalities/John Ranelagh.* New York: HarperCollins, 1991.

Rawls, John. *A Theory of Justice.* New York: Oxford University Press, 1999.

Reagan, Ronald. "Address to the Nation on the Explosion of the Space Shuttle Challenger." *The American Presidency Project.* Online at http://www.presidency.ucsb.edu/ws/index.php?pid=37646&st=&st1=#axzz1w0soEIeo (accessed May 26, 2012).

———. "Farewell Address to the Nation." *The American Presidency Project.* Online at http://www.presidency.ucsb.edu/ws/index.php?pid=29650&st=&st1=#axzz1w0soEIeo (accessed May 26, 2012).

———. "Inaugural Address." *The American Presidency Project.* Online at http://www.presidency
.ucsb.edu/ws/index.php?pid=43130#axzz1w0soEIeo (accessed May 26, 2012).

———. "Remarks at the Johnson Space Center in Houston, Texas." *The American Presidency
Project.* http://www.presidency.ucsb.edu/ws/index.php?pid=34875&st=&st1=#axzz1w0soEIeo
(accessed May 26, 2012).

———. "Remarks During a Visit to the Goddard Space Flight Center in Greenbelt, Maryland."
The American Presidency Project. Online at http://www.presidency.ucsb.edu/ws/index.php
?pid=40309&st=&st1=#axzz1w0soEIeo (accessed May 26, 2012).

Rearden, Steve, and Ann Smith. Interview with Paul H. Nitze (13 April 1983). Nitze papers,
box 119, folder 6. Library of Congress, Washington, DC.

Reynolds, Amy, and Brooke Barnett. "'America Under Attack': CNN's Verbal and Visual Framing of September 11." In *Media Representations of September 11,* edited by Steven Charmak,
Frankie Y. Bailey, and Michelle Brown, 85–101. Westport, CN: Praeger, 2003.

Ritter, Kurt, and David Henry. *Ronald Reagan: The Great Communicator.* New York: Greenwood
Press, 1992.

Rivera, Geraldo. *Good Night America.* TV. March 26, 1975. New York: American Broadcasting
Company (ABC).

Rodgers, Daniel T. *Age of Fracture.* Cambridge, MA: Belknap Press of Harvard University Press,
2011.

Rogin, Michael Paul. *Ronald Reagan, the Movie: And Other Episodes in Political Demonology.*
Berkeley: University of California Press, 1988.

Rousseau, Jean-Jacques. *The Social Contract, and Discourses.* Translated by G. D. H. Cole. New
York: Dutton, 1950.

———. *On the Social Contract, with Geneva Manuscript and Political Economy.* Translated by
Judith R. Masters. New York: Bedford/ St. Martins, 1978.

Rozario, Kevin. *The Culture of Calamity: Disaster and the Making of Modern America.* Chicago:
University of Chicago Press, 2007.

Salazar, Philippe-Joseph. "Rhetoric Achieves Nature: A View from Old Europe." In *Philosophy and Rhetoric in Dialogue: Redrawing Their Intellectual Landscape,* edited by Gerard A.
Hauser, 71–88. University Park: Pennsylvania State University Press, 2010.

Saunders, Dusty. "TV Captured Unfolding Terror." *Rocky Mountain News,* September 12, 2001.

Schumpeter, Joseph. *Capitalism, Socialism, and Democracy.* New York: Routledge, 2003.

Scott, Peter Dale. *Deep Politics and the Death of JFK.* Berkeley: University of California Press, 1996.

Sedley, David L. *Sublimity and Skepticism in Montaigne and Milton.* Ann Arbor: University of
Michigan Press, 2005.

Shelley, Mary Wollstonecraft. *Lives of the Most Eminent Literary and Scientific Men of France.* London: Longman, Orme, Brown, Green, & Longmans, 1838. Online at http://openlibrary.org
/books/OL7038222M/Lives_of_the_most_eminent_literary_and_scientific_men_of_France.

Shils, Edward. "The Theory of Mass Society." *Diogenes* 10, no. 39 (1962): 45–66.

Sidney, Sir Philip. "The Defence of Poesy." In *Sir Philip Sidney: A Critical Edition of the Major
Works,* edited by Katherine Duncan-Jones, 212–50. New York: Oxford University Press, 1989.

Siegel, Ed. "In Hollywood Style, the World Changed Before Our Eyes, but Spectacle Captures
Some of the Devastation." *Boston Globe,* September 13, 2001, D1.

Simpson, James. *Under the Hammer: Iconoclasm in the Anglo-American Tradition.* Clarendon
Lectures in English, 2009. Oxford: Oxford University Press, 2010.

Skinner, Quentin. *Reason and Rhetoric in the Philosophy of Hobbes.* Cambridge: Cambridge University Press, 1996.

Smith, Adam. *The Theory of Moral Sentiments*. New York: Cambridge University Press, 2002.

―――. *The Wealth of Nations/Adam Smith*. Introduction by Alan B. Krueger. Edited by Edwin Cannan. New York: Bantam Classic, 2003.

Snead, David L. *The Gaither Committee, Eisenhower, and the Cold War*. Columbus: Ohio State University Press, 1999.

Sontag, Susan. *On Photography*. New York: Farrar, Straus and Giroux, 1977.

―――. "The Image-World." In *A Susan Sontag Reader*, 349–67. New York: Farrar, Straus, Giroux, 1983.

Steger, Manfred B. *Neoliberalism: A Very Short Introduction*. Very Short Introductions, no. 222. Oxford: Oxford University Press, 2010.

Stillman, Edmund O., and William Pfaff. *The Politics of Hysteria; the Sources of Twentieth-Century Conflict*. New York: Harper & Row, 1964.

Stone, Oliver, and Zachary Sklar. *JFK*. Film. Directed by Oliver Stone. Burbank, CA: Warner Brothers, 1991.

Stout, Jeffrey. *Democracy and Tradition*. Princeton, NJ: Princeton University Press, 2004.

Sturken, Marita. *Tourists of History: Memory, Kitsch, and Consumerism from Oklahoma City to Ground Zero*. Durham, NC: Duke University Press, 2007.

Taylor, Charles. *The Ethics of Authenticity*. Cambridge, MA: Harvard University Press, 1991.

―――. *Hegel*. New York: Cambridge University Press, 1990.

―――. *Modern Social Imaginaries*. Durham, NC: Duke University Press, 2004.

―――. "The Politics of Recognition." In *Multiculturalism: Examining the Politics of Recognition*, edited by Amy Gutman, 25–73. Princeton, NJ: Princeton University Press, 1994.

―――. *Sources of the Self: The Making of Modern Identity*. Cambridge, MA: Harvard University Press, 1989.

Thatcher, Margaret. Interview for *Woman's Own* ("No Such Thing as Society"). September 23, 1987. Online at http://www.margaretthatcher.org/speeches/displaydocument.asp?docid=106689.

Thompson, Josiah. "Oral History Interview." Sixth Floor Museum at Dealey Plaza, 1998.

―――. *Six Seconds in Dallas : A Micro-study of the Kennedy Assassination*. New York: B. Geis Associates, 1968; distributed by Random House.

Trento, Joseph J. *Prescription for Disaster: From the Glory of Apollo to the Betrayal of the Shuttle*. New York: Crown, 1987.

Treuenfels, Rudolf L., ed. *Eisenhower Speaks*. New York: Farrar, Straus and Giroux, 1948.

Truman, Harry S. "Proclamation 2914—Proclaiming the Existence of a National Emergency, December 16, 1950." *The American Presidency Project*. Online at http://www.presidency.ucsb.edu/ws/?pid=13684.

―――. "Special Message to the Congress on Greece and Turkey: The Truman Doctrine, March 12, 1947." *The American Presidency Project*. Online at http://www.presidency.ucsb.edu/ws/?pid=12846.

Tsang, Lap-chuen. *The Sublime: Groundwork towards a Theory*. Rochester, NY: University of Rochester Press, 1998.

Tudda, Chris. *The Truth Is Our Weapon: The Rhetorical Diplomacy of Dwight D. Eisenhower and John Foster Dulles*. Baton Rouge: Louisiana State University Press, 2006.

Tully, James. *Strange Multiplicity: Constitutionalism in an Age of Diversity*. Cambridge: Cambridge University Press, 1995.

Turner, Frederick Jackson. *The Frontier in American History*. Tucson: University of Arizona Press, 1986.

Turner, Fred. *The Democratic Surround: Multimedia and American Liberalism from World War II to the Psychedelic Sixties*. Chicago: University of Chicago Press, 2013.

U.S. President's Commission on the Assassination of President Kennedy. *Report of the Warren Commission on the Assassination of President Kennedy*. New York: McGraw-Hill, 1964.

United States Department of State. *Foreign Relations of the United States, 1950*. Vol. 1. *National Security Affairs; Foreign Economic Policy*. Edited by S. Everett Gleason and Frederick Anadahl. Washington, DC: Government Printing Office, 1950.

Urbinati, Nadia. *Representative Democracy: Principles and Genealogy*. Chicago: University of Chicago Press, 2006.

———, and Mark E. Warren. "The Concept of Representation in Contemporary Democratic Theory." *Annual Review of Political Science* 11, no. 1 (2008): 387–412. doi:10.1146/annurev.polisci.11.053006.190533.

Venturi, Robert, Denise Scott Brown, and Steven Izenour. *Learning from Las Vegas: The Forgotten Symbolism of Architectural Form*. Cambridge, MA: MIT Press, 2000.

Wandel, Lee Palmer. *Voracious Idols and Violent Hands: Iconoclasm in Reformation Zurich, Strasbourg, and Basel*. Cambridge: Cambridge University Press, 1995.

Weaver, Richard M. *Language Is Sermonic: Richard M. Weaver on the Nature of Rhetoric*. Baton Rouge: Louisiana State University Press, 1970.

Weiner, Tim. *Legacy of Ashes: The History of the CIA*. New York: Anchor Books, 2008.

Wells, Samuel F. "Sounding the Tocsin: NSC 68 and the Soviet Threat." *International Security* 4, no. 2 (1979): 116–58. doi:10.2307/2626746.

White, Hayden. *The Content of the Form: Narrative Discourse and Historical Representation*. Baltimore, MD: Johns Hopkins University Press, 2009.

Whitfield, Stephen J. *The Culture of the Cold War*. 2nd ed. Baltimore, MD: Johns Hopkins University Press, 1996.

Williams, Raymond. *Television: Technology and Cultural Form*. New York: Routledge, 2003.

Wills, Garry. *Lincoln at Gettysburg*. New York: Touchstone, 1992.

Wilson, Rob. *American Sublime: The Genealogy of a Poetic Genre*. Madison: University of Wisconsin Press, 1991.

Wolin, Sheldon S. *Politics and Vision: Continuity and Innovation in Western Political Thought*. Berkeley: University of California Press, 1960.

Wrone, David. *The Zapruder Film: Reframing JFK's Assassination*. Lawrence: University Press of Kansas, 2003.

Yeager, Patricia. "The 'Language of Blood': Towards a Maternal Sublime." In *ReImagining Women: Representations of Women in Culture*, edited by Shirley Neuman and Glennis Stephenson, 87–110. Toronto: University of Toronto Press, 1993.

Young, Hugo, Bryan Silcock, and Peter Dunn. *Journey to Tranquility*. Garden City, NY: Doubleday, 1970.

Zakaria, Rafia. "The Tragedies of Other Places." *Guernica/A Magazine of Art & Politics.*. Online at http://www.guernicamag.com/daily/rafia-zakaria-the-tragedies-of-others/ (last modified April 17, 2013; accessed May 28, 2013).

Zapruder, Abraham. *Image of an Assassination—A New Look at the Zapruder Film*. Oak Forest, IL: MPI Home Video, 1998.

Zelizer, Barbie. *Covering the Body: The Kennedy Assassination, the Media, and the Shaping of Collective Memory*. Chicago: University of Chicago Press, 1992.

Zylinska, Joanna. *On Spiders, Cyborgs, and Being Scared: The Feminine and the Sublime*. New York: Manchester University Press, 2001.

Index